Elijah's Violin

& Other Jewish Fairy Tales

By Howard Schwartz

Poetry
Vessels
Gathering the Sparks

Fiction
A Blessing Over Ashes
Lilith's Cave
Midrashim: Collected Jewish Parables
The Captive Soul of the Messiah: New Tales About Reb Nachman

Editor
Imperial Messages: One Hundred Modern Parables
Voices Within the Ark: The Modern Jewish Poets
Gates to the New City: A Treasury of Modern Jewish Tales

Elijah's Violin

& Other Jewish Fairy Tales

Selected and Retold
and with an Introduction
by
Howard Schwartz

Illustrations by Linda Heller
Calligraphy by Tsila Schwartz

1817

HARPER & ROW, PUBLISHERS, New York

Cambridge, Philadelphia, San Francisco,
London, Mexico City, São Paulo, Sydney

Portions of this work originally appeared in *The B'nai Brith International Jewish Monthly, Corona, Dreamworks, Judaica Book News, Judaism, The Melton Journal, Midstream, Parabola, The Saint Louis Jewish Light,* and *World Over.*

FIRST EDITION

Designer: Abigail Sturges

Library of Congress Cataloging in Publication Data

Schwartz, Howard, 1945–
    Elijah's violin & other Jewish fairy tales.

    Bibliography: p.
    1. Jews—Folklore.   2. Fairy tales.   I. Title.
II. Title: Elijah's violin & other Jewish fairy tales.
GR98.S34   1983   398.2'1'089924   82-48133
ISBN 0-06-015108-0

83 84 85 86 87 10 9 8 7 6 5 4 3 2 1

For Shira and Nathan

How should we be able to forget those ancient myths that are at the beginning of all peoples, the myths about dragons that at the last moment turn into princesses? Perhaps all the dragons of our lives are princesses who are only waiting to see us once beautiful and brave.

Rainer Maria Rilke

Contents

Contents

Illustrations

Acknowledgments

The editor has been substantially assisted, in both the research and the editing of this book, by the beneficial contributions of many people. Foremost among these are Ted Solotaroff of Harper & Row, whose editorial guidance has been prodigious and invaluable, and Ellen Levine, who has given her support for this book from the first. Thanks are also due to my wife, Tsila, who willingly assisted in a multitude of ways; to Evelyn Abel and Jeremy Garber for research assistance; to Arielle North and Mary Ann Steiner for their valuable comments on the text; and to June Hilliard and Melody Newsom, who typed the manuscript. I am also indebted to the Israel Folktale Archives and its directors, Dov Noy, Aliza Shenhar, and Edna Cheichel, whose efforts have made possible a new renaissance in Jewish folklore. Support by the Senate Committee on Research and Publications of the University of Missouri–St. Louis is gratefully appreciated. Finally, I am very grateful to the following people, who graciously offered their assistance at various stages in this project: Dina Abramovitch of YIVO, Steve Anzalone, Alice Blankman, Robert A. Cohn, Bonny Fetterman, Laya Firestone, Nira Fratkin, Nissim Binyamin Gamlieli, Richard Gaugert, Karlene Gentile, Annette Harrison, Barry Holtz, Marjorie Horvitz, the Khanem family, Charles Larson, Luana Lewis, Lydia Link, Clarence Olson, Gabriel Preil, Mary Rapert, Nessa Rapoport, Michael Sagalyn, Rabbi Zalman Schachter, Charles Schwartz, Elsie Steimnitz, John Swanson, Bitite Vinklers, and Yehuda Yaari.

Elijah's Violin

& Other Jewish Fairy Tales

Introduction:
On Jewish Fairy Tales

Tales of magic and wonder can be found in every phase of Jewish literature, both sacred and secular. Among the post-biblical *aggadot* (legends) and the *maaysiot* (tales) of Jewish folklore are to be found a number of stories which can readily be identified as traditional fairy tales. Some of these are the universal type of fairy tale set in an enchanted land and populated with a variety of human and supernatural beings, both good and evil, and are Jewish solely by virtue of their source. But many others, perhaps half of the existing body of Jewish fairy tales, have fused some specific aspects of Jewish life and tradition with the archetypal fairy-tale framework. For the fairy-tale version of the world as a stage on which good and evil struggle is fully compatible with the Jewish view of the essential condition of this world, where faith in God can defeat the evil impulse, known as the *Yetzer Hara.*

The fairy tale is a very ancient genre, filled with marvels and enchantments, and typically concerned with kings and queens ready to give up half their kingdoms if they could only have a child of their own; with princes who set out on quests to waken sleeping princesses; and with witches who are prepared, at the slightest offense, to throw a fly in the ointment. Above all, the hero must overcome obstacles in order to prove himself and win his reward. And when all is said and done, good always triumphs over evil, and the prince and princess live happily ever after.

Yet despite the apparent simplicity and even childlike qualities of the fairy tale, much of its power derives from the timeless fantasies and human concerns it embodies, which we recognize primarily on an unconscious level when we read it, and which explain its primal and compelling power. This suggests why the fairy tale is found in virtually every culture, providing a medium of expression for the archetypes of the unconscious, embodied in such beings as witches, sorcerers, and enchanted princesses. For if fairy tales served merely as an outlet for the need to imagine ourselves as royalty, their spell would soon be broken, but instead these tales retain a remarkable power all our lives, not only when we are children. For just as the outer garments of Jewish ritual signify something much greater to observant Jews than mere custom, so too does the seemingly safe and familiar format of the fairy tale encompass some of the most elemental drives and emotions.

The pioneering work of Antti Aarne and Stith Thompson in this field, especially in *The Types of the Folk-Tale,* has demonstrated convincingly the parallel themes and patterns of fairy tales and other kinds of folktales found throughout the world. The fairy tales collected in the following pages from a wide range of Jewish sources and periods substantiate the thesis of Aarne and Thompson. There are even Jewish variants of such well-known fairy tales as "Cinderella," "Rapunzel," and "The Golden Bird," but at the same time they contain many unique qualities as a result of their origin. Especially those fairy tales which concern Jewish legendary figures have brought with them the customs and settings of the milieu from which they have emerged, and are valuable bearers of the Jewish tradition.

That fairy-tale elements can be found at the earliest stages of Jewish literature is demonstrated by the biblical Book of Esther, in which a queen, Esther, struggles with Haman, an evil minister of King Ahasuerus, who is trying to destroy her people, the Jews. The minister's plot is foiled by a wise old man, Mordecai, who is Esther's kinsman. Whatever the historical basis for this account, it has been cast in the mold of a fairy tale, for all of the characteristics are present except for the intervention of the supernatural, and there is even a happy ending. In fact, it is possible to recognize in the Book of Esther the direction taken by later Jewish fairy tales, especially those of the medieval period, which combine the universal fairy-tale format with a distinctly Jewish context.

Fairy-tale qualities can be found as well in the account of David and Goliath—the young shepherd boy David slaying the giant Goliath against all the odds. That this episode was indeed regarded as a fairy tale is made apparent by the tale of David and the giant Ishbi-benob, brother of Goliath, which is found in the Talmud, the most sacred Jewish text after the Bible. In this tale, "King David and the Giant," Ishbi-benob behaves exactly as do bellicose giants in fairy tales, attempting to crush King David beneath his olive press while his evil mother, Orpah, throws her spindle at Abishai, King David's general. Here the latent fairy-tale elements in the story of David and Goliath are made overt; whereas in the biblical tale it is David's skill and cunning that save him, here it is the supernatural power of the Name of God (known as the Tetragrammaton) which performs the magic of suspending David in the air so that he does not land on the giant's spear, making this much more of a fairy tale than its biblical forerunner. The use of divine intervention is characteristic of the Jewish fairy tale in general, where it replaces the usual devices of enchantment. Thus what other fairy tales attribute to magical causes, the Jewish vision interprets as a demonstration of the power and beneficence of God. King Solomon's primary source of power, for example, is his ring, on which is engraved the Name of God. Magical rings of enchanted origin are often found in fairy tales, but the power of Solomon's ring derives explicitly from the presence of God's Name: thus Benaiah, Solomon's general, need only hold up Solomon's ring and cry out "The Name of your Master is upon you!" and Asmodeus, king of the demons, is rendered powerless.

Fairy-tale elements can also be found in the accounts of the Garden of Eden, Noah's ark, and Joseph's rise to power under

Pharaoh, as well as in the many uses to which Moses puts his magic staff. Still, such elements do not play a prominent role in the Holy Scriptures, and it is only in the Talmud that the first clear-cut Jewish fairy tales are to be found. This is largely due to the more prominent role of fantasy in the talmudic legends, which make liberal use of poetic license. Yet as with virtually all of the *aggadot,* the fairy tales that are found in the Talmud and the Midrash have as their starting point an attempt to resolve a question raised in the biblical text. The workings of this process are especially apparent in "King Solomon and Asmodeus." The premise of this well-known talmudic tale is an explanation of how King Solomon managed to construct the stone altar of the Temple *with neither hammer nor axe nor any tool of iron heard in the house while it was being built* (I Kings 6:7). Since there was no known way to accomplish this, a magical creature, the Shamir, was created, which could cut through anything, and King Solomon sends his trusted general Benaiah on a quest to capture Asmodeus, king of the demons, who knows where the Shamir can be found, and then to obtain it from the bird that has possession of it.

All in all there are no more than a dozen fairy tales to be found in the Talmud, four of which are included here: "The Witches of Ashkelon," "King David and the Giant," "King Solomon and Asmodeus," and "The Beggar King." The first of these concerns historical figures, as do the tales about King David and King Solomon. There is little doubt that "The Witches of Ashkelon" is, in fact, based on a historical event: the hanging of eighty witches in the city of Ashkelon. Fabulous as the tale itself seems, in which the witches are deceived when their captors disguise themselves as would-be suitors wishing to dance with them, the Talmud also reports the fury of the relatives of the witches following their execution. And thus this tale offers an instance in which it is possible to follow the evolution of a historical event into a tale of the fantastic, whereas most legends have long since succeeded in discarding the historical kernel that brought them into being.

In a tale such as "King Solomon and Asmodeus" the distinction between legend and fairy tale has become substantially blurred. Legends are typically based upon historical persons, places, or events and usually possess some degree of realism, but while it is quite certain that King Solomon as well as his general, Benaiah, were historical figures, the quest described here is clearly drawn from the realm of fantasy. Such an approach is typical of most aggadic legends, which are free of most of the constraints of verisimilitude, including the portrayal of time. Yet because of the legendary intention that inspired them, the tales of the Talmud and the Midrash remain a unique form, functioning as both legendary tales and tales of the fantastic at the same time. And on occasion the rule of fantasy fully dominates the tale, bringing it into the realm of the tale of enchantment. That such fairy-tale elements are present in "King Solomon and Asmodeus" is readily apparent, enabling it to function both as a *drash* (biblical exegesis) explaining how the injunction that *thou shalt lift up no iron tool upon the altar of the Lord* (Deut. 27:5) was fulfilled, as well as a tale of enchantment concerned with a quest, the defeat and capture of the king of demons, the use of a magical ring to subdue him, and the discovery of a creature which can cut through the hardest stone. It is in this very tale, then, that the fusion of the uniquely Jewish aggadic tale and the universal fairy tale can be seen to take place. And it is worth noting that such hybrid creation is unusual—while most myths, legends, and folktales are colored, to a considerable extent, with the customs and setting of the culture from which they emerge, this usually is not the case with fairy tales, which exist in a timeless and spatially elastic world.

In the Talmud "King Solomon and Asmodeus" is followed by a companion tale in which Asmodeus revenges himself by outsmarting King Solomon, the wisest of all men. In this tale, "The Beggar King," Solomon's fall from glory is so complete he is reduced to being a wandering beggar, regarded as a madman when he insists he is a king. This tale exists as a brief coda at the end of "King Solomon and Asmodeus," but a considerable number of variants stemming from the Middle Ages are to be found, which expand on the wanderings of Solomon. This process of embellishment of an earlier narrative is characteristic of Jewish folklore in general, and demonstrates the manner in which the earlier tale was received as a story worthy of further development rather than as a fixed work that had to be retold in exactly the same way. Naturally, much of this narrative freedom derives from the nature of folklore, which belongs primarily to the people, and generally remains an oral rather than a written tradition. Although this is true of the folklore of most of the people of the world, the exceptional continuity of the Jewish tradition makes it possible to trace the evolution of many tales from their earliest written versions, preserved in sacred texts, through various retellings in later periods. And naturally the abundance of such variants often makes retelling the tale enviable in the possibilities of combination and variation.

Whereas the historical King Solomon was known as a great ruler and a man of surpassing wisdom, the legendary Solomon has been transformed into a sorcerer without peer, versed in all aspects of magic, including the knowledge of the languages of the birds and other animals, and able to call upon the demons and even the winds to serve his will. It is interesting to note, however, the ambivalence toward Solomon that emerges in many of these tales. On the one hand there is still admiration for his prowess and grandeur, but this is qualified by a recognition of his excessive pride. Such a portrayal of Solomon also reflects a hesitant attitude toward the realms of magic and the supernatural, for Jewish legend is filled with tales of those less wise and fortunate than Solomon who were destroyed by engaging in the occult.

This theme of chastisement is also found in the midrashic tale "The Mysterious Palace" when Solomon is riding his flying carpet. Filled with a sense of his own greatness, he is suddenly reminded of how fragile is the covenant that permits him to glide through the air, which God can withdraw as though it were the wind. The succeeding episode, concerning the palace of the eagles, teaches Solomon something of the lessons of eternity, not unlike those taught Ozymandias in Shelley's poem of the same title. The whole tale has a strong echo of a talmudic legend in which Solomon tries to enter the gates of the Sanctuary of the Temple, only to be rebuffed when the gates refuse to open, for he is not permitted to enter on his own merits, but only on those of his father, King David.

"The Princess in the Tower," a midrashic variant of "Rapunzel," demonstrates that even King Solomon, the wisest of mortals, could not outfox fate. Solomon attempts to circumvent the prophecy that his daughter will marry a poor man by isolating her in a tower on a remote island. But a giant eagle ends up carrying her destined bridegroom to the roof of the tower. This tale confirms the talmudic dictum that "Forty days before the formation of a child a voice goes forth out of Heaven to announce that this one will marry that one." And not even King Solomon can deprive a person of his or her destined match. A similar moral is found in a legend about two men Solomon attempts to assist in escaping the Angel of Death. In one version Solomon pronounces the Divine Name and suspends the men in the air, where, it turns out, the Angel of Death has been ordered to seize them; in another version he sends them to the city of Luz, which the Angel of Death is forbidden to enter, but the Angel still seizes them, at the gate of the city. As these parallel legends demonstrate, the same motifs are found throughout the Jewish legendary tradition, in which sacred legends and secular folklore, including fairy tales, are in many ways cut from the same cloth, and well-defined distinctions between them are often not possible.

This legendary city of Luz reappears in a medieval tale of the same title, which offers an opportunity to observe the evolution of a legend from its origin in the Bible through its development in the Talmud and Midrash until its crowning expression as a medieval folktale. There are four brief references to the city of Luz in the Bible. The first of these, that of Jacob's dream, identifies the city as one of the Gates of Heaven:

> And Jacob awaked out of his sleep, and he said: "Surely the Lord is in this place; and I knew it not." And he was afraid, and said: "How full of awe is this place! This is none other than the House

of God, and this is the Gate of Heaven." ... And he called the name of that place Beth-el, but the name of the city was Luz at first.

Genesis 28:16–17; 28:19

The Talmud identifies Luz for the first time as a city of immortals:

It has been taught: "That is the Luz against which Sennacherib marched without disturbing it, and even the Angel of Death has no permission to pass through it. But when the old there become tired of life they go outside the wall and then die."

Babylonian Talmud, Sota 46b

By the Middle Ages the city in which none of its inhabitants died had grown into a legendary place and the storytellers' art lay primarily in telling of the quest to reach it.

The quest for the blue dye (*tekhelet*) in the tale "The City of Luz," included here, derives from another biblical injunction:

And the Lord spoke unto Moses, saying: "Speak unto the children of Israel, and bid them that they make them throughout their generations fringes in the corners of their garments, and that they put with the fringe of each corner a thread of blue."

Numbers 15:37–38

By the time of the talmudic sages, however, it was no longer known which creature supplied the *tekhelet* dye. Some said it was derived from a shellfish, others a snail. Therefore the rabbis decided to leave the thread white rather than to dye it incorrectly. However, the Talmud states that the *tekhelet* dye can be found in the city of Luz. Thus the quest in this fairy tale is not only to locate the city of immortals, but to retrieve the dye with which to fulfill the *mitzvah,* or obligation, of the blue thread.

The most prolific period of Jewish folklore comes in the Middle Ages. It is in this period that the fairy tale first emerges as a prominent form of Jewish folklore. This abundance of folklore was brought about by the independent evolution of talmudic and midrashic motifs among the people, who were especially attracted to tales which demonstrated the greatness of the Jewish kings and prophets of the past. At a time when rabbinic formulations had become more allegorical and esoteric, especially as manifested in the kabbalistic literature, the common folk were drawn to tales with pronounced elements of fantasy and clear-cut morals. The fairy tales which are found in this medieval folklore demonstrate a considerable evolution in the genre, creating a form which in many ways is a hybrid, weaving the features of the typical folktale into the fabric of the fairy tale. For example, the hero in these tales is often a common Jew, but the characteristic link to royalty is usually retained by the presence of a king or queen (or prince or princess) of the opposite sex. In "The Princess with Golden Hair," the Jew Yohanan is sent out on a mission to locate the princess whose strand of golden hair has been dropped by a bird at the feet of the king, and the tale ends with the fairy-tale marriage of Yohanan and the princess and his ascension to the throne. Another example is found in "The Flight of the Eagle," in which the Jewish youth Shlomo becomes the beloved and then the husband of the daughter of the king of Spain. And in "The Demon Princess," a Jew even ends up wedded to the daughter of Asmodeus.

These medieval fairy tales also typically retain the moral basis of Judaism. A vow made to one's father is sacred, and Yohanan, in "The Princess with Golden Hair," honors it until he is left impoverished. When he has demonstrated his faithfulness, he is rewarded by the giant scorpion he has raised, and eventually he not only completes the quest to find his princess but even becomes king, a proper reward, the tale implies, for honoring a vow. It is interesting to note that in a version of this tale found in the *Maaseh Book,* which, according to Moses Gaster, dates from six hundred years later, the scorpion has become a frog and the principal figure a rabbi. But for the most part the story remains the same, another striking example of the continuity of Jewish tradition.

As Yohanan's fidelity makes him deserving of his great reward, so does the violation of such a vow unleash the punishments that overwhelm the man in "The Demon Princess." This tale, which is also known as "The Tale of a Jerusalemite," has been ascribed to Abraham, the son of Moses Maimonides, who lived at the beginning of the thirteenth century in Egypt. The Jew who breaks his vow to his father is portrayed as deceitful and manipulative, and makes other vows he has no intention of keeping to the daughter of Asmodeus. The man provokes the wrath of the king of demons and his daughter, which is not tempered with mercy.

This rare occasion of a fairy tale which does not have a happy ending indicates the extent to which the form has evolved. The notion of the kiss of death, with which the demon princess takes the life of the man who has betrayed her, is echoed in a talmudic legend which describes the death of Moses as having come from the Kiss of the *Shekhinah,* the Divine Presence and Bride of God. In this context it signifies a mystical union at the moment of death, whereas the man kissed by the demon princess simply has his breath snatched away. For those familiar with the talmudic legend, of course, its echo in the fairy tale is readily apparent, and enriches the resonance of the tale.

Of particular interest in "The Demon Princess" is the description of the religious life in the kingdom of the demons, which seems parallel, in every respect, to that of a devout Jew of the Middle Ages. This is not intended as mockery, for the *Yenne Velt,* the world in which demons and other spirits live, was believed to be a mirror image, somewhat distorted, of the world in which we live.

It is worth noting that the characterization of Asmodeus found in this tale is consistent with that in "King Solomon and Asmodeus" and "The Beggar King." Asmodeus is a characteristically Jewish demon who, like his nemesis, King Solomon, is one of the most popular figures in Jewish folklore. Spending part of his time in Paradise, where he studies in the Heavenly Academy, Asmodeus does not fit the mold of the typical demon of fairy tales—he performs good deeds, such as setting a blind man on the proper path, as well as mischievous ones. Further aspects of his character are found in the tales "Partnership with Asmodeus" and "The Magic Flute of Asmodeus." In the former, Asmodeus saves a man from suicide—again performing a *mitzvah,* or good deed—and proposes a partnership which brings the man great benefit until he proves to be an ingrate. Then Asmodeus turns on him, as does the demon princess on her dishonest husband, and puts him in grave danger. Or again, Asmodeus appears as a grateful father who rewards the shepherd in "The Magic Flute of Asmodeus" for saving his son and gives him every magical gift he requests. And it should be noted that even when Asmodeus is responsible for Solomon's fall from glory in "The Beggar King," it is for the purpose of teaching the king an important lesson. On the one hand Asmodeus is a worthy adversary, with some of the subtlety of Goethe's Mephistopheles. On the other hand Asmodeus plays a positive role in God's design, for His agency is seen ultimately in every event, whether good or bad.

Another strain of meaning in medieval Jewish fairy tales is found in those about Rabbi Adam, a Jewish sorcerer, who, like Solomon, was master of many mysteries. Rabbi Adam is perhaps best known for his role as the transmitter of the fabled Book of Mysteries to the Baal Shem Tov in Hasidic legend, but there also exist several independent medieval tales about him, including "The King's Dream," "The Magic Mirror of Rabbi Adam," and "The Enchanted Journey," which are represented here. In each case Rabbi Adam comes to the assistance of his fellow Jews either by interceding with an evil king or by directly aiding a Jew in danger. It is not difficult to recognize in these tales the deep frustrations, impotence, and isolation experienced by Jews in the medieval period, and to see how the fantasy mechanisms of the fairy tale operate. For it is out of the people's longing to be independent and secure that such tales emerged, and this is true of the tales from the Middle East and those from Eastern Europe, the lives of both the Sephardic (Middle Eastern) and Ashkenazic (East European) Jews being equally difficult. The tales about Rabbi Adam also served as models for some of the legends of Rabbi Judah Loew of Prague, the creator of the Golem. In both sets of tales the role of the Jewish hero is taken over by the *tzaddik,* the righteous man who owes his powers to his knowledge of the Torah and his trust in God.

The next important source for Jewish fairy tales, after the

Middle Ages, is in the Hasidic era of the eighteenth and nineteenth centuries in Eastern Europe. While the Hasidic masters, including the Baal Shem Tov, founder of Hasidism, had been the subject of a rich body of miracle tales, there are relatively few fairy tales, perhaps because the Hasidim identified their rabbis with the patriarchs and ancient sages rather than with the more fanciful heroes of fairy tales. However, there is a treasury of such fairy tales attributed to Rabbi Nachman of Bratslav, who lived in the nineteenth century. In the last four years of his life Rabbi Nachman, who was the great-grandson of the Baal Shem Tov, undertook to tell tales to his Hasidim as a method of transmitting his teachings. Four of Rabbi Nachman's tales are included here: "The Lost Princess," "The Prince Who Was Made of Precious Gems," "The Water Palace," and "The Pirate Princess." Although most of these tales seem, on the surface, to be traditional fairy tales, they are in fact complex allegories frequently linked to myths concerning the *Shekhinah* and the Messiah. In the tales of Rabbi Nachman the *maaseh,* the traditional Jewish tale, and the universal fairy tale fully merge and become inseparable.

A story such as "The Lost Princess," for example, appears to be a typical tale of the quest for an imprisoned princess, but, according to Rabbi Nachman's scribe, Rabbi Nathan of Nemirov, it is actually an allegory about the Exile of the *Shekhinah,* the Divine Presence, which becomes identified as a mythically independent feminine being during the kabbalistic period. According to kabbalistic myth, the *Shekhinah* went into Exile at the time of the destruction of the Temple in Jerusalem. The loyal minister who searches for her in this tale may be seen to represent the Messiah, who has been sent to bring her out of Exile, since tradition holds that the *Shekhinah* will be freed only when the Messiah has come. Or the minister may be seen as a *Tzaddik,* a righteous one, as the most elect among the Hasidic rabbis were called, who obeys the command of the King, the Divinity, to search for the lost *Shekhinah* so as to make it possible for the messianic era to begin. For those familiar with these kabbalistic myths, as Nachman's Hasidim were, this symbolism conveyed profound secrets, including, it is hinted, the means to hasten the messianic era.

This does not mean, however, that Rabbi Nachman's tales must be read allegorically to be appreciated. The tales have great power in themselves, for Nachman's figures, events, and images are, at once, so primary and so subtle that they evoke the numinous quality of the inner world. Furthermore, his allegorical intentions brilliantly exploit the fairy-tale form as a pure and spontaneous expression of unconscious states. So too does the kabbalistic concept of the *Shekhinah* naturally link up with the Jungian concept of the anima, the feminine aspect of the psyche of every man. The identification of the *Shekhinah* with the imprisoned princess does not differ very much from the way in which the figure of the evil stepmother in fairy tales serves as a mask for our own mothers, permitting the child an expression of fear or anger that might otherwise be repressed. Rabbi Nachman was thus especially remarkable because he recognized the vital symbolism in fairy tales, saw its link to the mystical imagery in the Kabbalah, and discovered a way to fuse the two.

From the perspective of the tradition of Jewish literature, then, it is possible to see how Rabbi Nachman's innovations represent a continuation of the development beginning with the *aggadot* of the Talmud and Midrash, the basic sources of postbiblical legends, where there is a remarkably complete identification with the primary biblical figures, such as Abraham, Jacob, and Moses, which made the legends modes of personal expression as well as of biblical exegesis. The rabbis not only freely provided missing episodes from the biblical narrative, such as that of Abraham's childhood, but also attributed to the patriarchs dreams of their own, such as an apocryphal dream Abraham is said to have had about a cedar and a palm tree, which warned him of the coming danger in Egypt. Such projections have always been the basis of fairy tales, in which the primary characters are often left unnamed, identified only as a king or queen, a prince or princess, thus inviting identification with the listener or reader of the tale. Beginning with the kabbalistic period of Jewish literature, the kinds of projections that were common for biblical figures came to include more abstract concepts, such as the *Shekhinah* and the Messiah. So for Rabbi Nachman the lost princess, or soul, in each of us must be sought after, for each of us must seek to accomplish the personal restoration and redemption that the Messiah represents on a cosmic scale. By linking these abstractions with the more concrete characters of the traditional fairy tale, Rabbi Nachman was making this process of spiritual projection a much simpler matter to envision.

Virtually all of the sources discussed so far have come down to us in written form. Nonetheless, all of them first existed as oral tales, which, except for the tales of Rabbi Nachman, were handed down for centuries before they were finally recorded. However, because of the low status of Jewish folklore among the rabbis, who were the primary keepers of the tradition, these secular tales were not scrupulously preserved, as were the sacred texts of the Talmud, Midrash, and Kabbalah. As a result a great many tales have been lost, which will almost certainly never be recovered. At the same time, many tales continued to be retold, and thus were preserved orally, especially in isolated areas such as Yemen, into the present century.

Among the early Jewish scholars who sought to preserve this oral tradition were S. Ansky, the Yiddish dramatist and author of *The Dybbuk,* and Y. L. Cahan, who collected Jewish folksongs as well as folktales. Ansky and Cahan went out into the countryside and wrote down the tales as they were told to them. Some of these tales had already been preserved in an earlier written form, but the majority had not. Often these tales were the purest kinds of fairy tales, which had been left unrecorded simply because they did not seem to bear a religious moral. But there were also examples of the fused Jewish folktale and universal fairy tale that emerged in its most complete form in the Middle Ages. Among the tales collected by Y. L. Cahan and recorded in Yiddish included here are "The Imprisoned Princess" and "The Exiled Princess." "The Imprisoned Princess" can readily be seen as another variant of the theme found in Rabbi Nachman's "The Lost Princess," while "The Exiled Princess" is a Jewish variant of "Cinderella." (The bulk of the material collected by Ansky has remained unavailable in a Russian archive, and promises to provide many treasures once it is released.)

One unusual format for the preservation of folk material, including fairy tales, was the ballad. Ballads were especially popular in Sephardic communities, such as those found in Greece, Turkey, and Morocco, and there are also Yiddish folksongs which have preserved similar material. In many cases the Judeo-Spanish ballads contain the only existing versions of the tales on which they were based. The fairy tale in a ballad format usually has been condensed to include only the primary episodes of the tale. But since fairy tales are in many ways predictable, it is not difficult to imagine the details suggested by the ballad's narrative. An example of a fairy tale reconstructed from such a source is "The Nightingale and the Dove," which comes from Salonika. Note that one of the subjects of the ballad/fairy tale is the beautiful singing voice of the young man, which enables him to court the princess against all odds.

While most of the fairy tales that have been preserved in the sacred literature of the Talmud and Midrash and the later medieval folklore are either specifically Jewish in content, or else parables and teaching-stories which have been transmitted for their allegorical intent, the universal fairy tale without overt Jewish elements also flourished during all of these periods. Some of the tales are very old indeed, but since they existed solely in the oral tradition, it is almost impossible to estimate their dates of origin. And while the outer garment of the tale cannot be identified as Jewish, there can be no doubt that the themes of many of these tales are parallel to the concerns of the more overtly Jewish ones. As with the identifiably Jewish fairy tales, the primary themes concern quests and imprisoned princesses.

What is it about these two themes that make them so compelling? The parallels of the theme of the imprisoned princess to the kabbalistic myth of the Exile of the *Shekhinah* have already been observed. The theme of the quest is often taken up in the midrashic literature, depicting, for example, the search for the legendary Book of Raziel, given to Adam by the angel Raziel, as well as the search for the Temple vessels, preserved from destruction by Jeremiah when the Romans overran the Temple in Jerusalem. And in his myth of the Shattering of the Vessels and the Gathering of the Sparks, the sixteenth-century kabbalist Rabbi Isaac Luria, known as the Ari, develops a method of restoration, or *tikkun,* which works very much like a quest. According to this kabbalistic myth, God sent out vessels filled with a primordial light (which itself is the subject of many midrashim), but these vessels unexpectedly shattered, scattering the sparks of light throughout the world. The role of the Jew, according to the Ari, was to raise these scattered sparks from where they had fallen, and so eventually restore the world to its pristine state. So it is that the Jew has been brought into this world, in the Lurianic view, to complete such a personal quest, and therefore has a stake in the ultimate destiny of this world and the next. This Lurianic myth is retold in "The Eternal Light," which itself is cast in the form of a quest.

That the standard fairy-tale quest and the myth of the Ari have distinct parallels is amply demonstrated in "The Princess and the Slave," where too the quest takes on religious significance. Here the slave Samuel seeks Moses in an endless wilderness, suggesting the wandering of the Israelites. As a result of the successful completion of his quest, Samuel discovers the secret of eternal youth, which in symbolic terms can be said to be eternal life, just as the reward for raising the fallen sparks that one is destined to gather is also eternal life in the World to Come. Likewise, the quest for Elijah's violin in the title story is of a religious nature. For the successful completion of the king's quest enables the violin's imprisoned melodies, emblematic of the Jewish spirit, to be set free.

Among the characteristics which these fairy tales and the midrashic literature have in common is their timelessness. That Samuel succeeds in his quest to find Moses in "The Princess and the Slave" indicates that this fairy tale is set in a timeless world indeed. In the midrashic tradition Moses is often viewed as an immortal figure, largely because his death is not recorded in the biblical narrative. So too does the appearance of Elijah in a multitude of post-biblical tales attest to the tradition that Elijah appears in each generation to assist those Jews with the greatest need. This tradition derives from Elijah's miraculous ascension into heaven in a chariot of fire. Yet while most of these stories concern the miraculous, very few are fairy tales in the traditional sense. "Elijah's Violin," however, is an exception, and the violin itself can be seen as a symbol for the positive attributes of the legendary Elijah, as well as a magical device exactly like those found so often in fairy tales—a Jewish equivalent of Aladdin's lamp.

The characteristic Jewish fairy tale, then, can best be seen as a fusion of the Jewish sacred legend or the Jewish secular folktale with the universal fairy tale, conditioned by the biblical and post-biblical tradition in which Divine Providence takes the place of magical devices and resolutions and the moral element is pre-eminent. The result is a powerful medium for the reaffirmation of Jewish faith and longing, sustained over one hundred generations. The archetypal and eternal nature of the fairy tale thus becomes particularly appropriate as an expression of continuity with the past, in which all the Jewish generations merge and mysteriously enter a single, timeless present.

Elijah's Violin

nce upon a time there was a king who had three daughters. Now he loved them dearly, but one day he had to leave them to go off to war. Before he left he spoke to his daughters and said: "If I am victorious in this war, I will bring each of you a gift. Tell me, what would you like?" The eldest spoke up and said: "I would like a diamond in the shape of a star." And the second daughter said: "I would like a gown woven from pure gold." But the youngest said: "I only want you to come home safely from the war." The king was pleased to hear this, and he said: "Thank you, daughter, for your good wish. But you must ask me to bring you something, as your sisters did. Think it over for three days, then tell me before I depart what it is that you want."

Now the youngest daughter was sitting alone on a rock next to the lake outside the palace, when there appeared before her an old woman, who asked her: "What is wrong, child?" And she replied: "I do not know what gift to ask of my father, the king." The old woman said: "You must ask your father for Elijah's violin." So the princess agreed that this would be her request.

At the end of three days the king said to his daughter: "What gift have you decided upon?" And the princess replied: "I would like you to bring me Elijah's violin." The king agreed and set out to war.

Now the king led his troops to victory in every battle, and after his triumph he sought and found the gifts for his two eldest daughters, the star-shaped diamond and the golden gown, but he was unable to find Elijah's violin anywhere. The king asked his generals if they knew where it could be found, but none of them had heard of it in any of the countries in which they had fought. And he asked his wise men, but none of them had read of it in any book. And he asked his soothsayers, but none of them could find it in the stars. So the ship of the king departed, and sailed until it came to land. The king ordered his crew to cast anchor there, to see if Elijah's violin was to be found in that place. And in this way he embarked on a long quest, which took him to the four corners of the world. After many trials and tribulations, he was led to an old man who lived in a cave, and the old man said: "Elijah's violin is in the possession of the king of this country." He also said that the king had a daughter imprisoned in stone and whoever freed his daughter from the stone would be richly rewarded. Then the old man gave the king three long hairs and he said: "These three strands are from the bow of Elijah's violin. Burn these when you are in the presence of the princess."

The king thanked the old man, and took the three hairs from the bow of Elijah's violin, and put them safely away. Then he asked the old man what he might give him in return. And the old man said: "There will come a day when you will repay me in full, for your daughter will set free the imprisoned melodies." And the king wondered at this, and he said: "Tell me, old man, what is your name?" The old man replied: "My name is Elijah." And then the old man returned to the shadows of the cave, and the king set off to rescue the princess who was imprisoned in stone.

When the king approached the palace in which the stone princess lived, he advised his generals and wise men and sooth-sayers that he preferred to proceed on his own, and that they should camp there and wait for him. And when he came to the gates of the palace and announced that his purpose was to set free the imprisoned princess, he was given an audience with the king and queen at once. For they had left orders that no one who offered to free her was to be refused, but that anyone who failed was to be put to death. That same day the visiting king was taken into the presence of the princess.

Now it was a great shock for him to see the princess, for she seemed to be alive and dead at the same time, as if she were a living sculpture. But much greater was his surprise when she began to speak—for the enchantment under which she had fallen permitted her the power of speech but no other. While the princess was speaking, it seemed as if she were alive. But when she fell silent, it was as if she had turned completely to stone. He could not bear her silence, so he asked her: "Tell me, how did it happen that you were turned to stone?"

The princess replied: "One day I was wandering through the palace, and I came upon a stairway I had never known about, and I followed it until I came to a room where there was a mirror with a golden frame. As I stood before it, my mirror image stole out of the glass and forced me to take its place within. And from that moment I found myself turned to stone, with only my power of speech remaining. No one has known how to set me free. Since then there have been reports that someone who looks exactly like me, and claims to be me, has been seen in the kingdom, but slips away like a shadow if anyone comes too close." And then the princess was silent, and it was the silence of stone.

The king remembered the strands from the bow of Elijah's violin that the old man had given him, and took them out and threw them into the fire that until then had done little to keep the room warm. Then the chill of the room seemed to melt, and at the same time the stone princess turned to flesh and blood again. And the king who had set her free said to her: "Now that you have been freed from this spell, your mirror image surely has been returned to its place in the mirror. To keep it there you must blindfold yourself and take a stone and shatter the glass. That way your mirror image will remain in its world of reflections, and will not take your place in this world again." The princess promised she would do this, and she did so before the end of the day. Her father, the king, was so grateful that he told the king who had broken the spell that he could have any gift of his choice. Nor did he refuse him Elijah's violin, for that is what he requested as his reward.

Now that the king had gathered the gifts for all three of his daughters, he sailed with his soldiers directly home. And because the winds were with them, it took them only seven days, and when the king arrived he gave the gifts to his daughters. The first two took their gifts and hurried off to try them on, but the youngest hugged her father first, and then took the violin to her room. And that is how the princess who was the youngest daughter of the king came to possess Elijah's violin.

Now when the princess first opened the case of the violin, what did she find? A small, perfectly carved violin that had been preserved for many centuries, and next to it a bow. And when she put the bow to the strings, a clear melody sailed forth, effortlessly. And while she played the violin, it seemed that the violin was playing itself, as if it had many melodies stored up, which sought to emerge from within. And even before she finished playing there appeared before her a handsome young man, who asked her: "Why have you brought me to this place?"

The princess was amazed to see him, and she said: "But how did you enter this room?" He showed her the window through which he had entered. Then the princess asked: "But where do you come from?" To which the young man replied: "From far away." And the princess asked: "Then how did you come to be here?" The young man answered: "The music of the violin brought me." Nor did the princess question him more than that, for she understood at once that the violin she had played was enchanted, and that she and the prince, for he was a prince, had been brought together through its magic.

After that, the princess would take out Elijah's violin whenever she missed the prince, and each time she would play it, the prince would arrive soon after the melodies floated outside her window. Before long the prince and the princess exchanged rings and vowed that one day they would be wed.

Then it happened, after some time had passed, that the eldest sister of the princess heard her speaking to the prince in her room. She hurried to the second sister, and said: "Someone has been visiting our sister in her room." They decided to search her room to see what they could learn, and so they persuaded the youngest princess to join them in the baths. When they arrived there the eldest said she had forgotten her soap, and left to fetch it. But instead she went to her sister's room and began to search through it. When she found the ring of the prince, she threw it and broke the window through which the prince entered the room. And when she saw the case of the violin, she opened it and began to play, but the melody that emerged was a dark one, filled with brooding. And as the music filled the air, the prince was compelled to appear. He sought to enter by the broken window, but was wounded by the sharp glass and was forced to turn back.

When the youngest princess returned from the baths, she could feel that something had happened in her room, but she did not know what it was. So she took out Elijah's violin and began to play, but this time the prince did not appear. Then she saw that the window was broken, and that three drops of blood were on the curtain. When she realized that her sisters must have discovered her secret, and brought harm to the prince, the princess became very sad and left the palace to sit on the rock by the lake. While she was sitting there the old woman appeared, and asked her what had happened. The princess told her all that had taken place, and the old woman said: "Pretend that you are ill, so that the doctor will order that no one be admitted to your room until you are well. Meanwhile, you must set out and find the prince who has been wounded, for only you can heal him. To do so you must pluck three strands from the bow of Elijah's violin, and take them with you. Then you must burn those strands when you are in the presence of the prince."

The princess did as the old woman had said, and the doctor ordered that no one be admitted to her room. She then set out on a quest to find the wounded prince, so that she might heal him.

So it was that the princess walked and walked through all of that kingdom and the forest surrounding it, until she grew tired and sat down to rest beneath an elder tree. She was so tired that she lay down to sleep. But no sooner did she close her eyes than she discovered she understood the speech of the doves that perched on the branches above her. When she opened her eyes, their speech sounded only like chirping, but when she closed her eyes once more, the language of the doves was clear to her, and she heard them say: "The prince has been wounded, and the way to his palace is impossible to find without a map. And where can a map be found? Only in the leaves of this tree."

Then the princess arose at once, and plucked one of the leaves from the tree. And when she looked at it, she read it like a map. She saw where she stood in the forest, and the way she must take to emerge from that labyrinth, and how she could reach the palace where the wounded prince waited to be healed. After this she followed the map directly to that kingdom. There she disguised herself as a man, and presented herself as a doctor before the king. The king warned her that thirty-nine doctors had already tried to heal the prince, and all had failed and been put to death. The fate of this doctor would be the same as that of the others if he did not succeed.

The disguised princess agreed to these terms, but requested that she be left alone with the prince. As soon as she entered the prince's room and saw him asleep on the bed, she was overcome with emotion and wanted to embrace him. But, remembering her purpose, she cast the strands from the bow of Elijah's violin into the flames of the fireplace, and as soon as they started to burn, the wounds of the prince healed, and he opened his eyes and saw the princess, who had cast off her disguise. Then she called in the king and queen, who were overjoyed to find that the prince had recovered, and they agreed at once that the prince and princess should be wed. So it was that they came to be married and that they lived together in great wealth, peace, and virtue for all the days of their lives, and many were the times when the melodies of Elijah's violin were heard drifting over that land.

Source: Egypt
Oral Tradition

The Witches of Ashkelon

ong ago, in the city of Ashkelon, the people were plagued by a coven of eighty witches who lived in a cave at the outskirts of the city. Those witches were sworn enemies of the people of Ashkelon, and saw to it that spells were cast that brought harm to them in ways large and small. Not only did they play nasty tricks, such as turning wine into vinegar, or causing the fire to go out, but they also brought about grave dangers, casting spells which kept the rain from falling, and causing the cows to go dry. And sometimes the vengeance of the witches was directed at one person, as when they caused a rabbi to become a bird, and his wife, a butterfly.

Now it happened that there were three witnesses to this foul deed, the three children of the unfortunate couple. They had seen the witches approach their parents and strike them with their magic wands, transforming their father into a bird and their mother into a butterfly, both of which had flown away and not been seen again. And after this event became known, the people of Ashkelon were outraged, and turned to Rabbi Shimon ben Shetah to rid the city of its curse. At first Rabbi Shimon seemed hesitant to move against the witches. But then it happened that one of his disciples dreamed that he was strolling in an orchard through which a river ran. In the dream this disciple saw Rabbi Shimon trying to reach the water but unable to do so, and he also saw Miriam, the sister of Moses, and she had an object in her hand. He asked her what it was, and she showed him an iron key, and said that she had been sent to deliver it to Rabbi Shimon. And when the disciple asked what key it was, she said it was the key to Gehenna, where the souls of the wicked are punished, the very gates of Hell, and that it would shortly be delivered to Rabbi Shimon unless he fulfilled his vow to rid the city of the curse of the witches.

Now when the disciple awoke, he wasted no time, but hurried to Rabbi Shimon and told him his dream. And Rabbi Shimon said: "I do not doubt that what you say is true. Surely this is a message from heaven that has been delivered to me, for I have told no one of my vow to eliminate the witches."

So it was that Rabbi Shimon thought up a plan. Then he waited for the rainy season to begin, and when it did, he gathered together eighty men. He told each of them to bring a large pot and a fresh garment, and when they had assembled, he told them to put their dry robes into the pots, and to place the pots upside down upon their heads. In this way he led them to the cave of the eighty witches. When they were almost there, he took them to a nearby cave and said: "When I whistle once, put on your robes, and when I whistle a second time, come together and enter their cave. Then each of you should take hold of one of the witches and start to dance with her. And while you are all dancing, lift the witches off the ground, as if this were part of the dance. But once you have raised them up, do not allow their feet to touch the ground again. For it is well known that when a witch's feet are not touching the earth, she is powerless."

So Rabbi Shimon went to the cave of the witches and knocked at the door. They called out: "Who is there, and what do you want?" He replied, "Open up! It is one of your own!" And the witches said, "Who are you?" And Rabbi Shimon said, "I am a sorcerer. I want to show you my powers, and for you to show me yours." "What can you show us?" they asked. "I can make eighty men appear, with dry robes, who will dance with you." And when the witches heard this, they said: "Come in, come in, for we would like to see you perform such a feat!"

Then the witches opened the door of the cave, and Rabbi Shimon entered. And when he was inside they saw that his robe was dry, and they could not understand this, since the rain was pouring outside. They said: "How is it that your clothes are dry?" And he replied: "I made myself small and walked between the raindrops." And they said: "Ah, you have great powers!"

Then the witches began to show him their powers: One of them made a table move to the center of the room without touching it, and another conjured up a tablecloth that descended from the ceiling onto the table, and it was covered with all the signs and symbols of the witches. Still a third pronounced a spell, and the table was covered with the finest food and drink. Then they said: "Now it is your turn to show us what you can do."

Then Rabbi Shimon said: "Yes, now I will show you the wonders I promised. For when I have whistled twice, eighty men as dry as I am will appear and will dance with you." Then he whistled once, and the men, hearing this, put on the dry robes, and when he whistled a second time, they all rushed into the cave. The witches shrieked with delight when the men appeared, their robes dry, exactly as he had promised. And each man chose a witch for a partner and began to dance with her, whirling wildly, and in a flash the men had lifted all the witches off the ground. At first the witches thought it was a part of the dance, but when the men did not put them down and began to carry them out the door, they began to shriek in fear, for witches are terrified of the rain. And just as soon as the witches were struck by the rain, all of them were transformed.

Those who had caused the wine to turn into vinegar were changed into grapes which were ripe on the vines, waiting to be plucked and crushed in the winepress.

Those who had caused the fire to go out burst into flames, and burned until they were ashes, which were scattered by the winds to the four corners of the world.

Those who had stopped the rain from falling were turned

into puddles, which formed into a stream, which flowed to a river, which flowed into the sea. And later these waters rose up into the sky and formed into clouds, and in time, when the clouds grew full, they fell down to earth as rain.

Those who had caused the cows to go dry became grass in the pasture, which the cows grazed upon, and from which they produced an excellent milk.

And those who had turned the man into a bird and his wife into a butterfly were turned into worms which scurried along the ground until they were swallowed by hungry birds which swooped down and picked them up.

And when all the witches were transformed, the spells they had cast were broken, and the bird and the butterfly again became the rabbi and his wife.

Thus were the witches punished for their evil doings, and the city of Ashkelon was rid of its curse for all time.

Source: Babylon
c. Fifth Century

The Golden Mountain

any years ago there was a king who ruled over a vast kingdom, and was believed by many to be the wealthiest man in the world. This king had a daughter who was curious to know about everything—why the sun rises and sets, why spring follows winter, why the moon is full at some times and is only a sliver at others. So it was that when the princess learned there was a wise old man in their kingdom, a soothsayer who knew how to read the stars, she begged her father to bring him to the palace to teach her what he knew.

Now the king's daughter was very precious to him, and he was very proud that she so loved to learn. Therefore he sent a messenger in a golden carriage to bring the old man to the palace. And while the messenger was still far away, the soothsayer read in the stars that he was coming, and he wondered what it was the king wished of him. When the messenger arrived he said to the old man: "You need not be afraid, for the king will do you no harm." So the old man accompanied the messenger to the palace.

When the old man arrived, he was given an audience with the king at once. The king said to him: "It is known that you possess the knowledge of how to read the stars. I would like you to reveal this secret to my daughter, the princess, who has a great thirst for such knowledge. As your reward, I shall build you the finest observatory in the world, from which you may gaze at the stars."

Then the old man said: "I agree to teach the princess on these terms, but there must be one more condition—that no one else be present while I instruct her." The king agreed to this condition, and the old man began to teach the princess how to read the stars. The princess listened carefully to everything he had to say, and she proved to be a fine student. At the end of one year the old soothsayer had taught her all he knew about the stars, and when he returned to his home he found the observatory had already been built, as the king had promised.

Now the princess was very pleased with all that she had learned, and she quickly put it to good use. For she read in the stars that an evil king in a bordering kingdom was planning a secret invasion. The princess warned her father about this, and he set a trap for the invading army, which was easily defeated. After this, the princess became the king's primary adviser, and he came to depend on her in many ways.

Some time passed, and one night the princess read in the stars of a mountain that had a vast treasure of gold hidden within it, and that only one person in the world knew how to enter it. And she also learned that this was none other than the old man who had taught her how to read the stars.

Then the princess reported what she had learned to her father, the king, and begged him to send for the old man again, so that he could reveal the secret of where the golden mountain could be found, and how it could be entered. The king agreed to his daughter's request, and sent a messenger in a golden carriage to bring the soothsayer back to the palace. And when the old man arrived, the king told him what his daughter had discovered in the stars, and asked him to reveal the secret of the golden mountain to her. As a reward, the king promised to have a telescope made for him that would bring the stars a thousand times closer to his eyes.

Now at first the old man hesitated, for he knew there were dangers associated with the golden mountain. But when the king insisted, he agreed to reveal the secret to the princess, but on the condition, as before, that no one else be present when he was with her. The king accepted this condition.

Then, when they were alone, the princess begged the soothsayer to take her to the golden mountain that very night. The old man told her that in that case they must hurry, for they had to be there exactly at midnight. So it was that the two of them made their way in complete darkness, and reached the mountain at the appointed time. There the soothsayer uttered a spell, which caused a large stone of the mountain to move with much rumbling, so that they could enter the cavern. But as they did, the old man warned the princess that the mountain would remain open for only half an hour, and that they must return before half past midnight, for then the stone would close over the mountain, and if they had not departed from it, they would be trapped inside.

Inside the golden mountain the princess beheld treasures unmatched in all the world, even in the treasuries of her father, the king. She saw golden apples, silver raindrops, and a multitude of diamonds in the shape of snowflakes. She was dazzled by the unimaginable splendor she saw there, and would not have remembered to take her leave had the old man not reminded her. And shortly after they took their leave, the stone entrance to the mountain closed. Then they returned to the palace, and the soothsayer received the telescope the king had promised him, and returned to his home. But before he left he warned the princess to take care if she ever returned to the mountain, and not to forget that she must leave it in time.

The following night the princess decided she wanted to return to the golden mountain, for just as they were leaving the night before she had glimpsed a golden seashell so exquisite that she had dreamed about it all night, and now she wanted to make it her own. She traveled there by herself, and when she reached the mountain it was almost midnight, and she repeated the spell that the old man had uttered, for she had listened very carefully while he had spoken. Once again there was a great rumbling, and the stone moved, and she was able to enter the mountain. But in the darkness her gown caught on a thorn bush as she entered, and a single golden thread became unraveled, although the princess did not notice this.

Inside the mountain, the eyes of the princess were again so dazzled by the golden treasury that she became dizzy. But she had not forgotten the golden seashell she had come there to seek out, and soon she held it in her hand. It was truly a miracle to behold, for it resembled an actual seashell of the most beautiful kind in every respect, except it was made entirely of gold. Knowing that real seashells echo the sea, the princess held the golden shell up to her ear, and to her amazement she heard voices speaking there. That is how she discovered it was a magic seashell in which she could hear anything being said anywhere in the world. If she held it in one position, she would hear one conversation, and if she moved it ever so slightly, another would take its place. Now the princess was fascinated by this magic shell, and did not notice the swift passage of time. Suddenly she realized it was time for her to leave the cavern, and she rushed to the entrance, but it was too late, for the mountain had already closed, and she was trapped inside it.

The next morning cries for help were heard from inside the mountain, and when it was discovered that the princess was missing, the king understood it must be the voice of his daughter that they heard. Then he commanded his soldiers to take pickaxes and other tools and to dig into the mountain to pull her out. But it was all in vain, for every pickaxe broke against the hard rock, and before long even the king conceded they would never save the princess that way.

Then the king recalled the old soothsayer who had taught the princess the secret of how to enter the mountain, and he immediately sent a messenger in the golden carriage to fetch him. But the messenger returned alone, and he told the king that the old man had passed away. The king was very grieved when he heard this, for now there was no one left who knew how to open the mountain and free his trapped daughter. Then the king announced that anyone who could free the princess would be wed to her, and would also receive half of his kingdom. Many journeyed to the mountain and sought to free the princess with one spell or another, but none of them succeeded in making the mountain open, and the princess remained trapped inside.

Now in that kingdom there was a clever lad whose name was Yousef, and although his family was poor, he always managed to find something so that they never went hungry. One day Yousef was walking in the marketplace when he heard an old woman cry out that she had an oud to sell. But everyone who looked at the oud only laughed in her face, for it was very old and battered, and besides, it was missing all of its strings. Now Yousef had only three copper coins in his pocket, but he said to himself: "The oud is old and worn, but I could polish it, and someday, when I have more money, I will buy strings for it and play it."

Then Yousef approached the old woman, and offered his three copper coins for the old oud. The old woman accepted his offer at once. After this she motioned for him to come closer, and she whispered in his ear: "This is a fine oud you have bought, my lad, for it is a magic oud. But for it to perform its magic, it requires golden strings, for no others will suffice." Then the old woman turned to go, and disappeared in the crowded marketplace. And even though Yousef ran after her, he could not find her, and he was sorry she had left before he could ask her what kind of magic the oud could do, and now it was too late.

It was at that time that the princess had become trapped in the golden mountain, and the king sought help in setting her free. And like many others, the boy Yousef liked to imagine how wonderful it would be if he was the one who freed her. And even though he had no idea how to do this, Yousef decided to go to the golden mountain to see for himself. So he took leave of his parents, picked up his only possession, the stringless oud, and set out on his journey.

Meanwhile the princess had begun to despair of ever escaping from the cavern. At first she had hoped that those trying to get her out would succeed, for she was able to listen to all their comments with the aid of her magic seashell. But in this way she soon discovered that they had failed, and that the king, in his desperation, had announced he was seeking the aid of anyone, and had offered her hand to whoever succeeded in releasing her. Then it occurred to the princess that she might be able to open the mountain from within by pronouncing the spell, but this too failed, for the spell was effective only from the outside. She had searched through the cavern of treasures to see if there was any-thing to eat or drink, and found a spring deep in the cavern, which had its source inside the mountain. So too did she find growing next to it a carob tree, which sustained her. And to pass the time she put the golden seashell to her ear, and heard in it all that her parents and others in the kingdom said about her, and learned how much they grieved over what had happened. So too did she listen to the lectures of wise men all over the world, for she had not lost her love for learning. And in this way several months passed, with the princess no nearer to freedom than she was in the first place.

Then one day the boy Yousef arrived at the golden moun-tain. He saw the crowds that gathered there during the day, be-cause what had happened to the princess had made it a famous place. But when it grew dark, they all left and returned to town, leaving Yousef alone outside the golden mountain, for he had nowhere else to go. He found a place for himself on the ground, and was about to go to sleep when he suddenly saw something glint in the moonlight. And when he arose and went over to see what it was, he was amazed to find a long, golden thread—the very one that had become caught in the thorn bush as the prin-cess had entered the cavern. Yousef carefully pulled the golden thread from the bush without pricking his fingers on the thorns, and when he had it in his hand it occurred to him that he might try to string his oud with it. For, after all, the old woman had told him its magic would work only with golden strings. And when he had strung the oud, he found that the golden thread was just long enough to serve for all its strings.

So it was that as midnight arrived Yousef plucked the strings of the magic oud for the first time. And all at once it sang out with a melodious voice, almost human, and each time he plucked a string, it sang out another word, of something that sounded to Yousef like a spell. Suddenly he heard a loud rumbling. Then the princess, who had heard every word pronounced by the magic oud with the aid of the golden shell, hurried outside, and ran straight to the boy who had released her, and embraced him, and thanked him again and again for setting her free.

Then Yousef and the princess returned to the palace of the king, he with his magic oud, and she with her magic seashell, and when the king saw that his beloved daughter had been freed, he was overjoyed. So too did he keep his promise, and soon there was a lavish wedding at which Yousef and the princess were wed. And the princess soon found out that the clever Yousef loved to learn as much as she did, and she taught him all that she knew, so that one day he became the wise ruler of that kingdom, where he was admired and respected by all.

Source: Morocco
Oral Tradition

The Princess and the Slave

n a faraway land lived a mighty ruler, whose name was King Nazim. Now this king had an exceptionally beautiful daughter, who was his only child, and the king loved her more than life itself. Her eyes were blue, her lips red, and her smile was like the sun at midday. Kings came from a great distance to meet her, and many wealthy princes requested her hand in marriage. But one and all, King Nazim turned them down, finding every suitor flawed and unworthy of his daughter. Still, those who wanted her were like bees buzzing around the hive, and for each prince he turned away two others arrived who sought her hand.

And it is true that the princess was worthy of all this attention, for she was not only beautiful and charming, but also very pious and pure. She loved to study so much that she had to have one tutor after another, for she soon learned everything they knew. So her father was understandably proud and protective of her, and demanded the highest standards of those who sought her hand.

Now despite all his efforts to see that the princess found a perfect match, King Nazim was haunted by a recurrent nightmare. In these dreams he was told that the lucky one who was destined to marry his daughter was none other than his Hebrew slave, whose name was Samuel. Now of course this was preposterous, for not only was Samuel a slave, but he was also an old man, more than ninety years old. It is true that he was of a great size, and was still strong as an ox, and capable of causing a hundred armed men to take to their heels by making a single move. But as a suitor he simply could not even be considered.

At first the king did not pay any attention to these dreams, but when they kept recurring, he became anxious. At last he called his wise men together and told them the dream and asked for their advice. They discussed many solutions, but at last they told the king to command the slave Samuel to go into the wilderness in search of his prophet Moses, since he was a Hebrew. And to send him on this quest with a riddle to which he must have the answer before he could return. The riddle was: "It is possible to contain a garden in the world. But how can the world be contained in a garden?" The advisers laughed heartily when they concocted this riddle, for they were quite certain it could not be answered. And the king agreed that this was a fine way to get rid of the worrisome fellow, for he would not dare return until he had completed the quest.

So it was that the slave Samuel was sent on his way the next morning. And although he had been given supplies to last him for many months, for he could carry a great load with ease, still he wept the whole way. For he understood that he was being sent into exile, but he could not imagine why, since he had been a faithful and dependable slave all of his life. And even though he felt that it was surely impossible to find Moses the Redeemer in this world, still he set out in search of him, since that is what he had been commanded to do.

Samuel traveled for many months on his quest, and all the time he was filled with grief. For every day it became more and more apparent that his mission was an impossible one, and all who heard of the reason for his quest laughed at him and took him for a fool. One day when Samuel was very tired, and began to feel like an old man for the first time, he sat down to rest under a large tree in the wilderness. He was about to fall asleep when he heard a voice whispering to him which said: "Where are you going?" Samuel quickly sat up and looked around, but there was no one to be seen. Then he became frightened, for perhaps he had been found by an enemy, and the most dangerous enemy is one who cannot be seen. Then the voice spoke again and repeated the question. This time Samuel found his voice and said: "Who is speaking to me?" And the voice replied: "It is I, the tree you are sitting beneath." Samuel could hardly believe his ears, but since there was no one to be seen in the wilderness, and no one was hiding in the tree, there did not seem to be any other explanation.

Just then the tree asked its question for the third time, and Samuel said: "I am searching for Moses, so that I may ask him a question." "If that is so," said the tree, "then I have one request to make—when you find Moses, please ask him why a giant tree such as I am does not bear any fruit. For if there were ripe and juicy fruit on my branches, a hungry man like yourself would have been able to break his fast and delight in it." "Yes," said Samuel, "I will certainly fulfill your request if I succeed in finding Moses."

After a good long rest, Samuel got up and continued on his endless way. He reached a hill overlooking a steep valley, and saw that there was something at the base of it, although he could not quite make out what it was. So he traveled down to the bottom of the valley, and there he found two marble pools, one next to the other. One pool had been built out of black marble and was filled with dark water, while the other was made of white marble, and was filled with clear water, but gave forth a repugnant odor, so that no traveler would risk tasting it, and if he did, he would discover it was bitter indeed.

Now when Samuel saw the two pools filled with water, his soul was filled with longing to rest there and satisfy his thirst. And when he realized that neither pool contained water that was any good for drinking, he was very disappointed. Then, as he was sitting there, he suddenly heard a voice speaking to him as if from far away. It was a muddled and murky voice, but Samuel could make out its words. The voice asked him where he was going. Again Samuel looked around and saw that no one else was there, and he was still trying to figure out who had spoken when the voice repeated its question. "Who is it that is speaking?" asked Samuel. "It is I, the voice of the two pools," came the reply. Then Samuel answered the voice's question and told it of his quest. "If that is the case," said the voice, "when you reach Moses will you please ask him why it is that we pools, made of the finest marble, have waters that are muddy and bitter? For if they had been clear and sweet a sad and exhausted traveler like yourself would have been able to quench his thirst." And Samuel said that he would gladly ask Moses this question, should he ever succeed in finding him.

After he had rested by the side of the two pools, Samuel got up and went on his way. He walked on for days and weeks and months, his tired body swinging from side to side, his hands rising and falling, his eyes blurry, his feet worn and aching. Tears washed over his cheeks, and his sadness ate away at his patience and strength. After all, who knew where Moses the Redeemer might be found? For since he had ascended Mount Nebo he had never been seen again, and now the poor slave Samuel had been commanded to seek him out!

Then it happened after many years had passed that Samuel reached a mountain in the wilderness. Since he did not have a map to guide him, he did not know where he was, but he was very pleased to find at the base of that mountain a fine fig tree, filled with ripe figs. He plucked one of them and tasted it, and it seemed to him as sweet as the very fruit of Paradise. Then Samuel ate his fill of those delicious figs, and lay down to sleep. He slept for a long time, and when he woke up he saw that he was sleeping in a shadow, where before he had been sleeping in the sun, and he assumed that the day had passed and the night fallen. He did not realize that he had slept through a day and a night, and that it was already the next day. And why did he not see the sun? Because someone was standing above him, who cast a long shadow. And whose shadow was it? It belonged to Moses, who had come down from the peak of that mountain where he made his home, because he knew that the slave Samuel had finally found him. And where was it that Samuel had come? To Mount Nebo in the wilderness of the Sinai, for that is where Moses makes his home.

So it was that when Samuel sat up and saw the man standing over him, whose face shone with a beautiful glow and whose long beard was pure white, Samuel suddenly knew that he had succeeded in his quest, for the dignified presence who stood there could be none other than Moses the Redeemer himself. Then Samuel lowered his eyes and said in a whisper: "Tell me, good sir, what is your name?" "Surely you know who I am," answered the old man. "I am the one you have been searching for all these years. And although you have doubted so many times that you would ever find me, you should know that it was destined before you were born that we should meet today. Now, tell me, are there any questions you want me to answer?"

For a moment Samuel was dizzy, since his long search had come to so sudden a conclusion, and for a moment the three questions that had been on his tongue day and night were lost to him, as if they had flown away. Then his memory was restored, and he said to Moses: "It is possible to contain a garden in the world. But how can the world be contained in a garden?" "That should be obvious to a man of the Hebrew faith, such as yourself," said Moses, "for is it not true that this world is God's garden?" And Samuel smiled when he heard this, for the riddle had tormented him all those years, and now that he knew the solution, it seemed so simple that he was amazed it had never occurred to him.

After this Samuel remembered the question he had brought from the giant tree, and asked Moses why it was that such a magnificent tree did not bear fruit. And Moses said: "It is true that the Holy One, blessed be He, did not bless this tree with abundant fruit, but that is because God gave it a very special virtue among all the other trees in the world. And what is that virtue? It is to be found in the leaves of that tree, for whoever takes a handful of those green leaves from its branches and cooks them in water and drinks the potion will be cured of any sickness or disease, and become a healthy man in his body and soul."

Then Samuel asked the third question he had promised to bring to Moses, that of the two pools. And Moses said: "It is true that the water of these pools is not intended for drinking. But that is because they have another purpose, unique among the waters of the world. And what is that? It happens that any man who immerses himself in the black pool, and then immerses himself in the white one, will in an instant become a young man of eighteen, and the same holds true for a woman, who will also become young again. But anyone who dips himself in the white pool first and then in the black will lose his youth and become a very old man full of days, very bent and worn."

Then Samuel kissed the hands of Moses and thanked Moses from the bottom of his heart for seeing fit to meet him there at the foot of Mount Nebo. Samuel then made his way back to the two pools. There he told the voice of the pools all that Moses had said, and then took off his clothes, and immersed himself in the black pool. After this he entered the white pool, and when he emerged from it he was a young handsome lad of eighteen, feeling stronger than he had ever felt in his life. So it was that Samuel left those pools singing and giving thanks to the Lord and to Moses for having revealed this secret to him, and making it possible for that miracle to take place. And every time he reached a body of water, he leaned over it to study his reflection, and at last he came to the happy conclusion that the wonderful transformation had indeed taken place for good.

Now Samuel felt light, and he ran like a deer. Before long he covered a vast distance and arrived at the great tree. When he stood beneath it, he told the tree the secret of its healing leaves, as Moses had told him, and then he climbed up the trunk of the tree and filled his bag with those green leaves, for he knew that such a wonderful cure would be invaluable. After this Samuel continued on his way, and his singing echoed in the empty fields, and there was no end to his happiness. For as much as he walked his feet retained their spring, and the way seemed shortened, and only a few days passed before he reached the gates of the city from which he had departed so long ago.

Now as soon as he had entered the city, Samuel saw that everyone was wearing black, and that their eyes were downcast and full of tears. He wondered what could have happened, and thought that perhaps the king had died. Then he asked one of the men he saw in the street, and he learned that not long after he had left on his quest the king's beloved daughter had fallen into a deep sleep, from which she could not be wakened. She had slept this way ever since, and it was as if a dark cloud had covered that city, for since then the lives of the people had grown sad and bitter, for they had dearly loved the princess. As for the king, his despair was so great that he had retreated to his chamber and was neither seen nor heard from. Of course doctors had come from all over the world, but none had been able to cure her. In his desperation the king had it announced that whoever cured the princess would be married to her, and would also receive half of the kingdom.

When Samuel heard this, he decided at once to bring about her cure. He quickly built a house near the palace, and on the door he hung a sign that identified him as a doctor. And when the messengers of the king passed the house and saw the sign, they came to the young doctor, whom no one, of course, recognized, and asked him if he was wise enough to cure the princess. Samuel told them that this indeed was the case, and he assured them that he could put a quick end to her long coma.

So it was that the next day Samuel went to the palace and when he arrived he was brought to the king at once. The king was surprised to see such a young doctor, but he was not about to turn down any possible cure. Then Samuel was taken into the presence of the princess, who slept on her bed with all the signs of life, although she was very pale. She was just as beautiful as ever, as if she had not aged, but she could not be awakened. So Samuel went about his work and took out a handful of the leaves of the giant tree and boiled them in water. And when the steam of the boiling water had filled the room, the princess breathed it in and began to stir. All of a sudden her eyes opened, and she smiled. And all who were present let out a cry of delight, for the princess had been saved at last, and brought out of her endless sleep. Then Samuel offered her a long wooden spoon full of the cool boiled water, and put it near her lips. And after she had swallowed it the princess regained her color and was no longer as pale as death. Then she sat up and looked at the handsome doctor, and in that moment she lost her heart to him.

So it was that soon the wedding between the young doctor and the princess took place, attended by everyone in the city. Never had there been a wedding such as that, and the people spoke of it for years to come. And after the wedding Samuel revealed his true identity to the king and his bride. At first they refused to believe what he said, but after he described every detail of his quest, and of the long years he had spent in the wilderness, they realized that what he said must be true. Then the king asked if Moses had solved the riddle, since the king and his advisers had considered it to have no solution. Samuel then told them what Moses had said: that the garden which could contain the world was this world, since it is God's garden. And the king was so moved by the wisdom of the reply that he decided then and there to become a Jew, and the princess also chose to make this her faith.

So it was that the king and his son-in-law Samuel began to study the Torah together every day. And from its holy words the king drew the wisdom to guide him in his judgments, so that his rulings were just and merciful. And when the king's life came to an end, Samuel and the princess ascended to the throne and ruled the kingdom together. Their love for each other was legendary, and they were the wisest rulers since the days of Joseph in Egypt, and the finest leaders since the days of Moses the Redeemer himself.

Source: Morocco
Oral Tradition

King David and the Giant

ne day, when King David was out hunting, Satan appeared to him in the guise of a deer. David took aim, but the arrows he shot did not reach the deer, and he continued the chase into the land of the Philistines, his enemies. In this way, Satan led King David past the cave of the giant Ishbi-benob, the brother of Goliath, whom David had slain when he was still a young shepherd. For David had volunteered to face the mighty giant Goliath when no one else came forth who was brave enough to meet him in combat. And to the amazement of all, David had defeated the giant with a well-aimed stone from his slingshot. Now Ishbi-benob had recognized King David as the one who had slain his brother, and gave chase until he caught him. And when King David was his prisoner, the giant, who was even more terrifying than Goliath, bound him and would have crushed him beneath an olive press, except that miraculously the ground softened beneath David, and he was saved, although he remained trapped beneath the press.

Now at that time Abishai ben Zeruiah, a general in King David's army and a friend of the king's, was preparing for the Sabbath, for the king's capture had taken place on a Friday. Abishai was washing his hands in a basin when he noticed some blood stains in the water. At the same instant he heard the cry of a bird, and when he looked outside the window he saw a dove perched on a branch, plucking its feathers and beating its wings. Then it occurred to Abishai that these might be signs that King David was in danger, for Israel is likened to a dove.

So Abishai left his house and went to look for King David. First he went to the palace, but he did not find him there. Then he looked for him in the House of Study and in the House of Prayer, but he was nowhere to be found.

Now King David possessed a magic mirror which revealed the location of anyone or anything that was lost. Abishai knew where the mirror was kept, and he also knew the spell that made it work, for he had once been present when King David had used it. But the king had forbidden anyone else to touch it. And King David also possessed a magic mare, which was as swift as the wind. But the king had forbidden anyone else to ride it.

Abishai then sought out the wise men of the kingdom, and said to them: "I am certain that King David is in great danger, and the only way to find him is to use his magic mirror, but the king has forbidden it, and the only way to reach him is to use his magic mare, but the king has forbidden this as well." Then the wise men consulted among themselves and said: "In a time of danger, such as this, it is permitted."

So Abishai took out the magic mirror and pronounced the spell, and asked to see where King David was to be found. And when he peered into the mirror, he saw David trapped beneath the olive press, while the giant Ishbi-benob stood above it, laughing horribly. Then Abishai mounted the magic mare and rode off into the desert. The mare galloped so swiftly that she did not seem to touch the ground, and in the twinkling of an eye they reached the house of the giant.

When Abishai arrived, he saw Orpah, the mother of the giant, sitting outside the door spinning. As soon as Orpah saw Abishai she knew he was there to try to save King David, so she broke the thread she was spinning, and flung the spindle at Abishai, intending to kill him. But the spindle fell short. Then Orpah told Abishai to bring the spindle to her. Instead Abishai threw it, striking her in the head, and that was the end of her.

Just then the giant Ishbi-benob came running up, and when he saw what had happened he grew furious and lifted up the olive press beneath which King David was trapped. He intended to fling David's body at Abishai, but he discovered, to his amazement, that King David was still alive. Then the giant flung David high into the air and set his spear in the ground, so that David might fall upon it and perish. But at that instant Abishai pronounced the Ineffable Name of God, and King David remained suspended in the air. Abishai then pronounced the Divine Name again, and then King David slowly descended to the ground, landing at a safe distance from the spear.

King David and Abishai then leaped upon the magic mare, and rode off as fast as they could. In his fury the giant ran after them, but he did not watch where he was going, and he tripped over the olive press, and fell beneath it and was crushed. And that is how King David was saved from a terrible fate, and he gave thanks to Abishai for his quick thinking, and to the Holy One, blessed be He, for protecting him in his hour of danger.

Source: Babylon
c. Fifth Century

The Princess in the Tower

ing Solomon had a lovely and charming daughter, whose name was Keziah. This daughter was the apple of his eye, and he often thought that he would let her marry only a great ruler, for no one else, he felt, would be worthy of her. Then it happened, during a war, when King Solomon's soldiers were crossing a river on a very hot day, that Solomon called upon the birds to protect them from the heat. In a moment the wings of thousands of birds beat above their heads, shielding them from the sun. And while this was taking place, an eagle, whose wings were sheltering King Solomon himself, whispered to Solomon, who understood the language of the birds, that it had overheard a voice from heaven which had announced that Solomon's beloved daughter Keziah was destined to marry a poor man before a year had passed.

Now King Solomon was very disturbed to hear this news, for he wished his Keziah to wed only another king. The words of the eagle consumed him day and night, until at last he decided to have a high tower built in the sea, where he would keep his daughter until the year had passed. That way, he believed, he could prevent the undesirable union from taking place.

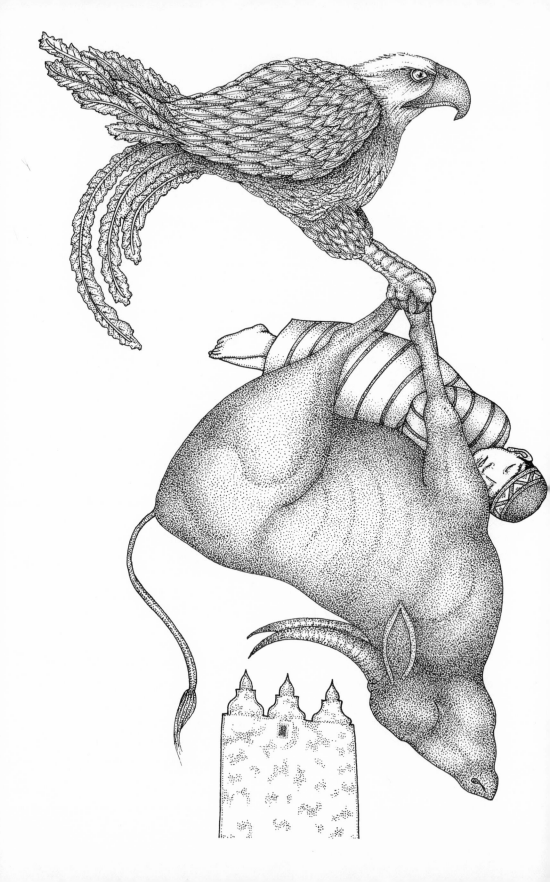

Therefore Solomon commanded that the building of a lofty tower be undertaken by his most trusted servants, on the farthest and most remote island of his empire. And he ordered the tower be built without entrances or doors of any kind, except for an entrance on the roof, and with only a single window in his daughter's chamber, from which she could look out on the sea. So too was the tower to be furnished with the finest furniture and many treasures, and seventy servants, all women, were to be sent to satisfy the princess's every wish and command, and there was abundant food to last a year.

Now with the great resources available to King Solomon, the tower was soon completed, and then Solomon called in Keziah and said to her: "I am sending you on a long voyage, to a beautiful island. I ask that you make your home there for one year. When you return I shall explain why I have sent you there. Meanwhile, I have seen to it that you will lack for nothing." And Keziah replied: "Your wisdom, father, is well known throughout the world. I know you love me, as I do you, and that you are sending me on this journey for a good reason. Therefore I will willingly go, and I do not doubt it will be for the best."

King Solomon thanked the Lord for having blessed him with such a wise and loving daughter. And a few days later the princess Keziah took her leave of the king and set sail. The ship sailed for forty days and nights, and at last arrived at the distant island where the tower had been built. To gain entrance a rope was put around the princess, and she was pulled up to the roof, where the only entrance to the tower was to be found. Once inside, the princess was met by the seventy serving women who had been sent there before her, and she made her home at the top of the tower in a room that overlooked the sea.

Meanwhile, far away, in the city of Acco, there lived a young man whose name was Reuben, a scholar and a scribe, who was poor in possessions, but rich in knowledge and learning. In order to support his poor parents and himself, Reuben wandered about in search of work. So it was that once he was wandering in the wilderness when night fell, and he had to sleep beneath the stars. However, as the night passed, it grew colder and colder, until he could no longer bear the chill, and he began to wander about, searching for some place where he could keep warm. There were no caves nearby in that barren wilderness, but in the dark the young man came upon the carcass of an ox that had been slain by a lion that very day. The carcass was torn open, and the ox was still warm, so he lay down inside it, and fell into a deep sleep. Then, during the night, a giant eagle swooped down and picked up the ox in its claws, and bore it away, with Reuben still sleeping inside it. As fate would have it, the eagle carried the ox to the roof of the tower in which the princess was living. There the eagle ate its fill of the ox, and then flew off back into the wilderness, while the young man was still asleep.

Now it was the custom of the princess to awaken very early and to go up to the roof of the tower to watch the sun rise over the sea. And when she came up to the roof that day, she found the youth asleep in the carcass of the ox, and her surprise was great. She gently woke him and said: "Who are you, and how did you come to be here?" And when Reuben opened his eyes and found himself in that place, on the high roof of a tower overlooking the sea, with a girl of peerless beauty standing before him, he assumed he was still dreaming. He rubbed his eyes, but nothing changed, and he realized that some kind of miracle had taken place. Then he said: "My name is Reuben. I am an Israelite of the city of Acco. Last night I was sleeping in the wilderness when it became very cold, and I found the carcass of this ox, and slept inside it to keep warm. But I do not know how I came to be here."

Then the princess noticed three very large feathers lying beside the ox. She picked them up and showed them to Reuben and said: "These are the feathers of a giant bird, perhaps an eagle, which must have carried the ox here to devour, and brought you along with it." And when he saw the feathers, Reuben realized the princess must be correct, and then he was even more amazed that such a thing had happened. Nor did he regret the turn of events, for from the first instant he had seen the beauty of the princess, he had bound his heart to her. So too was the heart

of the princess taken with the youth who had appeared so unexpectedly on the tower roof.

So it was that the princess invited Reuben into her chamber,
where she let him bathe and gave him a new robe to wear. And
when he emerged from the bath, she was greatly struck by how
handsome he was. Then she shared her breakfast with him, and
after they had eaten she told him who she was, and how she had
come to be there. Then she said: "This tower has been built so
that it is impossible to leave it, for there are no doors of any kind
except for the one on the roof where we entered. And even if
you succeeded in descending from the tower, nothing would be
gained, for no ship ever passes this secluded island. Perhaps it
was fated that you come here; therefore, stay until the day my
father, King Solomon, comes to fetch me at the end of a year."

Thus Reuben remained in the tower with the princess Keziah, and every day their love for each other deepened. Before
long Reuben asked the princess to marry him, and when she
agreed, he wrote out a marriage contract which they signed, and
then they exchanged vows and called upon God and the angels
Michael and Gabriel to be their witnesses. And thus they became
man and wife.

So it was that by the end of the year Reuben and Keziah had
become the happy parents of a beautiful child, a boy, whom they
named Solomon. And when the ship arrived to take the princess
back to the palace in Jerusalem, King Solomon disembarked
from it, for he had come to bring her back himself. Imagine his
astonishment when he discovered that his daughter was married,
and was the mother of a fine child, his namesake! Solomon was
overwhelmed, and understood for the first time how vain it was
to try to prevent the decrees of Providence from taking place.
And Solomon also recognized Reuben's fine qualities, and that
he was a scholar and a scribe, and he did not oppose him, but
welcomed him as if he were his own son.

Thereupon King Solomon accompanied his daughter and
her husband and their child to Jerusalem, where a lavish wedding was held for the princess and her beloved to share their joy

with all of the inhabitants of the kingdom. And afterward they lived together in joy and peace for all the days of their lives.

Source: Palestine
c. Eighth–Tenth Centuries

King Solomon and Asmodeus

ow King David had had a long and full life, and the time had come when he saw that he would soon take leave of this world, and that his son, Solomon, would take his place as king. So King David called in Solomon and said to him: "Solomon, my son, now that I am growing old there is a secret I wish to share with you, a secret I have been saving for many years. It concerns a dream that came to me on the night you were born. In the dream I was following a path at night, when I came upon a ladder that reached from earth into heaven. I knew at once that I must ascend that ladder, for I longed to know where it would lead me. And as soon as I stepped on the first rung, I heard a melody like a distant harp, more beautiful than any I had ever heard. And with each rung I climbed, the melody grew clearer and drew me closer.

"When at last I reached the top rung of the ladder, I found myself in a city that resembled Jerusalem in every respect, except that the stones of the houses and the streets were made of gold. I wandered through those streets in a daze, marveling at this mirror image of Jerusalem in the heavens, until I reached a Temple of great splendor in the center of that golden city. Just then an old man in a white robe approached me, and said: 'Welcome, King David. We have been expecting your arrival.' I asked the old man who he was, and he told me that he was Abraham, our first Father. He took me and led me to the entrance of the Temple, and there we were met by two other men, also robed in white, our Fathers Isaac and Jacob. They took me through the Temple, and showed me each and every aspect of it, and when the splendor of the Temple had been revealed to me in all its glory, Abraham said: 'The heavenly Jerusalem is like the earthly Jerusalem in every respect, except that the Temple that has existed here since the creation of the world has yet to be built on earth. It is for you, King David, to bring the vision of this Temple back to the world of men and, when the time comes, to share it with your son, Solomon, who is about to be born. For it is destined that Solomon shall bring the Temple on earth into being.'"

Solomon was amazed when he heard these words, and he understood that his destiny had been revealed to him. From that moment on he thought only of the Temple he would construct in the center of the city, which would resemble the celestial Temple in every way, exactly as King David had described it, so that the heavenly city would finally find its mirror image on earth.

Not long after, King David left this world and rejoined the Fathers in Paradise. And when Solomon became king and set out to build the Temple, he soon realized that he must find a way to fashion the stones that would be used in building the altar, for it is forbidden in the Torah to fashion the altar with iron, since iron is used in forging weapons of war. Solomon called in his wise men and asked for their advice. One of them recalled the legend of a creature no larger than a grain of barley, known as the Shamir, which could cut through mountains the way a knife cuts through butter, but the man did not know if it really existed or not. Solomon then used his powers to conjure up two demons, one male and one female, to see if they knew where it might be found. When the demons had been brought forth and questioned, they told Solomon that the Shamir did exist, but that they did not know where it might be found. Their king, Asmodeus, however, surely would know this secret, and might even have the Shamir in his possession. Solomon then asked them where Asmodeus could be found, and they told him that his palace had been built on the highest peak of the Mountains of Darkness, in the Kingdom of Darkness. There Asmodeus had an underground cistern, from which he alone drew his drinking water. Every day he sealed that cistern and covered it with a huge boulder. Then he left to rule the Kingdom of Darkness. When he returned he would check the seal to be certain no one had tampered with it, and when he was thus assured, he removed the rock and satisfied his thirst.

Now that Solomon knew where Asmodeus could be found, he summoned Benaiah, his most trusted minister, and sent him with six men to the palace of Asmodeus, in order to capture the king of demons and to bring him back. To assist them in their quest, Solomon first whispered a secret to Benaiah, and then gave him four things: a chain on every link of which the Name of God was engraved; his magic ring, on which the Ineffable Name was also inscribed; a large skin of wine; and a bundle of wool. Then Benaiah journeyed until he reached the Mountains of Darkness, and he and his men climbed the highest peak, where they discovered the cistern of Asmodeus. There they hid themselves in trees until Asmodeus left his palace and came to the cistern. But when they saw him, Benaiah and his men were terrified, for Asmodeus was very terrible in appearance—he was a winged giant with the feet of a cock, with the beard of a he-goat, and with fire shooting forth from his nostrils. Yet they put their trust in the power of the Name, and they did not lose heart.

When Asmodeus had finished drinking from the cistern, he sealed and covered it as usual and took his leave. Then Benaiah and his men climbed down from the trees and bored a hole in the cistern, letting all the water run out. Then they closed the hole with the wool they had brought with them. After that they bored a second hole, higher up, and let the wine flow in through there. Finally they covered both holes with dirt, so as not to arouse the suspicions of Asmodeus. Then they concealed themselves in the trees, waiting for him to return.

When Asmodeus finally appeared many hours later, he lifted the stone off the top of the cistern, checked the seal and saw it was unbroken, and lowered the bucket to drink. But when he drew up the bucket he was astonished to find that the water had turned to wine. At first he was reluctant to drink it, but since he saw no sign of tampering and his thirst was very great, he finally drank a bucketful of the wine, and then another and yet another. In this way he became drunk and fell to the ground in a stupor, and soon was deep asleep. Benaiah and his men then came down from the branches and drew the chain around the hands of Asmodeus, and around his neck.

On waking, Asmodeus discovered that he had been chained, and roared with anger. But when he tried to break the chain, he found that he could not. Just then Benaiah and the others came out of hiding, and as Benaiah held up Solomon's magic ring they shouted: "The Name of your Master is upon you!" And when Asmodeus saw that he was under the power of the Name, he ceased to resist, for his power flourished only in the absence of everything holy. And so he let himself be led away.

Nor did Asmodeus try to escape his captors during all of the journey to Jerusalem, but he did act in peculiar ways, of which Benaiah took note. When they passed a wedding, Asmodeus wept, and when they came upon a man who asked a shoemaker to make him shoes that would last for seven years, he laughed. Later, when they met a blind man who had lost his way, Asmodeus directed him back to the proper path, and when they came upon a magician who bragged of his great skill, Asmodeus had nothing but contempt.

After they reached the palace, Benaiah told King Solomon of Asmodeus's strange behavior, and Solomon decided to wait three days before receiving him. On the first day the king instructed his guard to tell Asmodeus he could not see him because he was drunk. When Asmodeus heard this he said nothing, but took two bricks and placed them one on top of the other. When the guard reported this to Solomon, the king laughed and said: "By this he means to say that you should give me more to drink." The second day the guard was instructed to say Solomon could not see him because he had eaten too much and felt sleepy. When Asmodeus heard this he again said nothing, but took one brick down from the other. "By this," Solomon explained, "he means to say that you should give me less to eat." Then on the third day Asmodeus was brought before Solomon. As soon as he stood before him, Asmodeus marked off four ells on the floor and said: "Tell me, King Solomon, why do you seek to conquer the world? Is not the kingdom you rule enough for you? Do you seek to rule over the Kingdom of Darkness as well? Do you not know that before long all you will need will be the four ells of a single grave?"

But Solomon ignored these questions and said: "Tell me first, Asmodeus, what was the meaning of your strange behavior on the way to my kingdom?" To this Asmodeus replied: "When I saw the wedding, I wept, because I knew that the bridegroom had less than a week to live. I laughed at him who wanted his shoes to last for seven years, since he would not own them for seven days. I set the blind man on the right path because he was one of the perfect pious ones, whom even demons must respect. And I had only contempt for the magician who boasted of his powers, since he did not even know that a buried treasure lay at his feet. Now, King Solomon, if you please, let me know why you have gone to all the trouble of having me captured."

Then King Solomon said: "It is my fate and destiny to build a great Temple in this holy city to honor the King of the Universe, who rules over us all, even kings such as you and I, Asmodeus. But I cannot fashion the stones for the altar without the aid of the Shamir, and you, I have learned, have possession of it."

"No, I do not possess the Shamir," said Asmodeus. "But I know it was created at twilight on the eve of the first Sabbath, and left in the care of Rahab, Prince of the Sea, who has entrusted it to the White Eagle." Then Solomon asked: "But what does the White Eagle do with the Shamir?" Asmodeus replied: "It places the Shamir on the high mountains and the Shamir splits and forms canyons, where wild fruit trees grow, and from the fruit of these trees the White Eagle is able to feed its brood." Then Solomon said: "And where can the White Eagle be found?"

Asmodeus answered: "It makes its nest on the peak of the mountain where I make my home." When Solomon heard this, he directed Benaiah to return to the Mountains of Darkness, in order to recover the Shamir.

This time Benaiah went alone, and took with him only a plate of glass. And when he reached the nest of the White Eagle on the highest peak of the Mountains of Darkness, he covered it with the plate of glass. Then he hid himself behind a huge rock and waited. When the White Eagle returned to feed its brood and found it could see them, but could not reach them because of the glass, it flew off to its hiding place, and soon returned with a small object in its beak. This was the Shamir, which it then set down on the plate of glass. At that moment Benaiah came out shouting and making a great clamor, and so frightened the White Eagle that it flew off. Then Benaiah took the Shamir, lifted the plate of glass off the nest, and returned triumphantly to his king. So it was that King Solomon was able to fashion the stones of the altar, and thus complete the House of the Lord in the Holy Land that was the mirror image of the Temple in the celestial city on high.

Source: Babylon
c. Fifth Century

The Beggar King

uring the construction of the Temple in Jerusalem, King Solomon kept Asmodeus, the king of demons, as his prisoner, to prevent any of the forces of evil, which Asmodeus commanded, from interfering with the building of the Temple. When the Temple was completed, King Solomon called in Asmodeus, and told him that he was prepared to set him free if Asmodeus would first reveal a single secret to him. Asmodeus said: "Tell me first, O king, what secret it is that you want to know." Solomon said: "Of a great many mysteries am I master, Asmodeus, of the language of the birds, of the secrets of the wind, and of the mysteries of the Ineffable Name. But there is one secret that has eluded me so far—that is the secret of Illusion. And it is of great importance that I learn this secret, for as king I often am called upon to distinguish truth from illusion."

Asmodeus nodded when he heard these words from King Solomon, and he said: "I agree, King Solomon, to reveal this secret to you. But I cannot do so while I stand here in these chains, nor unless you surrender the ring you wear, inscribed with the Ineffable Name. For in the presence of the Name my lips are sealed." When Solomon heard this, he found the words of Asmodeus plausible, and for the sake of learning the secret he had Asmodeus released from his chains, and surrendered his ring to him. But no sooner was Asmodeus free and in possession of the ring than he flung it a great distance, so that it was soon lost on the horizon, and sank into the sea. Then the king of demons approached King Solomon, who stood before him unprotected, and setting one of his vast wings into the heavens, and the other into the earth, he picked Solomon up from where he sat on his throne, and hurled him hundreds of miles.

Now Solomon flew through the air like an arrow, and at last fell down in a field in a foreign country. When he stood up he was like a drunken man who has lost his way, who does not know where he is going or what he is doing. He wandered this way for a long time, until he became thirsty, and at last he came to a pool. But when he bent down to drink and saw his reflection in the water, it was not the reflection of a great king he saw, but that of a miserable beggar. For the light that had lit up his face had vanished, and there was no longer a crown upon his head. Overwhelmed with the vastness of his loss, Solomon lay down in sorrow and slept. And while he slept he dreamed that the evening star, the first to be seen, the very ruler of the heavens at night, fell from its place and sank like a meteor into the sea. When Solomon awoke from this dream he trembled, for he recognized its meaning. And in the morning he set off on his wanderings, which lasted for many years.

So it was that, deprived of his kingdom, King Solomon made his way begging for his daily bread. At first, it is true, he insisted he was a king everywhere he went. But those who saw him in his rags paid no attention, and believed him to be merely another beggar gone mad. Then, after three years of wandering, Solomon reached the kingdom ruled by King Ammon. One day, while he stood in the streets of the capital city, the royal cook passed by him, bearing baskets laden with food of all kinds. The beggar king offered to help carry these baskets, and in this way he found favor with the royal cook. For many weeks after that Solomon worked as a laborer in the king's kitchen, until one day he pleaded with the cook, who had become his friend, to let him prepare the royal meal. The royal cook granted his wish, and Solomon prepared a sumptuous feast. When King Ammon tasted this food, he summoned the royal cook and said: "Who was it who cooked this food? For never before have you brought me food so exquisite." Then the cook admitted that the meal had been prepared by Solomon, and thereupon the king ordered that Solomon alone should prepare his meals.

As the head royal cook, Solomon soon came to the attention of Naamah, the daughter of the king. And before long Naamah recognized that she loved Solomon, and wanted him for her husband. Solomon, too, fell in love with the princess, and at last a day came when she announced to her father that she wished them to be wed. But when King Ammon heard this he was consumed with anger that his daughter, the princess, should choose a cook for her husband, when princes from all over the world were at her feet. And in his anger he commanded that the couple should be taken to a desert, and left there to die.

So it happened that Solomon and Naamah found themselves alone in a vast wilderness. They had no supplies of food or water, and the sun overhead was like a fire burning on their bodies. All they possessed were the clothes on their backs and the walking stick that Solomon carried with him. But it occurred to Solomon that this staff might serve as a divining rod, and by using it in this way he found an underground stream, which flowed beneath the sand. There he dug a well, which the clear waters of the stream filled with fresh water, and it was there that Solomon and Naamah made their home. With the fruit they found, they sustained themselves, and with the stones they gathered Solomon built a stone hut in that place, and digging furrows into the earth he used the waters of the stream to fertilize the land. There Solomon planted every species of fruit which was to be found scattered throughout the wilderness, including every variety of cactus which bore fruit.

So it was that over a period of years, Solomon and his wife established a home in that desert, and turned it into an oasis. Together they were the parents of three children, two boys and a girl, whom they brought up there. In time Solomon forgot about his life as a king, and came to think of himself as one who made his home in the desert. Nor did he miss his former life, for his days were full, and his nights were peaceful, while as king he had passed many sleepless nights trying to reach just decisions. In this way many years passed, twelve in all.

Then one day it happened that from out of nowhere a dark cloud covered the desert as far as they could see in every direction, and the rains poured down in great sheets. In a short time a great wave was rolling through the desert, and when this wave struck Solomon's hut it tore it to pieces, and carried off Solomon's wife at the same time. Solomon fought off the waves, with one child held in his left arm, and the other two in his right. A moment later another wave struck them, and at that moment the child in his left arm was torn away from his grasp. Solomon reached for that child, and in this way he lost his grip on the other two, so that all three children were lost at the same time. Then the world went dark around him, and he was carried a great distance by the currents.

When Solomon awoke he found that his arms were chained. Looking up, he discovered that he had been captured by thieves, who had found him unconscious after the flood. The thieves took Solomon with them, to sell as a slave, but Solomon did not care that this was his fate. He was filled with grief at the loss of his family. So it was that Solomon was sold as a slave to a caravan, which brought him across the burning desert, and finally sold him as a slave to a blacksmith in a foreign kingdom.

As the slave of a blacksmith, it was the duty of Solomon to work the bellows, so that the fire would continue to burn, and since Solomon was a steady worker, the blacksmith soon came to trust and respect him. Now this blacksmith had a son who wished to become a goldsmith, and who was already quite accomplished at this craft. It happened that among Solomon's many skills he was a highly accomplished goldsmith, and in his free time he taught the son of the blacksmith, whose skills grew so considerable he was able to take a position in the court of the king.

Once, when the young goldsmith was visiting his father, he

spoke to Solomon, who begged him to let him fashion a treasure for the king. The son agreed, and in this way Solomon came to fashion a golden dove, set with rubies, moonstones, emeralds, turquoise, mother-of-pearl, and diamonds. In the beak of the dove he placed a golden twig, and from the twig he hung three golden bells like buds. Now when the goldsmith presented this treasure to the king, he was overwhelmed with its magnificence and the great skill of its creator. He asked the goldsmith how it happened that this treasure was so superior to anything he had previously created. Then the goldsmith confessed that it had been created by a slave who worked for his father, the black-smith. So it was that the king ordered Solomon to be purchased from the blacksmith, and made chief goldsmith in his palace.

In this way Solomon came to the attention of the king, who recognized that he possessed great wisdom. Little by little, the king came to Solomon to discuss the affairs of his kingdom, and to seek his advice in matters great and small. Now it happened at that time that the king's daughter was possessed by a dream that haunted her night after night. In this dream she saw a man climbing into a cave high in a cliff that faced a cove shaped like a half moon. She never saw the face of the climber but, as often happens in dreams, her eyes were able to see him as he entered the cave, and she watched him take out of a crevice in the wall a jewel of immense beauty, illumined from within, as if by a flame.

Now the princess became possessed by the idea that she must somehow make that jewel her own, and while she pined away over it, her health declined, and she refused to leave her chamber in the palace. At last there came a night when she was able to glimpse the face of the man who climbed up the cliff in the recurring dream, and the face she saw was that of Solomon.

When the princess reported this dream to her father, the king, he understood at once that he must ask his wise goldsmith, Solomon, to set off on a quest to find that cave, and to bring back the jewel his daughter craved so terribly. Nor did Solomon hesi-tate to undertake this task, but set out at once. And how did he proceed? He remembered that the cove in the dream of the prin-cess had been shaped like a half moon. It was there that she had envisioned the cliff, with the cave in its side, which he must seek out.

So it was that Solomon journeyed for many years, and at each place he came to he asked if there was a cove shaped like a half moon, but nowhere had anyone heard of such a place. Then one day Solomon heard a child call out to another in the street: "Let us go to the cove of the half moon." Now when Solomon heard these words he could hardly believe his luck, and he went to the child and asked him if he knew the way to such a cove. The boy told him that he did, and he led Solomon to that place.

When they reached the crescent-shaped cove, and Solomon saw the cliff and the cave in its side, he was delighted, and he gave the child a piece of silver and then set off to climb the cliff. It took him over an hour to reach the cave, high up the cliff, and when he crawled inside he was worn out. Still, he searched through every crevice in the cave, but he could not find anything resembling the jewel in the dream of the princess. All he found was a rough rock in one crevice, and there was nothing to distinguish that rock from any other. But since there was no other clue, Solomon struck the rock against the wall of the cave, and it broke in two. At that instant a beautiful, glowing jewel fell from inside the rock, and Solomon knew his quest was complete. Putting the jewel in a pouch that was strapped to his body, he lay down in the cave and fell asleep.

So tired was Solomon from his efforts that he slept for several hours. When he woke up he found that the cave was no longer lit from the light outside, for the sky had grown dark. Then Solomon went to the entrance of the cave, and when he looked down he saw that the tide had come in, and that the waters had risen, and lapped near the entrance of the cave. Just then another wave came in and started to flood the cave, and Solomon realized he was in great danger of drowning. He clung to a rock as the next wave washed in, and as it started to recede he threw himself from the entrance of the cave into the waters, and in this way he was carried a great distance.

When the wave at last set Solomon down, he saw that it had

returned him to the kingdom from which he had set out on the quest for the glowing jewel. With great joy and relief, Solomon hurried to the palace of the king, and presented the jewel and reported all that had happened on his quest. And when the princess saw the jewel of her dreams her sadness turned to joy, and her recovery was swift and complete.

Now the king of that kingdom was so grateful to Solomon for making possible the recovery of the princess that he told him he could have whatever he wanted. Solomon then told him, for the first time, his true history, and the fact that he himself was once a great king. So it was that Solomon asked only for his freedom, in order to recover his kingdom. The king granted his wish at once, and ordered a ship to be made ready and well stocked for the voyage.

That night there was a great feast and many happy toasts were offered. Solomon's ship was launched the next day, and he left to search for his lost kingdom. To occupy himself on the long voyage, Solomon decided that he would take up fishing. And the first time he cast his rod into the water, he found at the end of the line a magnificent golden fish, unlike any he had ever seen. Solomon was so delighted with this fish that he decided he would not entrust it to the ship's cook; rather, he would prepare it himself. But when Solomon cut the fish open, he was astonished to find in its belly his own magic ring, engraved with the Ineffable Name, which Asmodeus had cast into the sea. Solomon rejoiced to recover the ring, and placed it on his finger, and in an instant he found himself seated on his throne in Jerusalem, with the demon Asmodeus standing before him. And Asmodeus said: "We have been waiting for you for almost an hour, O king. Tell me, now, have you learned something of the secret of Illusion?"

Solomon was staggered to learn that he had been absent only such a short time. It had seemed like many years to him. But when he asked his ministers, they confirmed that barely an hour had passed since his departure. Then Solomon commanded from his throne that Asmodeus be set free, since he had fulfilled Solomon's request. And no sooner did Solomon say this than Asmodeus flew away, and he was not seen again in that kingdom during the rest of King Solomon's reign, in which Solomon demonstrated a wisdom unmatched among men, and an evenhanded mercy that was remarked upon by all.

Source: Babylon
c. Fifth Century

The Eternal Light

ow it was well known that in the palace of King Solomon there were to be found treasures unmatched in all the world, so precious and unique were they. And whenever a merchant who sold precious items came from another kingdom, he was taken directly to the king. In this way Solomon had gathered in his palace the most rare and treasured vessels, which had been handed down from earlier ages.

So it was that King Solomon was very curious when the Queen of Sheba told him she had heard of a treasure more precious than any to be found in his palace. Solomon laughed, for he did not believe this was possible. Still, he asked her to describe this treasure, and she said it was a precious glass vessel illumined from within by an eternal light, and that anyone who stood in its aura was filled with a sense of peace. King Solomon asked her if she had ever seen this treasure, and she confessed she had not, although she had often heard of it. Nor had she sought it out, since she did not yearn for a life of peace.

Now Solomon could not rest after this, for he longed to know if such a vessel truly existed, and he was determined that he must somehow obtain it, for it would serve as the jewel in the crown of his treasures. Thereupon Solomon called in his minister, Benaiah, and told him to gather ten men together, and to set out on a quest to discover if such a vessel of light, illumined from within, was anywhere to be found. Solomon gave Benaiah his magic ring, with the Ineffable Name of God engraved on it, in case its assistance might be needed. Nor did Benaiah delay any longer, but he set out at once to undertake this quest, for he recognized how important it was for his king.

So it was that Benaiah and his men began their journey by traveling south, toward the kingdom of the Queen of Sheba. And wherever they went they asked everyone they met if they had ever heard of such a vessel of light, but none of them had. At last they traveled so far south they reached a desert, and the men wanted to turn back, for the desert was so vast and barren it seemed to them they must have reached the end of the world. It was a dangerous desert, filled with snakes and scorpions and many low-flying birds looking for prey. But Benaiah insisted they had to search in the desert as well, for no stone could be left unturned in their quest.

In this way Benaiah and his men walked for thirty-nine days in the desert, until their supply of food had almost been exhausted, and only a small amount of water remained. And by then even Benaiah was afraid that the desert was boundless, and that they were lost there in vain. Then it happened on the fortieth day that they reached an oasis, where they found a fresh spring and many carob and date trees with ripe fruit. There they refreshed themselves, and gave thanks to the Lord for having rescued them from certain death. And after they had eaten and rested, Benaiah and the men traced the stream to its source, for they wondered whence it might flow in such a barren place. So it was that they traced it from the oasis into the desert, where it spouted forth from a great rock, which stood by itself among all the barren waste, the water flowing from it as if it were endless. And in the other side of that rock they found the mouth of a cave, and entered there and made their way through it. And when they emerged from that cave they found themselves in another kingdom.

Not long afterward they saw campfires, and when they approached close enough they heard the speech of the inhabitants. They were amazed to hear them speak in Hebrew. Then they did not hesitate, but came forth and revealed themselves, and in this way they discovered one of the ten lost tribes of Israel, that of the Levites, the children of Moses, which had lost contact with their brothers in the days of the wandering in the wilderness in the time of Moses. And they were as amazed to hear Benaiah and his men speaking Hebrew as were Benaiah and the others to discover them. And after they had prayed and eaten, Benaiah asked them to describe what their lives were like. He learned that they were strong in faith and well-versed in the Torah. They lived to one hundred and twenty years of age, and no son of theirs died in his father's lifetime. There were no robbers among them, nor wild beasts, nor demons, and they did not lock their houses at night. They also had six springs whose waters gathered into one lake, and from this they irrigated their land. And the lake teemed with all kinds of fish, and they also had all kinds of fruit trees that grew in their orchards. And for each measure they sowed, they reaped a hundred.

From all that they told him, Benaiah saw that they were saintly, and stood in the sanctity of Moses. That is why the Holy One, blessed be He, had given them such abundance. Still, they had been isolated for so long, and were curious to know how their fellow Jews were faring. So Benaiah told them of King Solomon and his kingdom, and of the wondrous Temple he had built in the holy city of Jerusalem, and of the lives of the Jews who lived there, and they followed his every word with wonder. After this Benaiah told them of his quest, and asked if they had ever heard of the eternal light he sought. And, to his amazement, they had all heard of it, for they had a legend among them that such a vessel had illumined the Tabernacle which Moses had carried through the desert. But like the Tabernacle itself, it too had long been lost, and none of them knew what had become of it. Then Benaiah spoke to the High Priest among them, who served as their leader, and asked that he join them on their quest, so that the eternal light of the Tabernacle could be recovered and cast its aura of peace over both of their kingdoms, which could at last be reunited. And so it was that this High Priest agreed to accompany them.

Now the name of this High Priest was Aaron, just as Aaron was the name of his ancestor, the brother of Moses. And he told them the legend of how that vessel of light had come into being. And this is the story that Aaron the High Priest told: "Once, long ago, there was a kingdom which had been blessed with a sacred light which pervaded the entire realm. And each of the inhabitants of that kingdom knew peace in his heart, for peace reigned supreme in its presence, and everything flourished. Then, somehow it happened—no one knew why—that the soothsayers and astrologers of that kingdom divined that a time was shortly to come when the kingdom and its precious light would cease to exist.

"Then the king of that kingdom ordered that a way be sought to preserve at least some of that enchanted light, for it was their greatest blessing, so that it would continue to exist after the kingdom had disappeared. And all of the king's sorcerers and wise men consulted together in the spirit of peace, since they lived directly beneath that divine presence. Yet they were unable to find a solution, for how can light be captured? But then one of them recalled seeing the marvelous work of a craftsman who created treasures out of glass that he himself blew into many astonishing and remarkable shapes. It was said there was nothing to be found in this world that he was unable to give form to with his breath. And all of the other sorcerers and wise men agreed that he might well be the one who could succeed in finding a way to preserve the precious light, so that at least a small part of it could be saved.

"So it was that a messenger was sent forth to bring this craftsman to the palace of the king, and when he arrived no expense was spared so that he might succeed in his task. Before long the master craftsman had begun to seek ways to capture the light in his glass creations, but although he succeeded in capturing the air, the light eluded him. Then one night he was shown in a dream the secret of how to capture light, a secret that has since been lost for many generations. All we know is that he acted on his dream, and utilized the secret, and succeeded in capturing the light in ten perfect vessels, which emerged from his lips in succession. And he brought those ten vessels before the king, and demonstrated that they were illumined from within, for they continued to glow in the dark. And all who stood in the aura of those vessels of light were overcome by a feeling of peace that took root in their souls.

"Now by the time the ten vessels of light had been formed, only a few days remained before that kingdom was destined to come to its end. Then the king called in his sons, the three princes, and bade them make ready the finest ship in the king's fleet, and to set sail on the Sea of Darkness, beyond the region illumined by the sacred light, where no one had ever dared to go. And he bade them to seek out a kingdom beyond their own, in which they might establish a new life, where the vessels of light, which he entrusted to them, might survive into another age, beyond their own.

"So it was that the three princes set sail, and had passed only beyond the circle of light that contained their kingdom and entered into the realm of darkness, when they saw all trace of their kingdom disappear, as if it had been only a mirage, and darkness was everywhere to be seen. Now it would have been impossible to steer the ship in that darkness, and they would have had to abandon themselves to the currents of fate. But fortunately they had been blessed with the ten vessels of light, and when they carried them from the hold onto the deck, the darkness around them was illuminated, and they were able to sail surrounded by an aura of light.

"In this way the princes were able to discover an island, which was not recorded on any map, for no map had ever been made of the Sea of Darkness. And the people of that island had lived their lives in darkness, for they had never seen light. Nevertheless, they had been born with eyes, although they did not know how to open them, for they had never been used. But when the ship of the three princes cast its aura around the island, the eyes of the people opened, and they hurried to discover the source of this great blessing, and that is how they found the three princes, and invited the eldest to serve as their king. In this way the royal family was re-established, as the princes found lovely maidens among these people to take for their wives, and they were soon rewarded with beautiful children. And so too was the precious light preserved on that small island, and men were once more able to find shelter in its divine presence.

"That island kingdom existed for many ages, and flourished in its aura of abundance. Then its wise men detected signs that revealed the coming of the end of its era. The king of that kingdom, who had descended from the eldest of the three princes, called in his two younger brothers, and directed them to set out in the ship that their ancestors, the first king and his brothers, had sailed in, which had been carefully preserved by each of the succeeding generations. And this king directed them to take with them one of the ten vessels of light. For he feared the people would despair in that terrible time if more than one of the sacred vessels were taken away. And the two princes set sail, and had not gone very far when they saw the island disappear. And when that happened, the nine vessels that had remained behind were all shattered, and their sparks were scattered across the Sea of Darkness, where some became the stars, and others clustered together, and in this way there came to be a sun that shone in the day, and a moon that illumined the night."

Then Aaron, the High Priest, who had told this tale, explained that the fate of the two princes was unknown, and all that was certain was that the last vessel of light had somehow come into the possession of Moses, who had discovered it beneath the burning bush. For this light shone from below, illuminating the bush, and making it appear to be burning, although it was not consumed. And eventually Moses had placed that eternal light inside the Tabernacle that the Israelites carried through the wilderness. But since the time of Moses the vessel of light had again been lost. And Aaron, the High Priest, told them of a legend that held that this eternal light had become hidden at the source of the River Sambatyon. But in order to reach the mouth of this river, it was necessary to cross it. Yet this was impossible for them to do, since the river was too wild to be crossed during all of the week, throwing up rocks as high as a house, and spreading a mist as thick as a fog. Nor could they cross it on the Sabbath, although Friday at sunset the waters would subside and disappear, and it would resemble a lake of snow-white sand. And why could they not cross it then? Because to do so would be to desecrate the Sabbath, and this, of course, could not be done. And at the close of every Sabbath it would resume its torrent of rushing water, stones, and sand.

Aaron also explained to Benaiah and his men that since the lost tribe could not cross the River Sambatyon on the Sabbath, any more than they could on the other days of the week, when the waters were running, they had given its existence much thought, since it perpetuated their exile. In general there were two schools of opinion about its purpose. There were those who insisted that the river had been formed to remind them of the unchanging nature of the eternal laws, and to assure them that they had not been forgotten in their exile. Then there were those who had concluded the river had been created to keep them in exile from their brothers, since the Sabbath is also their day of rest. Those who regarded the river from this point of view were certain the exile would end on the day when the river stopped flowing and they were permitted to come across.

Finally Aaron, the High Priest, told Benaiah and his men the legend of the origin of the River Sambatyon. For that river had come into being only in the time of Moses—in fact, it was said to pour forth from the rock that Moses had struck in the desert with his staff, from which waters flowed. For those waters had never stopped flowing, and from them had emerged that remarkable river, which had become impassable during the week, just as it was on the Sabbath.

Now Benaiah listened to these tales with fascination. And when he heard about the rock from which the waters of that river flowed, he recalled at once the rock he and his men had found in the desert, with water spouting from it, and the cave in the other side of the rock, which had led them to that kingdom. And he suddenly realized that the rock from which the water flowed must be that which had been struck by Moses, and that in discovering that rock and cave, they must have stumbled on the way to cross beneath the River Sambatyon, for that was the only way it could be crossed. None of the lost tribe had ever detected the entrance to that cave that was to be found in their kingdom, for it was too well hidden. But Benaiah and his men had discovered the cave from the other side.

Then Benaiah led the High Priest Aaron to that cave, and he accompanied them to the entrance. But when he was about to enter the cave, he saw before him a flaming sword that turned in every direction, and he jumped back in fear, although, to his amazement, the others saw nothing. Then Aaron understood that the way was barred to him, and that the Holy One had not yet declared the exile of the lost tribe to be at an end. Therefore Aaron and Benaiah took leave of each other, and the High Priest returned to his people, asking only that Benaiah reveal the existence of the lost tribe to the rest of the world.

It was then, before they proceeded to return through the cave, that Benaiah wondered if the vessel of light might be hidden in that cave, as the legend had it. Therefore he took out the magic ring that King Solomon had given him, on which the Ineffable Name of God had been engraved, and he put it on his finger. It was his hope that the ring might signal the presence of the sacred vessel in the event that it was truly hidden in that place. After this Benaiah and his men returned through those secret caverns that ran beneath the River Sambatyon.

Now for most of the way Benaiah did not notice any sign, but when they had almost reached the other end of the cave, Benaiah felt the ring gently pull him in one direction, and before long it led him like a magnet to a rock-covered crevice, and when Benaiah pulled away the stones that covered it, the cave was suddenly filled with light—for he had been led to the right place, and there, for the first time since the era of Moses, a man stood in the divine presence of that sacred vessel of light. But no sooner did he take it in his hand than the floor of the cave began to rumble, as though from an earthquake. Then Benaiah hurried out of the cave, with his men close behind, and he had just emerged with the eternal light safe in his hands, when the ground shook, and the entrance to the cave collapsed, so that it could no longer be found.

Benaiah realized that the only route to the lost tribe had been cut off, and that the tribe would remain in exile until the day the River Sambatyon would permit them to come across. But he was greatly relieved that at least the eternal light had been saved, and that their quest was almost complete. With the light to guide them, Benaiah and his men succeeded in only six days to return the distance that had taken forty to travel without it. And on the seventh day they rested in Jerusalem, where King Solomon shared the peace of the Sabbath in the glow of that sacred vessel of light. And as soon as the building of the Temple was completed, Solomon placed the eternal light in the Tabernacle. And that light shone in the Holy of Holies, and in this way shed its light of peace over all Jerusalem. And there it remained until the Temple was destroyed by those who were blind to its light.

And what was the fate of that sacred vessel of light? No one can say for certain. Most assume that when the Temple was destroyed, it too was shattered, and its sparks of light scattered throughout the Holy Land, where they are found in abundance to this day. But there are still a few who believe that the eternal light was saved by the prophet Jeremiah, who concealed it in a cave along with the other sacred Temple vessels, where it still remains hidden.

Source: Palestine
c. Sixteenth Century

The Mysterious Palace

ow King Solomon possessed a carpet with intricate designs, interwoven with fine gold and green silk. It is said that he hung this carpet in his bedroom, where it served as a mirror in which the future could be read. But whenever he wished to travel to a distant place, it was only necessary to take down the carpet and place it on the roof of the palace, and as soon as Solomon spoke the Ineffable Name, it would rise up in the air.

One day King Solomon invited his adviser, Asaph ben Berachiah, and Ramirat, a demon prince, to accompany him on a journey. They seated themselves on the flying carpet, Solomon pronounced the Name, and the winds picked up the carpet, making it rise higher and higher, until they flew through the heavens with the earth far beneath them. As they sailed through the air, Solomon thought to himself: "There is none like me in the world, for the Holy One, blessed be He, has given me wisdom and understanding and has set me to rule all of his creations." But no sooner did these thoughts cross Solomon's mind than the wind ceased, and the flying carpet began to fall. Then Solomon and the others grew terrified they would tumble to the earth from that height, and Solomon shouted to the wind: "Return, O wind, return!" And the wind replied: "First you must return to your God and not be proud, and then I shall return to you." And the words of the wind made Solomon ashamed of himself. And when he grew ashamed, the wind returned, and they continued their flight.

So it was that they flew through the heavens for ten days and nights, and it was then that they glimpsed a glorious citadel far below, and Solomon was very curious to know what it was. So he said to the wind: "Descend," and the flying carpet descended beside the citadel. Now the palace was even more beautiful when they stood beside it, but it was also very mysterious, for not a soul was to be seen anywhere. Solomon and his companions walked around it, and they were amazed that there was not any gate or entrance to be found, and this too seemed very strange.

Thereupon Solomon turned to Ramirat, the prince of demons, and said to him: "Call upon the hosts of demons, and let them determine if there are any living creatures to be found here." This Ramirat did, and soon there were demons searching everywhere, but they found nothing. Then Solomon said: "Let them also ascend to the roof, and search there as well." This the demons did, and when they returned they reported that although no man was to be found there, there was a giant eagle who had made its nest in that place. Solomon then commanded that the eagle be brought to him, and the demons departed and shortly returned accompanied by the noble bird.

Then Solomon greeted the eagle and said: "What is your name?" "Elenad," said the eagle. "And how old are you?" asked the king. "Seven hundred years old," came the reply. "Tell me," said Solomon, "is there any entrance to this palace, for there is none we have found." "My lord king," said the eagle, "there is none that I know of, but perhaps my brother, who is two hundred years older than I am, could be of help to you."

Then Solomon summoned the second eagle, who turned out to be even larger than the first. The king greeted it and said: "What is your name?" And the eagle replied: "Aleoph." "And how old are you?'' asked Solomon. "Nine hundred years old,'' was the reply. "And do you know of any entrance to this citadel?'' The eagle answered: "I do not know of such an entrance, my lord king, but I have a brother who is four hundred years older than I am, and perhaps he will know.''

Then Solomon summoned the third eagle, and it was even larger than the other two. Solomon greeted the eagle and said: "What is your name?'' "Altamar,'' the eagle replied. "And how old are you?'' asked Solomon. "Thirteen hundred years old,'' said the eagle. "And do you know of any entrance to this mysterious palace?'' The eagle answered: "I do not know of any such entrance, but I do remember my father, the king of eagles, telling me that there is an entrance on the western side, although it has been covered by dust during all the ages it has been abandoned.''

Solomon was very glad to hear this, and without hesitation he immediately summoned the winds, who were at his command, and ordered them to blow against the western side of the citadel. The winds blew once, twice, and three times, and thus removed all the dust that had accumulated there, so that the entrance was finally revealed. It was a very large gate of iron, which had been greatly worn down over the ages. On it there was a lock on which was written: "Let it be known to you, sons of men, that we dwelt in this palace for many a long year. Yet when the famine came, we ground our pearls instead of wheat, but they could not sustain us. Therefore we have left this palace to the eagles for all the days to come, and no man shall be permitted to enter here unless he is a king. But if this be the case, and he desires to enter, let him dig to the right of this entrance. There he will find a glass box, and within it the keys to this gate and the doors beyond it.''

In this way Solomon came into possession of the golden keys that fit the doors of that palace. He first opened the iron gate, and found beyond it a gate of silver, and beyond that a gate of gold. Inside the golden gate he found a pavilion made of precious stones, with a dome of ruby, and a courtyard paved with bricks of gold and silver. There, in the center of the pavilion,

Solomon saw a large silver scorpion. He lifted it up, and found there an entrance that led down golden stairs to rooms that were underground. Solomon and the others descended those stairs, and they found stored there all kinds of pearls, jewels, and golden objects in great profusion. And at one end of the room there was another door that was locked, and on the lock was written: "The king of this palace once lived here in power and might, and reigned upon his throne. Yet his hour came to perish, and so he did, and the crown fell off his head. Enter here, and look around and wonder!"

Then Solomon took out the golden keys and opened that door, and there inside he saw a statue seated at a golden table. Now Solomon and the others were astonished when they saw this, for anyone who looked at that statue would think it was alive. Solomon approached the statue and reached out his hand to touch it, and when he did, fire and smoke suddenly shot forth from its nostrils, and it cried out in a giant voice: "Awake, ye children of Satan, for King Solomon has come to destroy you!" Then there was a frightful rumbling and great outcry, and all of the statues in the room started to move, as if they were alive once more, with a terrible look in their eyes. But King Solomon was not afraid, and pronounced the Ineffable Name, and all at once the statues grew silent, and fell upon their faces with a loud crash.

Then Solomon approached the statue that was seated, which had also grown silent, and took from around its neck a silver tablet on which words were written. But Solomon, who was familiar with seventy languages and with the languages of the birds and the beasts, did not recognize that writing. He turned to Asaph and Ramirat and said: "You know very well how much we have toiled in order to reach this palace, and now I do not know how to read what is written here."

Then Ramirat, the demon prince, spoke and said: "Let me see if I can decipher this language, O king." And he took the silver tablet from Solomon, and looked at it and said: "Yes, this is a language that has been lost to men for many centuries. But it is still known among the demons. I will tell you what it says here." And these were the words that he read: "I, Shadad ben Ad, ruled over a thousand times thousand cities, and rode on a thousand times thousand horses, and slew a thousand times thousand warriors. Yet when the Angel of Death came, I could not prevail against him."

And it was also written there: "Whosoever may read this message, let him remember that in the end all things must perish, and that nothing remains of a man's possessions but a good name."

And when he heard these words, Solomon understood why he had been led to that palace on the flying carpet, and that what had happened to that king would come to pass for him as well. And he also understood that his purpose in life should not be to amass possessions or wisdom, but, above all, to make a good name for himself. And so he returned to Jerusalem greatly humbled, and never forgot what he had learned that day.

Source: Palestine
c. Eighth–Tenth Centuries

The Flight of the Eagle

ong ago there was a rabbi in the city of Guadalajara in Spain who was often called upon to pray for barren women to be blessed with a child. Now this rabbi and his wife were themselves childless, and his wife could not understand why he did not pray for a child of their own. But each time the rabbi's wife would ask him about this, he would reply: "If it is God's will, there is no need for a prayer." At last, however, the rabbi decided to seek a reply to his wife's burning question, and he immersed himself in the *mikvah* seven times, and prayed that their destiny as parents be revealed.

That very night an angel appeared to the rabbi in a dream and said: "You are destined to be blessed with a son, but when he reaches the age of eighteen he will disappear, and it will be many years before you see him again." Now when the rabbi awoke, he told his dream to his wife; on the one hand they were greatly relieved to learn they would have a child of their own, but on the other they were frightened of his fate. But the rabbi reminded his wife that everything God does is for a purpose, and if that was to be their son's fate, there was surely a reason for it. And after a year the rabbi's wife gave birth to a son, and he was circumcised as a Jew according to the laws of Moses, and they named him Shlomo, which is Hebrew for Solomon.

His father raised Shlomo so that he was very well versed in the Torah, the Talmud, and the other sacred texts, and he could be counted among the scholars. So it was that time passed, until the boy reached the age of eighteen. In the summer it was very hot, and Shlomo went up to the roof of their house to study. Then one day, while he was there, an eagle of gigantic proportions passed over their house and swept up the boy in his talons and carried him off. And with the terrified boy held tightly in its grip, the eagle flew with him until they arrived at the city of Madrid, the capital of Spain, and there the eagle dropped the boy on the roof of the palace of the king of Spain.

Now at that time the king was asleep, and when he heard a loud thumping on the palace roof he was very frightened, for he feared it might be the sound of a cannon, and that the palace was under attack. He quickly ordered his servants up to the roof to see what had happened, and they found, to their amazement, the boy Shlomo, who had fainted. And when the servants came back and reported what they had found, the king himself went up to the roof, and when he saw Shlomo's face shining like an angel of God, the king tried to wake him up.

At last, when Shlomo opened his eyes, he found himself lying on a bed in a luxurious chamber, and he did not know where he was. After all, only a few hours earlier he had been studying peacefully on the roof of his father's house, and now he found himself surrounded by opulence. So it was that Shlomo was truly amazed to learn that the eagle had carried him to the palace of the king of Spain. In reply to the king's questions, he told the king that he was a Hebrew of the Spanish city of Guadalajara many miles away. And after this the king had food brought for him, but Shlomo explained to the king that the only food he could eat had to be kosher, and the king said: "Tell us what you need, and we shall bring it to you." And Shlomo replied: "I will need new dishes and all kinds of vegetables and fruits, and I will prepare the meal myself." The king ordered that these things should be brought, and Shlomo cooked the meal with his own hands and ate it. And the king was greatly taken with the fine qualities of the boy, and had a house built for him inside the palace garden, furnished with everything he might need.

Now when Shlomo's parents did not find him in the house, they called for him to come down from the roof. But when he did not reply, they went up there and discovered that he was gone. They searched for him everywhere, and at last they realized that the prophecy of the angel had come true, and that he had disappeared. Then they greatly mourned over losing him, although they did not abandon all hope, for the angel had also prophesied that one day he would return.

Meanwhile the king came to visit Shlomo every day, for he greatly enjoyed his company. For the truth is that while this king had a very lovely daughter, whom he greatly loved, he did not have a son, and Shlomo had many of the fine qualities he had hoped to find in a son of his own. So it was that he soon recognized that Shlomo was unhappy, and he asked him what it was that he was lacking. Then Shlomo explained that he had always devoted himself to the study of the Torah, but in that place he did not have the books he needed to study. The king then had him make a list of the books he wanted, and he sent a servant to a nearby city in Spain where there were Jews, and the servant brought the books back for Shlomo. After that Shlomo spent all of his time studying the books and memorizing them, and he was happy in his heart.

One night the king's daughter could not sleep and took a walk in the palace garden. And there she saw a house in which candles were still burning. She wondered who might live there, and when she came closer she heard the voice of Shlomo chanting prayers. Then she went up to the window and peered inside, and when she saw Shlomo's handsome face she fell in love with him at first sight. Then the princess tapped on the window to draw his attention, but Shlomo did not stop praying. Twice more she tapped on the window, but Shlomo pretended not to hear anything. Finally, when he had completed his praying, she tapped again, and he said: "Who is there?" And she replied: "It is I, the daughter of the king." And when Shlomo learned who it was, he hurried to the door and let her enter. And when he saw how beautiful the princess was, he too lost his heart. Then she asked him: "Why did you not reply when I tapped on the window the first three times?" And Shlomo said: "I was afraid that you might be a demon trying to tempt me away from my studies." Then the princess told him that she would never do such a thing. In fact, she asked Shlomo if she might study with him, and he agreed to become her teacher.

After this the princess came every day to study Torah, and Shlomo greatly enjoyed teaching her. Because she was very bright, the princess learned very quickly, until she was as knowledgeable as Shlomo himself. And after they had studied together for a year, the princess confessed to Shlomo that there was nothing she would like more than for them to marry. But Shlomo replied: "That is impossible, since you are a princess and I am a Hebrew." Then the princess said: "I will convert and become a daughter of Israel." And Shlomo said: "If it is God's will, it will happen. But who will convert you and marry us according to the law of Moses?" Just then there was a knock at the door, and when Shlomo answered it, three figures entered whose faces shone with such great light that Shlomo and the princess had to shield their eyes. And these were three angels, Gabriel, Michael, and Uriel, who had descended from Paradise to confirm the princess as a daughter of Israel. This they did, bestowing on her the name Sarah, and then they wrote up a wedding contract for the two of them and served as witnesses to it. And before the angels departed they made the Seven Blessings for Shlomo and Sarah, who exchanged rings, and so they became man and wife in the eyes of the Holy One, blessed be He. But they did not reveal their marriage to anyone else out of fear that the king might object to the match, nor did Sarah reveal her new name.

In this way three years passed, which were filled with happiness and bliss for the loving couple, who succeeded in keeping their marriage secret. Then one day, while Shlomo studied in the palace garden on a hot day, the gigantic eagle reappeared and swept up Shlomo in his talons and carried him off, dropping him on the roof of his parents' house, so far away. Now when Shlomo's mother heard the loud crash on the roof, she told the maid to find out what had happened. When the maid returned and told her that it was her son, Shlomo, who was lying on the roof in a faint, his mother could not believe her ears and went to see for herself. And when she saw that it was truly her long-lost son, the light of her eyes, she embraced him and almost swooned herself. After that she ran and brought garlic and held it under Shlomo's nose, and in this way she brought him out of his faint. When he awoke, Shlomo was very surprised to find himself there, to say the least, and he told his parents all that had happened.

Now at first Shlomo was very happy to be reunited with his family, but as each day passed he found that he missed his Sarah more and more. And at last he fell sick with longing for her, and was too weak to get out of bed. Day after day his sickness grew worse, and at last his parents began to fear that he might die if he was not reunited with his beloved.

So too did it happen that the princess was heartbroken when she discovered that Shlomo had suddenly disappeared. She did not believe he had abandoned her, but she was certain that something terrible had happened, although she did not know what. And she too became ill and grew weaker by the day, and none of the finest doctors in the kingdom were able to do her any good. Her father, the king, began to grow desperate, and he told the guards at the gates of the city to bring every doctor who entered the city to the palace at once.

Meanwhile, Shlomo's father decided to make an effort to reunite the couple. And he said to Shlomo: "Don't worry, son, for soon you and your wife will be back together. I am going to go to Madrid to bring her back to you." After this Shlomo's father bought the clothes of a peasant and took a few provisions and began to walk to Madrid. And when he arrived at the city gates, the guards asked him what it was that he did, and he said he was a doctor. Then the guards brought him directly to the palace, where he was soon taken to see the princess. And when he was alone with her, he whispered: "Sarah, I am Shlomo's father. And as a sign that I am telling you the truth, here is the ring which you gave him." And when the princess heard her Jewish name, and saw the ring, she knew that it was truly Shlomo's father who had come to her. And she began to get better at once. Then the rabbi gave her some dove soup he had brought with him, and after she had finished it, she was able to sit up in bed for the first time in several weeks.

After this Shlomo's father returned to her every day and gave her the soup and other things to eat and drink, all of them kosher. Before long the color returned to her face, and everyone could see that she had recovered. The king was very happy, and very grateful for the good work of the doctor who had cured her. At last Shlomo's father came to the princess and said: "Now, what must we do so that you will be able to accompany me to our city, where Shlomo is pining away over you?" And the princess replied: "You are a very wise rabbi; surely you can find a way to make this possible."

So the rabbi thought up a plan, and he brought her curry, which is one of the thirteen spices used in the Temple in Jerusalem. And she smeared it over her body, so that it appeared as if she had become inflamed. And when her father saw her, he wondered what had happened, and the princess told him that she had pain in all parts of her body. Then the king called in the rabbi and asked him to examine her. And after he did, the rabbi said: "The sickness of the princess can be cured only if she travels to a place near the sea. And if she is exposed to the sea air for a few weeks, she will make a complete recovery." Then the king said: "I am entrusting my daughter to you, for you are like a father to her. Take her to the sea so that she may recover."

So it was that the princess and the rabbi departed from Madrid and returned to the city of Guadalajara. But when they reached the rabbi's house, they found that a crowd had gathered there and that the people all had tears in their eyes. Sarah asked them what had happened, and they replied: "The soul of Shlomo, the son of the rabbi, has taken leave of this world." Then the princess and the rabbi ran inside the house and found Shlomo lying on his deathbed. And when she saw that terrible sight, the princess fell on Shlomo's chest and wept and prayed to

God, saying: "My God, I left my father and mother, I left my kingdom, I converted, and all for Shlomo, the love of my life. Please, God, return Shlomo's soul to him!"

Then it happened that the angel Gabriel came and prayed before the Lord for the return of Shlomo's soul, and the Holy One, blessed be He, who sat on his throne of Mercy, gave his consent. Then Shlomo's soul returned to him, and reentered his body, and Shlomo opened his eyes. And when the princess and all the others saw this, they were thunderstruck, and cried out: "Blessed be He who brings the dead to life!" Then they said the Seven Blessings, and there was a great celebration, for Shlomo and Sarah had been reunited at last. And after that they lived together in love all the days of their life, and every day was more precious to them than all the riches in the world.

Source: Spain
c. Twelfth–Fourteenth Centuries

The Wooden Sword

ong ago, on a hot summer night in Afghanistan, the king decided to leave the palace and go out into the city for some fresh air. So he took off his royal garments and put on the clothes of a peasant, and went by himself to wander through the streets of his city. At first he went to the center of town, and from there he walked until he reached a poor section on the outskirts of the city. After a while the heat began to bother him, and he saw that one of the houses there had a light in the window, and a pleasant singing voice reached the king's ears. The king came closer and peered through the window of that house, and there he saw a man sitting at the table beside his wife. On the table were different kinds of fruits and salads and a small bottle of arak. The man drank a glass of the arak and tasted the fruits and sang praises to God.

The king stood at the window for a few minutes, astonished by the peace and serenity of this poor man, and he wondered what might be the source of his joy. So the king knocked on the door, and when the man inside asked who it was, he told him that he was a wanderer, and he asked if he might be accepted as a guest. Then the man immediately opened the door and invited the king inside, and offered him food and drink, and the man himself resumed his joyful ways. After a while the king asked his host what he did to earn a living, and the man replied: "I am a poor Jew. I wander in the streets during the days and fix shoes, and with whatever I earn I buy enough to sustain my wife and myself." And the king said: "But what will happen to you when you get old and won't be able to work?" And the man replied: "I don't have to worry, for there is someone who looks out for me." This reply surprised the king, and he said: "Who is this guardian? I see that you and your wife are home alone and that you don't have children. And if you do have children, it will be many years before they grow up." At this the man laughed and said: "It is not a man who protects me, but God, may His Name be blessed and praised forever." The king laughed when he heard this, and he got up and said: "It is late and I must go. But if I come here again, will I be welcome?" And the man told him he would be welcome any time.

The king went back to his palace and decided to test this man, to see how he would fare in times of adversity. So he issued a command forbidding anyone to fix shoes in the streets. And the next day, when the Jew got up and came to the city, he was astonished to see an order denying him his livelihood. Then he lifted his eyes to heaven and said: "God, the door to my livelihood has been shut. But I am confident that you will open another one to take its place." And when he looked around him he saw a man carrying a water pitcher, and he said to himself: "From now on I will be a water carrier." So he went to the market and bought a water jug, and then he went to the well and filled it and carried it into town until he found someone who needed the water, and he did this all day long. And by the time evening came he found that he had as much money as usual, which was enough to purchase food for his wife and himself.

That night the king returned to the house of the Jew to see how he was faring after the order he had given. And the king was astonished when he peered through the window and saw that the man was as happy as ever. So he went to the door and knocked, and the man invited him to join them at the table. Then the king said: "What did you do today? For surely you saw the announcement of the king." The man replied: "The Holy One, blessed be He, did not abandon me, and just because the king closed one door to me, God opened another to take its place." And the man told the king about how he had become a water carrier, and how well his work had gone.

After a while the king took his leave and returned to the palace. The next day he gave an order that made it forbidden for water to be sold to anyone, and from then on each person had to draw water for himself.

When the Jew returned to the well, he discovered that his new occupation had been outlawed by the king. And while he stood there, trying to think of what he might do, a group of woodcutters passed by him on their way to the forest to cut wood. He asked them if he might go with them and cut wood to earn his daily bread, and they welcomed him. So it was that he worked hard all day long cutting wood, and in the evening, after he had sold what he had cut, he found he had earned as much as he did when he was a shoemaker and a water carrier.

In the evening the king returned to his house, curious to know how he had done that day. And when he learned that the Jew had found a new occupation, he decided on a new plan to test the man. The next morning the king ordered the captain of his guards to come to him, and he said: "Take your soldiers to the road that leads to the forest, and stop all the woodcutters who pass and bring them to the palace. Then dress them as palace guards and give them swords, and order them to guard the palace." The captain of the guards did as the king had commanded, and among the woodcutters who were brought to the palace was the Jew. The woodcutters were made to guard all day, and in the evening the new guards were all sent home with their new uniforms and their swords. But they were not paid anything, for the guards received their wages only once a month.

So it was that the Jew returned home empty-handed, and he was very puzzled, for he did not have enough to live for another day, much less for another month. Then he saw his new sword hanging in its sheath, and he had a clever idea. First he made a sword of the same size and shape out of wood, like the kind he had when he was a child, and put it in the sheath. Then he took the sword of the king and sold it, and the money he got for it was enough to live on until the end of the month. After this he went to the market and bought food and drink for himself and his wife and returned home, a happy man.

What a surprise it was for the king that night, when he returned to the Jew's house and found him sitting as usual, singing happy songs in praise of God, as if he did not have a worry in the world. The king asked him what he had done that day, and the man told him all that had happened. Then the king said: "And what are you going to do if the king hears about the sword?" And the man replied: "I don't worry about things that haven't happened. I simply trust in God not to abandon me, and my confidence in Him is strong."

The next day, when the palace guards came to their posts, the king ordered that they report to the center of the city, for there was to be an execution that day, and it was the custom for all the citizens to go to see the sentence carried out. And when everyone was assembled and the execution was about to take place, the king ordered that the Jew be called upon to cut off the head of the condemned man, who had stolen a melon from the palace garden. Now when he heard this, the Jew became very afraid and said to the officer who had given him the order: "Do not ask me to do this, for I have never even killed a fly!" The officer said: "It is an order of the king that you must obey, and if you do not it will cost you your life!" And when the Jew saw that there was no escape, he asked to be given a few minutes to pray to God to give him courage, and then he would do what he was told.

Then the Jew stood up in front of the large crowd and prayed silently. After this he lifted his eyes to heaven and said in a loud voice: "My Lord, you know me very well, and you know that I have never killed anyone in my whole life, and now I am commanded to do so by force. Please, Lord, if this man in front of me is guilty, let me take my sword from its sheath and cut off his head in a single blow. But if he is not guilty, let my sword turn to wood, as a sign of his innocence." And by then all eyes were on the Jew, and he reached into his sheath and pulled out his sword and held it up high. And when everyone saw that it was wooden, the crowd gasped and then clapped and cheered, for they assumed that a miracle had taken place. The king was delighted when he saw the wisdom of the Jew, and called him over and said: "Do you recognize me?" The Jew looked at the king closely and at last he said: "You are my guest! It is you who have visited my house four times!" And the king said: "That is right, and from now on you will be my guest, for I see that you are a man of wisdom, whose confidence in God is strong and unwavering. I intend to make you my right hand and to listen to your advice."

So it was that the Jew and his wife came to live in the palace, where the Jew became the trusted adviser of the king. And all this came about because of his unshakable confidence in God, may His Name be blessed forever and forever.

Source: Afghanistan
Oral Tradition

The Magic Flute
of Asmodeus

here once was a shepherd who served a wealthy king. It was this shepherd's duty to take the king's numerous herds of sheep and cattle to the meadow every day to graze. One day, while the shepherd was in the fields, he heard dogs barking, and saw that they were chasing a young man. Then he acted at once, using his shepherd's staff to chase off the dogs, and thus saved the young man from their teeth. But when the young man came closer, the shepherd was astonished to see that he did not cast a shadow, and he knew at once that although he had a human form, he must be a demon. This, indeed, was the case, and the demon was very grateful and said: "You have saved me from the clutches of the dogs, who otherwise would have torn me to pieces. My father Asmodeus is the king of demons, and if you will accompany me to his palace he will surely reward you. But do not be distressed if he does not speak to you for three days, for on the third day he will surely ask you to name the reward you would like for having saved me, his son. And then you will surely receive whatever it is that you request."

The shepherd agreed to accompany him, after he had returned the herds to the stable. Then he set off with the prince of demons and they walked until dark. They built a fire and the demon cooked delicious dishes of a kind the shepherd had never tasted, for demons eat and drink like men, but have their own dishes, and do not share the secrets of how they are prepared. While they were eating there was a loud chorus of birds chirping in the tree above them, and the shepherd said to the demon prince: "I have heard that demons like yourself know the language of the birds, but I have never believed it to be true." "Oh, yes, it is certainly true," said the demon. "In fact, the birds in this tree are talking about you." "If that is the case," said the shepherd, "prove it by telling me what it is they are saying." Nor did the demon resist the challenge, but said: "One of the birds said to the others: 'The lucky shepherd is going to receive a great reward. If he were smart, he would ask for a hat that would make him invisible. That way he could go anywhere he wanted to without being seen.' 'No,' said a second bird, 'I think he should ask for a magic tablecloth which would become covered with food whenever it is spread open. That way he would never have to go hungry.' 'You are both foolish,' said a third bird. 'Surely he should ask for a magic sack which would always remain filled with gold. That way he could buy anything his heart desired.' 'Not so,' said a fourth bird. 'If he were clever he would ask for a magic stick, able to open any door. That way no gate could remain closed to him.' 'In fact, all of you are wrong,' said a fifth bird. 'If he were truly clever, he would request the magic flute of Asmodeus, which he uses to summon the demons and spirits who serve at his command.' 'You are all fools,' said a sixth bird, 'for if he were a clever man indeed he would ask for all five of these magical gifts. After all, he did save the son of the king of demons, and he deserves a great reward.' "

Now when the shepherd heard what the birds had said, he decided at once to follow the advice of the last bird, and to ask for all five of those magic gifts. Then he thanked the demon for translating the words of the birds, and he admitted that the demon was capable of understanding the language of birds after all.

The two continued on their way until they came upon a female demon, who was asleep at the side of the road. The shepherd asked the demon who it was, and he told him that she was a relative of Asmodeus. Then the shepherd saw that the demon had a precious ring on her finger, and he was so charmed by the ring that he wanted to steal it from her. But the demon prince said to him: "Do not steal the ring. While it is true that whoever wears that ring will be protected from any danger by turning it, it is also true that whoever steals it will die within three days." Nevertheless, the shepherd decided to take the risk, so precious was the ring, and he took it from the sleeping demon's finger, and placed it on his own. Then the two continued on their way until they came to the palace of Asmodeus, king of demons. There the demon prince told his father how the shepherd had saved his life. But although Asmodeus nodded his approval, he said nothing at all; nor did he speak to the shepherd for three days. But on the third day Asmodeus said at last: "What reward do you ask for the great favor you have done by saving the life of my son?"

Then the shepherd replied: "I ask to be rewarded with five gifts: a hat which will make whoever wears it invisible; a magic tablecloth which will be covered with food whenever it is spread open; a magic sack which will always be filled with gold; a magic stick empowered to open any door; and, last of all, your magic flute, with which you summon the demons and spirits who serve your will." Now Asmodeus was surprised that the shepherd was so well informed as to what he should ask for, but at the same time he noticed the ring that he wore on his finger, and he recognized it. Thus he did not question the reason for these choices, or attempt to barter with him, but provided him with all that he had asked for and sent him on his way. For he knew that the time remaining to him was short.

Now Asmodeus also saw to it that the shepherd was returned to his home that day, with all of his wondrous gifts. But before he could tell his wife and son all that had happened, the demon's prophecy regarding the stolen ring came true, and the shepherd fell to the floor, dead. So it was that his wretched widow and son remained impoverished, for they did not know the true value of the gifts, and merely placed them in a corner of their poor cottage. And to sustain the family, the son of the shepherd took the place of his father, and became the king's shepherd. For all that his father had left him was the ring he had worn, which the boy now wore as his own.

One day when the young shepherd went out to the pasture he asked his mother to give him a small tablecloth on which to place his bread. Now they were so poor that they did not own a tablecloth, but then his mother remembered the tablecloth that had remained folded in the corner until then, which the shepherd had brought with him the day he had died, and this is what she gave her son. And when the lad reached the fields and opened the tablecloth, he found it suddenly covered with platters of silver and gold that were filled with delicacies more wonderful than anything he had ever tasted. The youth was amazed at this, but still he ate everything with a hearty appetite. And when he returned home, he told his mother about the wonderful tablecloth, and from that time on they had the finest foods to eat at every meal.

Not long afterward, the boy asked his mother to give him a hat before he left for the fields, for the sun was scorching hot that day. His mother gave him the hat which his father had brought as a gift from Asmodeus, and as soon as he put it on, he disappeared, and his mother could not see him. But when he took off the hat, she saw him again. "It is a magic hat!" the youth rejoiced. And then he asked his mother for his father's flute as well, so that he might play to the sheep in the meadow.

Now when the young shepherd went out into the meadow and began to play the flute, there appeared before him spirits and demons, who bowed down before him and asked him what it was that he wished. Then the lad asked them to tell him where his father had obtained those magical objects, and they told him the tale of how his father had saved the son of Asmodeus, and how he had been rewarded. And but for his error in stealing the demon's ring, he would have been alive to enjoy their benefits. But now they belonged to the boy, including the ring, and they would surely serve him well. And when the young shepherd learned this, he vowed that he would make good use of the treasures that his father had obtained at such a cost. Then he picked up the flute of Asmodeus and turned it over, and at that moment all the demons disappeared. So it was that in this way he discovered that to summon the demons he need but play on it, and to send them away he need but turn it over.

Now because of all these treasures, the fortunes of this lad and his mother were greatly improved, and for the first time they were able to gather savings. Then the boy asked his mother to give him a sack in which he could put away all that they had saved, and she gave him the sack from the corner, which his father had obtained from Asmodeus. But as soon as he opened the sack, he found it already filled with golden coins, making the boy and his mother almost as wealthy as the king. And when the lad poured out the coins to count them, he discovered, to his amazement, that the bag was inexhaustible.

After that the boy gave up being a shepherd, and purchased a large shop in the city and began to sell food and clothing at very low prices. Soon the people stopped buying from the other merchants, and bought only from him. The merchants were incensed about this, and they complained to the king that the boy was selling his goods so cheaply that no one bought their own. The king heeded their words, and decided that the boy must be stopped. He turned to his daughter, the princess, for help, since she knew the charms and spells of demons, and she said: "You can leave the matter to me. I will see to it that he is stopped."

That night the princess had the youth invited to her chamber. No sooner did he arrive, however, than she commanded her servants to throw him out the third-floor window. This they did, but the boy turned the magic ring as he fell, and the spirits and demons caught him before he reached the ground, and made certain that he was safe and sound.

Now that the lad had seen the great beauty of the princess, he decided that he must have her for his own. And the next day he returned to the palace, but its heavy iron gates were locked. Then he knocked on the gates with the magic stick, and the gates immediately opened before him and he went inside. Now when the princess saw him coming, she could hardly believe her eyes, and she quickly ordered her servants to throw him out of the fourth-floor window. But once again the boy turned the ring, and the demons saw to it that he landed without coming to any harm.

The following day the determined boy went back to the palace, this time wearing the hat that made him invisible. No one saw him, of course, and in this way he came into the chamber of the princess without anyone knowing he was there. Then, all at once, he removed the hat and revealed himself, and the astonished and frightened princess screamed for her servants, who came running, and this time she ordered that he be thrown out of the window of the fifth floor. But when this had been done and she looked out of the window, she saw that the boy was alive and well, laughing on the ground.

The next day the youth came to the palace and played the magic flute of Asmodeus. All at once a multitude of demons appeared and crowned him with a royal crown, placed him on a throne, sounded trumpets, and carried him into the palace. When the king heard the tumult he fled to the palace roof and announced that he would give the boy anything he asked for. Then, without hesitating, the lad said: "Let me have your daughter, the princess, for my wife." Now the king had not expected this, and he wanted to refuse, but the princess whispered to him: "Agree to let him marry me and send him to my chamber. This time I will succeed in taking care of him for good."

So it was that the lad came to the chamber of the princess, and this time he was welcomed with open arms, and no one attempted to throw him from a window. Instead she offered him wine to drink, and when he was quite drunk, and did not know his right hand from his left, she said to him: "Tell me, what is the source of your great power?" And being drunk, the boy foolishly revealed this secret, and told her of the magic flute of Asmodeus, and of all the other magic treasures—the hat that made him invisible, the stick that opened the door, the magic tablecloth that supplied him with food, and the magic sack filled with golden coins. Then the princess asked him where he kept these treasures, and the drunken boy confessed that they were hidden beneath his bed. Then the princess ordered one of her servants to bring them to her, and when she had all of the treasures in her possession, she turned over the flute, as the boy had explained, so that the army of demons disappeared. After this she tied the lad with ropes, and called in a giant servant and ordered him to throw the drunken boy into the sea.

But the lad had meanwhile emerged from his stupor, and saw that his life was in danger. Then he was greatly relieved to find he still had the magic ring on his finger, for in his drunken state he had forgotten to tell the princess about it. He turned it, and at once demons appeared and spirited him away from the giant servant, and carried him off to the woods in which they lived, setting him down near two large apple trees. On the one tree grew large red apples, of the most delicious kind, and on the other tree grew green apples that looked very bitter. From where he was hidden behind the trees, the boy saw a passerby pick one of the ripe apples and bite into it. Immediately the man sprouted two long horns, which reached the sky. Then he picked one of the green apples and took a bite of it, and the horns immediately disappeared.

After that the boy picked a basket full of red apples and took a few green ones as well, and traveled to the market, disguised as an apple merchant. There he was easily able to sell the red apples to a servant of the king, and in this way the apples were soon served to the king and his ministers, and when they ate them, they all sprouted long horns. Then they were terribly upset, and summoned all the doctors and wise men in the land, but none knew a way to rid them of the horns. Meanwhile the princess had herself tasted one of the red apples, and she too had grown long horns and was sorely distressed. Then the boy again donned a disguise—this time that of a doctor, and came to the palace and promised to heal everyone on the condition that the princess be made his wife. This promise he received in writing from the king himself, signed with the royal seal, and then he gave each of them one of the green apples, and as soon as they took a bite out of them the horns disappeared, and they were completely cured. After this the boy revealed his true identity, and married the princess, who saw that it was futile to struggle against such a clever lad, and in this way he won her over, and her feelings for him turned to love, and they lived together happily ever after.

Source: Persian (Iranian) Kurdistan
Oral Tradition

Partnership with Asmodeus

n a town in Libya there lived a Jew who was plagued by bad luck. Whatever he did turned out poorly. He seldom earned a dinar, and things went from bad to worse. Nor was his wife a source of happiness—for whenever she saw her husband her mouth was full of curses and she roared like a lion. And one day, when everything seemed to be going wrong, this poor man decided to take his life. He left the town walls behind him, and climbed a nearby mountain outside the city, intending to cast himself down from the top of it. And when he reached the top he took out a kerchief and tied it around his eyes. But before he could jump, two strong arms took hold of him. The man removed the kerchief and saw standing before him a winged giant with the feet of a cock, a beard like that of a goat, and fire shooting forth from his nostrils. And even though the man had been about to kill himself, he was terrified when he saw this giant, and his legs began to tremble.

All at once the giant spoke and said: "Why would you want to kill yourself? You are still young." "I am sick of my bad luck," said the man, "and my wife torments me. All day long she's after me. I have no rest, neither day nor night. I have decided to leave the world and be finished with all my woes." "Don't be hasty, my son," said the giant. "I am Asmodeus, king of the demons, and I often find myself in situations similar to yours. My wife, Lilith, is very troublesome, and yet I have not despaired. I'll tell you what—let us join together and become partners. In working together we will become rich and solve our problems. Here is what I suggest: leave your town and go to the city, rent a store, and hang up a sign in large letters which reads 'Doctor for All Complicated Illnesses.' Then I will enter the bodies of wealthy persons and cause them to have fits, and I will speak from their bellies, so that they will think they are possessed by dybbuks. At first they may try various remedies, but when they find that they cannot be cured, they will come to you. You will ask for a hand-some sum to heal them, and later we'll divide the fee between us equally."

The man thought over this plan and decided it was a good one. Then he asked Asmodeus: "But how will I know that you are inhabiting the patient's body?" And the demon replied: "When you enter the sick man's room, cough three times. I will answer you from his belly and cough three times as well. Then you will know that I am the dybbuk inside the patient."

So it was that the two shook hands and became partners.

Now in the city there lived a wealthy man who was as miser-ly as he was rich. All that he really cared for besides his money was his only daughter, who was young, lovely and wise. He kept her at home almost all of the time, for he did not want her to fall in love with a poor man, whom he might have to support. One day this girl seemed to go crazy. She stopped eating and drink-ing, and when she spoke, another voice could be heard coming from her belly. Her father sought a doctor who could cure her of this illness, but none could be found. Then one day the miser was told that a new doctor had come to the city who specialized in complicated illnesses. The miser immediately went to him, and learned that a cure for his daughter would cost a thousand dinars. The miser hated to part with a single dinar, but since he had no choice, he agreed to the fee after all.

Soon the doctor found himself in the girl's room and the

first thing he did was to cough three times. And lo and behold, three coughs could be heard coming from the girl's belly. Then the man commanded the dybbuk to depart from the girl's body at once, and Asmodeus did, crying out as if he were being forced to go. And the next day the girl awoke healthy and whole, and the miser paid the fee. That same day the doctor met Asmodeus in the city square and divided the money, honestly and fairly.

A few weeks later Asmodeus possessed the son of the mayor. Early in the morning the mayor's eldest son went hunting, but when he came home he fell off his horse, and a strange voice was heard speaking from inside him which terrified everyone who heard it. After that the boy stopped eating and drinking, and mumbled like a madman. His father's servants locked him up in a room, and sent for the new doctor to cure him. And this time, too, the doctor managed to exorcise the dybbuk, and for his services he was paid twenty thousand dinars, which he divided with his partner, who took his share and vanished.

Soon after that Asmodeus entered the body of the Great Vizier, and the doctor who had made a name for himself as an exorcist was called upon to cure him. This time he set a price of fifty thousand dinars, and after he had healed him he did indeed receive this sum in full.

Wandering gaily through the streets, the man sang to himself, for his partnership with Asmodeus had done well, and his money was in a safe place. From now on, he thought, he could live in peace and quiet in the house he intended to build in his home town. He hoped his wife would rejoice at his good fortune, change her manners and no longer curse him. Suddenly he got an idea—he would keep this last sum all for himself. Why share it with a demon? What would Asmodeus do with all that money?

The man took down his shingle and prepared to leave the city. But before he could depart, Asmodeus appeared and demanded his share—twenty-five thousand dinars. The man refused to give him the money. Asmodeus became angry and said: "I will get my revenge!" Then the demon disappeared. And hardly any time had passed, when a messenger arrived summoning the "doctor" to the palace at once. For the lovely princess had suddenly become possessed, and a strange voice was heard speaking from her belly. The man realized that he could not refuse the king, and he reluctantly accompanied the messenger to the palace.

After visiting the princess, the doctor announced that her case was more complicated, and that the cure would take ten days. For he knew if he refused outright to treat the princess, the king would have him hanged.

Each day the man went into the room of the princess and pleaded with the demon inside the girl to leave. But each day Asmodeus replied from her belly: "I am waiting to see how you are put to death. You forgot I saved your life, and you repaid my kindness with treachery. Now I will stay here a few more days. It is nice and warm in the body of this girl, and that way I will see you led to the gallows."

The tenth day arrived, the time limit set for curing the princess, and still Asmodeus stood firm and refused to leave under any circumstances. So the man decided to use cunning. He went to the king that morning and asked to speak to him face to face in a remote hut in the palace garden. When they met there, the man told the king: "The demon that has entered your daughter's body is none other than Asmodeus himself, the king of demons. Against him, special action is required. You must bring all the cannons in the capital to your palace, three hundred in all, and when I take your daughter for a walk outside the royal palace, you must command that all the cannons be fired in succession. When Asmodeus hears the explosions, he will panic and take leave of your daughter's body."

The king promised to do as the man asked. And later that day the man took a walk with the princess leaning on his arm. Suddenly a tremendous explosion was heard, followed by another, and then another. "What is that terrible noise?" cried Asmodeus from within the body of the princess, as still more explosions were heard. "It is your wife and mine who are coming after us!'' the man shouted, as if terrified. And in a flash the king of demons fled in fear and never returned, and thus was the princess cured of her dybbuk, and the life of the "doctor" saved for the second time.

Source: Libya
Oral Tradition

The Demon Princess

ong ago there was a wealthy merchant who had only one son, whom he instructed in the Torah and all of the other sacred books. Now his son grew older and married, and the merchant saw his son's children in his own lifetime. And when the merchant lay on his deathbed he called his son to him and said: "Know that I possess great riches, and I am leaving all of these to you on one condition—that you swear never to sail across the sea. For I have made my fortune through sea voyages, and I have learned all too well the dangers lurking at sea. Therefore, if you should break the vow, then I bequeath all my property to heaven instead." Then the son solemnly swore that he would never undertake a voyage at sea, and shortly after that his father passed away from the world.

A year or two later a ship reached the harbor of that town, loaded with gold, silver, and many precious gems. When the men of that ship had disembarked, they tried to seek out the rich merchant, and when they discovered that he had died, they came instead to his son. They told him that the ship they had arrived in and all of its treasures had belonged to his father, who had entrusted it to them. And now that he had died, it belonged to his

son. So it was that the happy man went with them to the ship, and carried back many loads of riches to his home. And afterward he had a great feast for the sailors of that ship, and thanked them many times for their honesty, for less scrupulous men might have kept the treasures for themselves once they had discovered that the merchant who had hired them had died. And while they feasted, one of the men said: "What did your father tell you about his properties beyond the sea?" And the man replied that his father had said nothing about them, and furthermore had made him vow never to set foot in a ship. "In that case your father was not fully conscious of what he was doing," said the sailor, "for his holdings over the sea are immense, ten times more than the treasures we brought with us on this voyage." And they tried to convince the merchant's son that in such a case the vow he had made was null and void, and that he should accompany them across the sea to recover the properties that were rightfully his.

Now at first the merchant's son resisted their entreaties, but eventually he decided that it made no sense to abandon such riches, and in the end he accompanied the sailors, and set sail on a voyage across the sea. And the Holy One, angered at the breaking of an oath, raised a great storm, causing the ship to founder and sink. So it was that all of the sailors who had convinced the merchant's son to accompany them were drowned, and as for the young man who had broken the vow, he was cast up upon a desert island at the end of the world. There he found himself naked and barely alive, and he knew that he had roused the wrath of the Lord.

In his great exhaustion the man fell into a deep sleep, and when he finally woke up he realized that he was very hungry and thirsty, so he set out to explore the island on which he had been exiled. After wandering for a day he reached an immense tree, whose boughs hung over the sea, and he wondered who might have planted it. That night he slept in the boughs of the tree, and kept warm by wrapping himself in its large leaves.

Around midnight the man was suddenly awakened by a great roaring, and he discovered, to his horror, a lion prowling at the bottom of the tree. And when the lion roared again, the man began to panic and climbed higher into the branches of the tree, until he was out of reach of the lion. But there he suddenly found himself confronted with a mighty bird, as great in size as the legendary Ziz of old. And when this bird saw him, it opened its mouth and tried to swallow him, and the man saved his life only by quickly mounting upon the back of the bird, and taking hold of the feathers around its neck with both hands. But then the bird, startled to have this strange being on its back, immediately flapped its wings and took flight, hoping to shake the rider off into the sea.

Thus the terrified man found himself flying on the back of a giant bird, with nothing but the sea beneath him. And as he clung to that bird's crown of feathers, he prayed to God to deliver him in his hour of peril. The bird continued to fly all day, and toward evening the man saw that they had reached a country, for he saw land beneath him on which houses had been built. And as the bird flew low over the land, the man threw himself from its back and went tumbling to the ground. There he lay hurt and bruised by the fall, and he shivered with cold all night. And by dawn he was very faint, since he had not eaten for more than two days. Still he raised himself and began to walk until he reached a town, and there he found a synagogue, and when he saw it, he wept with joy, for he knew that he had found Jews, who might take pity on him and help him to return to his home.

Entering the synagogue he found only the shammash, and told his tale to him. And he was very shocked when the man did not reassure him but said: "I am sorry to tell you that all the trials you have suffered so far will be as nothing compared to those which await you in this land." Now the man could not understand this at all, for Jews are commanded by the Torah to be merciful, and he asked the shammash to explain what he meant. Then the shammash said: "The country you have reached is not a land of men, but the kingdom of demons, which is ruled by Asmodeus, king of demons. And when it is discovered that a man of flesh and blood has come here, your life will be as good as

lost. For humans are not permitted to set foot in this kingdom."
And when the man heard that he had reached the land of demons, he began to tremble and almost fainted. Then he fell at
the feet of the shammash, and pleaded with him to help him
escape. And the shammash, who was a pious demon, took pity
on him, and placed him under his protection.

Soon afterward other demons began to arrive for the morning services, and before long one of them suddenly cried out: "I
smell the smell of one born of woman!" and all of the others
shouted in agreement and they soon discovered the man among
them. But then the shammash spoke up and said: "You must not
harm this man, for he is under my protection." And because of
the respect they had for that demon, they agreed not to harm
him, but they wanted to know how he had reached their kingdom, so remote from all human habitation.

Then the merchant's son told them his sad tale, without
omitting anything that had happened. And when the demons
learned that he had broken the vow he had made to his father,
they were filled with wrath and said: "How can we permit one
who has broken a holy oath to remain among us? For the penalty
for this transgression is death!" But the shammash replied: "He
cannot be killed until he has been brought before our king to
decide his fate." And the others said: "Well spoken." So it was
agreed to leave his fate in the hands of Asmodeus, their king.

Now it had been a very long time since any other human
being had been in that kingdom, and Asmodeus invited him to
spend the night in his palace until he had reached a decision
concerning him. There Asmodeus spoke with the man and asked
him if he had studied Torah, and when he discovered that he was
well versed in all of the sacred texts, the demon king said: "Because you are a scholar, you have found grace in my eyes, and I
will spare your life. For the Holy One has already seen to it that
you have been well punished for the sin of breaking the vow you
made to your father. And if you will swear to me that you will
teach my son all that you know, you may remain in the safety of
my palace." Now the man was very grateful and relieved to hear

this, and he swore to that effect. So it was that Asmodeus took him into his palace, presented him to his son, and treated him with the reverence due to a teacher.

Three years passed, during which the man diligently taught the son of Asmodeus all the Torah he knew. Then it happened that Asmodeus had to go off to war, and before he left he placed the man in charge of the palace, for he had grown to trust and respect him. Asmodeus gave him the keys to all of his treasuries, and ordered the servants to obey him. Then Asmodeus said: "Now you have the keys to every room in this palace except one, and you are permitted to enter every room except that one." And after that Asmodeus went off to war.

In the days that followed the man took charge of the palace, and happened to pass by the room which Asmodeus had forbidden him to enter, and he wondered what might be in there, since Asmodeus had permitted him to enter every other room. So he went to the door and looked through the keyhole, and saw the daughter of Asmodeus seated upon a golden throne, with servant girls dancing and playing around her. And when the man saw the great beauty of the demon princess, he could not tear his eyes away from her, and at last he decided to enter there. So he tried to open the door, and discovered that it was unlocked. But no sooner did he enter than the daughter of Asmodeus pointed to him and said: "O foolish man, why have you disobeyed the command of my father? For no man is permitted to see my unveiled face. My father is already aware of your transgression, for he sees in his magic mirror everything that takes place, and he will soon arrive to punish you with death!" And when the man heard this, he threw himself at the feet of the demon princess and implored her to save him from her father's anger. And the princess took pity on him and said: "When my father arrives, tell him that you entered here because of your love for me, and say that you wish for us to be married. I know that this will please him, because he has often mentioned that we should be wed, since you are such a learned man." And the man thanked her with all his heart for this advice.

Before long the enraged king of demons returned to the palace and demanded to know why the man had disobeyed him and entered his daughter's chamber. Then the man said what the princess had told him to say. And when Asmodeus heard that this was his reason for disobeying the order, his anger vanished, and he smiled and said: "I shall gladly give you my daughter for your wife." Then he commanded that a festive wedding be prepared, and he invited not only all of the demons who inhabited that kingdom, but also all the birds and beasts as well. So too was a marriage contract written, and the man received as the dowry innumerable treasures, which made his wealth second only to that of Asmodeus himself. And after the wedding, when the man was alone with his bride, he promised her that he would love her always and never forsake her. The demon princess had him swear to this, and write down the oath, which he did, and give it to her for safekeeping.

Before a year was out the demon princess gave birth to their child, a boy whom they circumcised on the eighth day and named Solomon. One day, as the man sat playing with his child, he suddenly sighed deeply. "Why do you sigh?" she asked. He replied: "For the wife and children I left so far behind in my native land." Now the demon princess was deeply hurt when she heard this, and she said: "Is there anything you want for? Am I not beautiful in your eyes? Are there any riches or honors that you long for? Tell me, and I will fulfill your wish." Then the man said: "There is nothing that I lack. It is just that when I hold my son Solomon, I am reminded of my other children."

So it was that more and more often the daughter of Asmodeus found her husband sighing for the family he had lost. At last she decided that she must let him return to them for a while, for otherwise he would never be satisfied. So she said to him: "I will grant you one year to spend with your family. All I ask is that you take an oath to return to me at that time, and put it in writing." The man was exceedingly grateful for this opportunity, and he made the vow and set it down in writing. Then the demon princess commanded one of her servants to fly the man to his country, for demons have wings, and can travel great distances in the wink of an eye. So too did she command the demon to accompany him while he was there. And the servant demon swept up the man in his arms, and in a flash they stood before the door of his home in his long-lost country. There the man had a joyous reunion with his family, who had given him up for dead.

Now as soon as the servant demon had arrived in that country, he had taken on human form, and appeared to be as normal as any man. When the man saw that this change had taken place, he decided not to inform his family of the demon's true identity, for fear that it might frighten them. So too did he decide not to reveal the fact that he had married the daughter of Asmodeus, king of demons. He preferred to regard his trials and tribulations as a bad nightmare, which at last had come to an end.

So it was that the merchant's son resumed his old life, and his days were joyous and full. But one thing darkened his life: each time he encountered the servant demon in the marketplace or synagogue he would be reminded of his vows to the demon princess. For the disguised demon had taken up residence in the Jewish section of that town in order to keep an eye on the man, and to ensure his return at the end of the year. One day when the man could not bear it any longer, he went up to the demon and said: "You are wasting your time here. I will never return with you to the land of demons." The demon said: "And what of the marriage vows you have made, and the oath that you would return to your wife at the end of the year?" "Those vows were forced on me, and I only made them to save my life. Therefore they are null and void, according to the law." When the demon realized that the man was not about to change his mind, he departed from that town and returned to the kingdom of demons. There he informed the demon princess of her husband's intentions. But the daughter of Asmodeus grew angry with the servant demon and insisted this could not be true, as the man had signed an oath. And she told the demon that they would wait until the end of the year to see if the man would keep his vow.

At the end of the year the demon princess sent for the same servant demon, and told him to go to the man and to remind him that it was time to return to her. This the demon did, but when he approached the man as he was leaving the House of Study, the man shouted for him to depart at once, for he had already made it clear that he would never return with him. So the servant demon came back to the princess, and reported what the man had said. Still, the princess could not believe he would dare to break a written oath. And she went to her father, Asmodeus, and asked him what she should do. Asmodeus thought the matter over and said: "Take your son with you and go to this man, and I will send my army with you to his city. First send his son, Solomon, to ask him to return to you, and if he refuses, go to the synagogue and make your case known before the congregation. And tell them that if they do not force him to accompany you, the army of demons will demolish their town, and their lives will be lost. And when he who has betrayed you has returned, I will see to it that he is properly punished for his crime!"

So it was that the demon princess did as her father said, and traveled to the man's city with her son and the army of Asmodeus. First she waited outside the city gates and sent the boy Solomon into the city, to approach his father. The boy came to his house while the man was sleeping, and gently woke him. The man was astonished to see his demon offspring and embraced him and then asked him what he was doing there. Solomon told him that he had come there accompanied by his mother and the army of Asmodeus, so that the man would accompany them to their kingdom. When the man heard this, he grew terrified, but he still insisted he would never return. And despite all of the boy's pleading, the man could not be moved. So the sad boy took his leave and returned to his mother and told her what his father had said. After this the demon princess bid the army to wait there until she saw if she would receive justice from the town. If she did, she would spare the inhabitants, but if she did not, she would order them all to be killed. Then she went directly to the synagogue, and arrived there just as services were about to begin. She walked up to the pulpit, and stood before the congregation, and told them who she was and why she had come there. And she showed them her wedding contract and the written vow the man had made that he would return to her at the end of a year. And she bid that a *Beit Din,* a court of rabbis, be called together, to determine if the man should be forced to return with her or not.

Now when the documents were examined and found to be valid, it was realized that a *Beit Din* must be convened to settle the matter. This was done, and the demon princess entered first, and when she faced the court she said: "This man came to be in our land because he broke the oath he made to his father. My father, the king, showed him great favor and saved him from those who were determined to take his life. I have also saved him from certain death, at the hands of my father, whose command this man disobeyed. And after this my father gave me to him as a wife, and made him a prince and commander over his armies. So it was that this man married me according to the laws of Moses, and this boy, Solomon, is our child. And when he wished to return to his family for a visit, I permitted him to go, and he vowed never to forsake me. Here are all the documents that prove what I have said to be true. And now this man wants to repay good with evil, and prefers to abandon his wife and son."

Then the judges examined the documents, and when they proved to be authentic, they turned to the man and said: "Why do you not return to her, after she has done so much for you? And how can you justify breaking a vow that you yourself have signed?"

Then the man said: "I have sworn and acted under constraint, for I feared for my life. Therefore the vows I signed are null and void. Furthermore, it is unnatural for a man to be married to a demon, and I prefer to remain with the wife of my youth."

Now after the man had said this, and it was apparent to all that he would not voluntarily accompany the demon princess to her kingdom, she spoke up and said: "All will agree that if a man wishes to divorce his wife, he must first give her a bill of divorcement and return to her all of her dowry." And the judges replied: "Yes, that is the case." Then the princess showed them that it was written in the marriage contract that in the event of divorce the man must pay her an immense amount of money, more than was possessed by any king. And when the judges saw this, they said to the man: "According to the law, you must either pay her in full or go with her."

Then the princess said: "I see that you are honest judges, who act according to the law. But since it is apparent to all that this man refuses to accompany me, I hereby renounce the right of compelling him to return by force. Instead, if you will ask him to give me one last kiss, I will depart from him and return to my home."

Then the judges said to him: "Do as she asks, and give her one last kiss, and then you will be free from all obligations toward her." So the man went and kissed her, hoping to be free of her at last, but instead she kissed him with the kiss of death, and snatched away all of his breath, so that his lifeless body slumped to the floor. Then the demon princess turned to the judges and said: "This is the reward of one who transgressed the will of his father and broke an oath. Now if you all do not wish me to die, take my son Solomon and raise him in the laws of God and when he is grown, marry him to the daughter of the greatest among you, and make him chief among you. For I do not wish to remain with the son of such a husband, who will always remind me of him. I shall leave him riches enough that nothing will be wanting, and you shall also give him half of his father's property." Then the congregation vowed to do as she told them, and promised that when the boy Solomon had grown they would proclaim him their chief. After this the demon princess departed and returned to her kingdom, taking her father's army with her. And never again did she return to the land of men, but remained in the kingdom of demons ruled by her father, Asmodeus, where she lives to this very day.

Source: Byzantium
c. Thirteenth–Sixteenth Centuries

The Enchanted Fountain

he king of Bozrah had only one son, who was very precious to him. For this reason he did not permit him to travel outside the city, for fear that something might happen to him. But the prince had a strong desire to go hunting, so he pleaded with the king's minister to take him. The minister sought permission from the king, who agreed that the prince could go hunting with him, but he warned the minister to take care that no accident befell him.

So it was that the prince accompanied the minister to the forest, and they spied a stag and pursued it. Then the minister said to the other hunters: "Let the prince go after the stag by himself, for that is how he will best learn to hunt." So the prince pursued the stag on his horse, and rode deep into the forest before he realized that he had lost his way and did not know where he was, nor how to return to the others. He rode on and on, trying to find his way out, but he only became more confused. Meanwhile the minister and the others began to worry about him, and searched for him in the forest, but did not find him. At last, as it was growing dark, they returned to the king, and the minister told him that a lion had sprung upon the prince and devoured him, for he did not want to confess that he had left him on his own during the hunt. Then the king was crushed to think that he had lost his only son, and he rent his clothes and mourned for many days.

Meanwhile it came to pass that as the prince was wandering in the forest, he chanced upon a beautiful maiden there. He asked her: "Who are you?" And she replied: "I am a princess. I was riding on an elephant, and I grew drowsy and fell asleep, and shortly after that I fell off. And the soldiers and servants of my father, the king, knew nothing of it. For the past week I have not seen another human being, and I have eaten only the fruits and nuts that grow in this forest." Then the prince told the princess who he was, and how it had happened that he too had become lost there, and they were both happy to find each other.

Then the princess said: "I think I can find the way out of the forest. Let me ride behind you on your horse, and we will search for the road together." She mounted behind him on his horse, and they rode together until they came to a ruin in the forest. The princess said: "If you please, I would like to go into the ruin to see if anything of value is to be found there. I will be back shortly." And the prince said: "Go, if you wish." Then the princess dismounted and entered the ruin.

But when it seemed to the prince that she had tarried there for a long time, he dismounted and came up to the ruin, for he wanted to be certain that she had not come to any harm. When he reached the ruin he peered into a hole in the wall, and there he saw that the appearance of the princess had changed, and that she no longer appeared to be a person, but was instead a demon. And she was saying to the other demons in the ruin: "Lo, this time I have brought you a prince, and you can work your will upon him in any way that you please. And afterwards you can make him into a rock that you can place in the wall of this ruin— for every rock represents another fool who has crossed my path." Then the other demons said to her: "If you will bring him into the ruin, we will begin to sport with him, and then we will be happy to change him into a rock. For if we do not find more such rocks, this will always be a ruin, and will never serve as a palace."

Now when the prince saw what he saw and heard what he heard, he grew very frightened. He quickly mounted his horse and was about to ride away, when lo, the demon emerged from the ruin, and once more she had the appearance of a beautiful woman. But when she looked at the prince, she saw that he looked very anxious, and was reluctant to come with her into the ruin. Therefore she did not insist that he join her there, but sought to allay his fears, and said: "Help me to mount the horse, and we will be off." Then the prince did not know what to do, so he let her mount behind him on the horse, and they rode off.

When they had traveled a short distance, the girl said to him: "What caused you to become so frightened?" The prince replied: "I have an enemy, and I am afraid that he may try to harm me when we reach the road. That is why I am so upset." To this the princess replied: "But you are a prince. Why should you fear him?" The prince said: "He is stronger than I am." "Perhaps," said the girl, "you could pay him to leave you alone." "No," said the prince, "he doesn't want money." "In that case," the girl replied, "you had better call upon your God to rescue you from your evil enemy."

Then the prince cried out: "I pray to you, O Lord, O great, mighty, and just God! Rescue me from this demon, and take from her the power to do me harm!"

Now the demon was confused and frightened when she heard this, for she realized that the prince had discovered her true identity, and she knew as well that her power flourished only in the absence of good, and that the power of the Lord could protect the prince and destroy her. And in her fright she threw herself from the horse, and when she struck the ground she disappeared in a puff of smoke, and all that remained was a pile of ashes, which were soon dispersed in the wind.

Greatly relieved, the prince rode on through the forest, seeking a way out of it. By then he had become very thirsty, and thus he was delighted when he spied a fountain flowing there.

He did not know that this was an enchanted fountain, and that any male who drank from it became a female, and any female who drank there became a male. He drank from the fountain, and suddenly discovered that he had been transformed into a woman, and his heart sank. Then he said to himself: "I, too, have become a demon," for he had no other explanation.

Just then this "maiden" saw other maidens in that place, who were sporting among themselves. Then the prince—for he still felt like a prince, even though he now had the body of a woman—was approached by one of the maidens, who said: "Who are you, and where do you come from?" Then the poor prince told her everything that had happened since he had become lost in that forest.

When he had finished telling her this tale, the girl said: "If you will swear to take me for your wife, I will save you, and return you safely to your father, the king." The prince swore to her that if she saved him she would become his wife, and she said: "Drink again from the fountain." This the prince did, and at once he became a man again, as he was before. Then the girl led him out of the forest, and they rode together back to the palace of the king. There the prince told his father all that had happened to him, and the king welcomed the girl and thanked her many times for saving his son, and ordered that a magnificent wedding be prepared for them at once. But the king was very angry with the minister who had abandoned the prince, and ordered that he should be left in the forest by himself, as he had done to the prince. And it is said that before long that minister became another rock in the demons' ruin.

Source: Byzantium
c. Fourteenth Century

The Nightingale
and the Dove

n a faraway kingdom there lived a king and queen whose palace had been built by the shore of the sea. This king had a daughter by his first wife, who had since died, and he had remarried, but his second wife was an evil woman, who despised the princess because of her great beauty. This king loved above all to lead his army in conquests, so he was rarely home, and he was so bewitched by the new queen that he left all decisions concerning the princess to this jealous woman. Now the queen was determined that the princess should not marry, because if she did she might have a son who could come to challenge the queen's right to rule should the king die. So she found fault with every suitor who showed an interest in the princess, and saw to it that the princess remained within the palace at all times.

Yet despite the best efforts of the evil queen, it happened one day that a young man was walking along the seashore and looked up and saw the princess in the balcony of the palace tower. And the moment he set eyes on her he lost his heart, and he knew that he could never rest until she had become his bride. Yet what chance did he have to win the hand of the princess? He was only a Jewish youth who spent most of his time studying to be a cantor. Since many richer and mightier princes had been refused by the queen, he realized that he would not be considered a proper match even for a moment. Yet there was one treasure that this youth possessed which made him unique. For his singing voice was as sweet as honey, and all who heard it thought that they were in the presence of an angel.

So it was that this youth decided to stroll along the beach at midnight and raise up his voice in song so that the princess could hear it. It happened that the princess was lying awake that first night, and all at once she heard a song sweeter than that of any nightingale. She could not imagine who it was who sang with such a wonderful voice, so she stepped out to her balcony. And there, by the light of the full moon that shone that night, round and full, she saw that young man strolling along the beach, singing. When she saw how handsome he was and heard his voice as it rose up with the waves, she gave her heart to him as well. For three nights the young man strolled along the beach and sang, and the princess listened from her balcony. And on the fourth night she took off her royal ring and tied it in her scarf, and threw it as hard as she could, so that it landed on the beach near where the young man stood. And when he untied the scarf and saw the ring of the princess, he knew that she loved him as much as he loved her.

After that the young man returned to the beach every night, and sang the ballads that were so familiar to him, but which the princess had never heard before in her life. And one night it happened that the evil queen also was awake at midnight, and heard the beautiful strains of his song. This caused her to wonder greatly, for never had she heard such a sweet voice, and she thought it was so beautiful that it must be unearthly. Therefore she decided it was the voice of a mermaid, who had emerged from the sea.

Now it happened the next day that the queen mentioned to the princess the marvelous song of the mermaid she had heard in her chamber at night. And the princess replied that it was not a mermaid, but a young man who was courting her, although he would not win her hand. The queen grew furious when she heard this, and said that she would order him to be killed. Then the princess grew very pale and protested that if he were killed, she also wished to die. In this way the queen discovered the deep love of the princess for this youth. Then she turned to the princess with hatred in her eyes, and told her that if she ever tried to run away with him she would get her wish and lose her life. And when the princess saw that the intentions of the queen were evil, and that she could not turn to her father for help, since he was not expected to return for several years, she decided to try to escape with her loved one as soon as possible.

That night the princess wrote out a message to the youth and cast it from her window wrapped in a scarf, with a coin enclosed to make it heavy enough to reach him. When the young man read the letter of the princess, he burst out in a song that was filled with joy, and the next day he made preparations to meet her as she climbed down from her balcony by a rope, for that is what she told him that she would do.

Now the evil queen recognized how deeply in love was the princess, and she expected that she would try to elope. Therefore she warned the guards to watch her window both day and night, and if they ever saw the princess trying to escape, to arrest her and anyone else who was with her as well. Thus it happened that the princess and the young man were caught that night as they tried to run off together, and they were brought before the queen. Of course the evil queen did not intend to pass up this chance to do away with the princess, whom she so hated, and she commanded that the two lovers be put to death.

Shortly afterward the princess and the young man were dragged out to the courtyard, and as they were being blindfolded they cried out to each other, swearing that their love would last for all time. And it happened that at the very instant the sword of the executioner descended, each of them was transformed into a bird, the princess into a dove and the young man into a nightin-

gale, who quickly flew away together. The astonished guards reported this miracle to the queen, who fell into a terrible fury.
Just then she heard song birds singing in the tree outside her
window, and when she looked outside she saw two birds sitting
in the tree, a nightingale and a dove, who were singing together
in perfect harmony. Then she did not hesitate, but ordered her
guards to capture those two birds at once, and they hurried out
to do as she had commanded. And before long both birds were
captured in a single net and brought to the queen, who ordered
that their throats be slit on the shore of the sea. She herself went
along with the guards to be certain that this was done, and so it
was that she saw how in the instant the knife took their souls
each of the birds turned into a fish, the nightingale into a perch
and the dove into a flounder, who swam off together.

Now when the queen saw that the princess and her lover
had escaped her clutches once more, she screamed for the
guards to go out in boats and to fish until they had captured the
perch and flounder that were swimming together. And before
three days had passed a great many fish had been caught, and at
last the guards came back with the two fish flapping together in
one net. Then the queen ordered the fish to be killed and
cooked, because she intended to eat them herself, to be certain
that the two of them were out of her life at last. And when this
was done, the queen sat down to a meal of the perch and flounder that were the princess and the youth. But she took only one
bite before one of the bones became caught in her throat, and
she choked to death while the servants stood helplessly around
her.

After this the king's minister took over the kingdom until
the return of the king, and directed the guards to bury the two
fish together, since the king would surely want to know where
the grave of the princess could be found. This was done, and to
the amazement of everyone it happened that the next day a car-
nation and a rose bush were found growing from the grave of the
princess and the youth, which grew so closely together that the
beautiful flowers stood side by side. But from the grave of the

evil queen nothing ever came forth except for smoke, which arose for many years, although it did not last nearly as long as the two plants, which eventually grew so closely entwined that they could not be separated from each other at all.

Source: Greece
Oral Tradition

The Golden Tree

ne of the Emperors of India had five wives. Four of them each bore him a son, but the fifth, the youngest and most beautiful of all, was childless. The other wives took every opportunity to insult her because of this, and to incite the Emperor against her, so that she might be banished. For a long time they did not succeed, because the Emperor greatly loved this wife. But in the end they harped on it so often that his resistance broke down, and he agreed to their demands. So he banished his youngest wife, and sent her from the palace alone, without providing her with any silver or gold or the least amount of food or water.

In great shame the queen left the capital of that kingdom, and walked wherever her legs carried her. In this way she came at last to a dense forest. She roamed there a whole day without food to eat or a drop of water to drink, and in the evening she began to be afraid. With the last of her strength she climbed a tall tree in order to protect herself from beasts of prey, but because of her hunger and fear she could not fall asleep. When at last the dawn appeared, she was exhausted and barely managed to climb down from the tree. She tried to walk, but after an hour she felt ill and sat down to rest. Suddenly she heard a rustling in the trees and there appeared before her an aged wanderer. The queen panicked and started to flee, but the old man said: "Why are you afraid? I will not harm you." Then the queen, who had no strength left, stopped and burst into tears.

"Don't cry, my daughter," said the old man. "My house is not far from here. There you can rest undisturbed and eat as much as you like. I am poor, but the forest has always supplied me with all that I need."

The young queen looked at the old man, and she saw that his eyes were clear and honest, and that his face had a light of its own, and she agreed to follow him. Less than an hour later they arrived at a hut which looked miserable from the outside, but inside was neat and clean. The old man quickly gave the queen water to drink and to bathe in, and then bread to eat and wine to drink. The queen ate, drank, and fell asleep. And while she slept she dreamed she was walking in a beautiful garden, where there was a lovely pool surrounding a golden tree. She gazed at the golden tree with wonder, for she had never seen anything like it in her life. The leaves were of the thinnest gold, resembling the leaves of no other tree, and the blossoms on it were clusters of diamonds that lit up the surroundings with a strong and beautiful light. While the queen gazed at the tree she noticed an old man approaching her, who wore white robes, and it was the same old man who had helped her in the forest. When he stood before her, the old man handed her a golden amulet on a chain, and that amulet was in the shape of a golden tree. Without their exchanging any words, the queen understood that the amulet was meant for her, and she took it and placed it around her neck. Then she awoke.

The queen did not know how long she had slept, but when she opened her eyes she was astounded to find she was still wearing the amulet of the golden tree, which she had received in the dream. Then she understood that the old man, who sat in the next room praying, had been sent to guide and protect her, and she was no longer afraid.

"Good morning, dear father!" she said to the old man.

"Good morning," he replied. "Come, let us eat."

The queen came to the table, which she found set with all kinds of foods of the forest. Then she ate a meal of tender greens and various nuts and berries, and she was surprised to find that each of them was as tasty as the delicacies that had been prepared in the palace, while the water of the stream had a rich taste almost like that of wine. After they had eaten, the old man asked the queen to tell him about herself. She then told him about how the other wives of the Emperor had conspired against her because she was childless, and how the king had banished her because of this. She added that it was all the more unjust because, according to the signs, she was pregnant.

"Stay here until the king realizes his error and his recklessness," said the old man. And the queen agreed to stay.

So it was that she spent her days living in that hut, gathering nuts and berries with the old man, and assisting him in his work—for this old man was a great craftsman, who created beautiful objects out of gold and other precious metals, which he himself mined from a rich lode in a cave he knew of in that forest. And he purified the metals himself, and cast them into treasures of many sizes and shapes. But the most beautiful of all were those he fashioned in the shape of a golden tree, like the amulet of the queen. The queen watched the old man work with fascination, and greatly admired his creations. But she wondered how the old man sold his treasures, for she never saw him leave the forest, and why, since he was such a great craftsman, he remained so poor. At last she asked him about this, and he said: "I do not create these objects to be sold. Rather, when I have finished one, I beat it down and begin again. For it is the creating that matters to me, and nothing else."

At last, when the time came, the queen gave birth to a healthy and handsome son. Her joy and that of the old man, whom she called "Grandfather," was great indeed. And it was on the night the child was born that the Emperor had for the first time a vivid dream in which he found himself standing beside a golden tree. And the leaves of that tree looked like beaten gold, its blossoms were clusters of diamonds, and its trunk was the purest gold he had ever seen. The Emperor caught his breath and came closer to the tree, and there in the golden trunk he saw the reflection of the queen whom he had banished from his sight. Then he was filled with remorse at having sent her away, for he understood that she had been precious to him, and he tried to take hold of the trunk. But as soon as he touched it, it disappeared, and he awoke.

Now when the Emperor awoke from this dream he was filled with grief—both at the loss of his queen and at the loss of the golden tree. The dream continued to haunt him all that day, and that night the dream recurred, and once again he sought to grasp the golden tree in which he saw the reflection of the banished queen, but at the instant he touched it, it vanished, and he was never able to take hold of it, although the dream continued to haunt him every night. At last the Emperor called in his vizier, and ordered him to call together all of the dream interpreters in the kingdom, so that he might know what this dream meant. But when the Emperor met with the dream interpreters, he found they were divided as to the meaning of the dream.

Some of them thought the dream revealed how much the Emperor longed for his banished wife, and they suggested that he send messengers throughout the kingdom to search for her and to bring her back, for in this way the dream would surely stop haunting him.

But others among the dream interpreters felt that the king need only command his goldsmith to recreate the golden tree of his dreams, so that he might make it his own, and in this way he would be freed from the recurring dream.

Finally, there were those among the dream interpreters who insisted that no such simple solution would suffice, and that the Emperor must set out alone in search of that golden tree and find it for himself, for until then the dream would continue to recur.

Now the Emperor hoped that he might succeed in finding his banished queen, for he greatly longed for her, and was deeply ashamed of what he had done. Therefore he sent messengers throughout the kingdom who announced that he was seeking her, and that she was welcome to return. But these messengers failed to find the queen, and returned empty-handed, and the king began to fear that the queen might have starved or otherwise met her death, and he was filled with grief. Meanwhile the dream of the golden tree in which he saw the reflection of the queen continued to torment him every night, so that he woke up shaking and covered with sweat. For every time he approached that golden tree it vanished, and always continued to elude him.

Then the king ordered the gold to be brought from his treasury, and the golden bracelets of his wives collected as well—for he was angry with his wives for having convinced him to expel the youngest queen. He had all of this gold melted down, and had his goldsmith attempt to create a golden sculpture like that of the golden tree. And even though this goldsmith was known to be the greatest in the kingdom, the tree he created failed to resemble that of the Emperor's dream, and he ordered that it be melted down, and that the goldsmith begin again. When this was repeated three times, without success, the Emperor concluded that the goldsmith could not duplicate the golden tree of his dreams, nor did his creations cause the nightmare—for that is how he had come to think of it—to end.

At last, out of desperation, the Emperor announced that he would give half of his kingdom to whoever could help him find that golden tree. Many days passed, and no one was able to help him, for none knew of such a golden tree. Then the Emperor fell ill because of his bitterness, and he finally concluded that he must undertake the quest to find the golden tree himself, as the last group of dream interpreters had advised him. His sons, the princes, offered to undertake the search for him, but he reminded them that the dream interpreters had insisted he alone undertake the quest. And that is what the Emperor did—leaving the eldest prince in charge of the kingdom until he returned, and disguising himself as a beggar, so as not to attract robbers, he set off on the long journey by himself. For he knew he would have no peace until he had seen the golden tree for himself, and held it in his grasp.

So it was that the Emperor traveled throughout the kingdom,

and everywhere he went he asked if anyone knew of such a tree. But no one had ever even heard of it, and all his efforts were in vain. After many months had passed, he despaired of ever finding the golden tree, and thought of returning home, resigned to being cursed with the recurring dream until the end of his days. Then, as he traveled through the forest, he saw an aged wayfarer, and decided to ask him if perhaps he had ever heard of the golden tree. The old man nodded in reply, and said: "First come home with me, to rest from your journey. Then shall we speak of the blessed golden tree."

Now in the hut of the old man the Emperor saw a woman, whose face was hidden behind a veil (which also hid the amulet of the golden tree that she wore), and with her was a young child, but he did not recognize them as the queen and his son, although he did think to himself that the child was unusually beautiful. Of course, the queen recognized her husband, even though he was disguised as a beggar, but she did not reveal herself, nor their son. The Emperor joined them for a meal, and afterward the old man said: "The golden tree you are seeking can be found only in this vast forest. To reach it you must continue to walk in the forest until you come to a large stream, deep and wide. Follow that stream until it becomes a river, and its waters grow warm. Then keep following it until you reach its source, and there you will find the golden tree. But take heed—as you come closer to the source, the waters of that river will grow turbulent and boiling hot, for they emerge from a great fountain that has its source deep within the earth. And the golden tree grows within that fountain, surrounded by it on all sides. Many have tried to reach it, but all have failed and drowned in the boiling waters. But if you take my shoes, and wear them when you enter the waters, the heat of the waters will have no effect. Then you may succeed where others have failed, but if you do, be certain to return my shoes, for if you do not the golden tree will be lost to you once more." Then the old man took off his shoes and gave them to the Emperor, who thanked the old man many times, and promised to return the shoes as soon as his mission was complete. Then he tied the shoes to his waist, to wear only when he reached the source of the river, and he set out to continue his quest.

Before he had traveled very far, the Emperor came upon the stream the old man had described, and he followed it from there on, noticing that as it widened the waters grew warmer and more wild. And at the same time the forest grew more dense, and the ground became warm beneath his feet as he made his way through the thicket that covered the banks of the river. But even though he had to struggle to make his way, he did not think of turning back.

At last the Emperor reached the river's source, where the waters rose up as high as a house, and gave off great clouds of steam, which covered the entire area in a thick fog. And when he saw how wild the waters were, he lost heart, for he was certain they could never be crossed. Still, he held out hope that the sandals the old man had given him might make it possible to reach the golden tree, which could faintly be seen through the heavy fog as a bright light glowing from within the fountain.

So it was that the Emperor put on the old man's sandals and stepped into the waters. Then, instead of being hot, the waters were cool to his touch, and the fog disappeared. Now, too, he saw the golden tree revealed before him, in the very center of the fountain, even more beautiful than it had appeared in his dreams. And when he slipped into the waters, he found that he could not sink in them below his waist, and in this way he floated to the fountain, carried by the currents, until at last he was swept into the fountain itself, where he found a circular rock on which to stand, surrounded by a wall of gushing water.

There, in that sacred circle, the Emperor saw the golden tree face to face, as had happened so often in his dreams. But now he was astounded to discover that the golden tree was not a motionless object created out of gold, but was itself a golden fountain that sprang up in that place, with molten gold that formed the shape of a golden tree. And with a strange certainty, an intuition that came to him from nowhere, the Emperor reached out and grasped the molten trunk of the golden fountain, and it did not burn his hands, nor did it disappear. Instead, a portion of it solidified at his touch, as long as his outstretched arm. Then, with the golden tree firmly in his grasp, the Emperor stepped out of the fountain, and slipped back into the currents, where he found the gold to be weightless, so that it floated like a log. Then, as he floated away, he looked back and saw for the last time the golden glow formed from the light of the molten tree, and he understood that the golden fountain never stopped flowing, but that it formed another golden tree every instant. And all of those trees were different, but at the same time they all had the same essential form, and he marveled at the infinite shapes that a golden tree could take. Then he returned his gaze to the golden tree that carried him through those waters, and he saw that it too had retained the essential form of the molten tree, even though the gold had hardened, and he knew that he had finally resolved the unfinished dream that had haunted him for so long.

At last, when the Emperor emerged from the fog with the golden tree in his hand, it took on its proper weight. Exhausted, he sat down on the bank of the river and examined his treasure. Then it happened, to his amazement, that he saw in it the reflection of the banished queen, and once again he was grieved at her loss. Finally he arose and used all of his strength to carry the golden tree back downstream, until he reached the hut of the old man. For he did not doubt that if he failed to return the shoes of the old man the golden tree would be lost to him again, this time for good. And when he entered the hut, bearing the wondrous treasure in his hands, the old man and the boy marveled at it, and even the queen examined it through her veil. Then the Emperor thanked the old man for all he had done for him, and out of his remaining grief over what he had done to his queen, he confessed to the old man about how he had banished her, and how he rued the day he had given in to his wicked wives. It was then that the queen removed her veil, and the Emperor found himself face to face with his youngest wife again at last, and he also saw the amulet of the golden tree that she wore. Then he prostrated himself at her feet, and begged for her forgiveness, and for her to return with him to the palace. And when the queen saw how bitterly he regretted banishing her, she accepted his apologies. Then she introduced him to the child, their son, about whom he had never known. The king was over-whelmed at his good fortune, for all that he had sought after had been given to him at the same time.

The next morning the Emperor and the queen and their child took their leave of the old man with many fond farewells, and set off to return to the palace. And when the Emperor went to pick up the golden tree, he discovered that it had become almost weightless, and that he could carry it without effort. When they had returned, the Emperor wasted no time, but quickly divorced his other wives, and treated the queen with the greatest love and respect for all the rest of their days. As for the golden tree, he planted it in the royal garden outside their window, where the child often played.

Source: India
Oral Tradition

The Golden Feather

here was once a wealthy man who had twelve sons; eleven of them were clever but the youngest was regarded as a fool. Now this man had a fine mare, which had twelve colts; eleven were handsome, and one was ugly. And it came to pass that when the colts were one year old, the man decided to give a colt to each of his sons. Each son, according to his age, was permitted to choose the colt he wanted for his own. Naturally, the eleven clever sons chose the eleven handsome colts, so that the twelfth colt, the ugly one, was left for the youngest son. He started to weep because of his bad luck, when the colt suddenly spoke to him and said: "If you will stop crying and do everything I tell you to do, I will show you how to make me handsome."

Now the lad was stunned to discover his colt could talk, and he began to realize that he might have been fortunate after all for having received this colt rather than any of the others—for he was not as foolish as they thought. Then he replied to the colt and said: "Of course I will listen to you."

"In that case," said the colt, "get on my back and let us ride together into the forest."

The lad did this, and let the colt lead him. In this way they arrived at a fountain hidden deep within the forest. Then the colt said: "Let me stand beneath the waters of this fountain, and then dry my coat and comb it, and I will become the handsomest colt of all." The lad did everything the colt said, and after its coat had been washed and combed, the boy was amazed to see how handsome the colt had become—far more so than the eleven other colts. And when his brothers saw it, they too were amazed, but there wasn't anything they could do, for each brother had chosen his colt fairly.

One day the youngest brother rose early in the morning, got on his horse, and took a long ride. At first he trotted the horse slowly, but when he reached the open fields he increased the speed until he reached a gallop. After he had ridden for some distance, he saw something nearby that sparkled on the ground. And when he came closer he stopped the colt, dismounted, and picked up the object and, to his amazement, he found it was a golden feather, radiating many colors in the sunlight.

Just then the colt spoke up and said: "Don't take that feather. Leave it where it lies, or you will have many troubles."

Now the lad was taken aback at this, for he had come to respect the wisdom of the colt. But at the same time he saw that the feather was very precious and unique, and he decided to ignore the warning. He picked up the golden feather and put it in his pocket.

As he rode away, the lad tried to decide what he should do with the golden feather. He did not need to sell it, although it was surely valuable, for his father was already wealthy, and he did not lack for anything. Then he considered keeping it for himself, but if he did, who would marvel at its splendor? And at that moment he was struck by a thought: "I will present the golden feather to the king, for it is truly fit for a king. He will display it in his palace, and all who visit there will be enchanted by its splendor and beauty."

Night began to fall as the young man returned home, happy with his decision to give the golden feather to the king. He slept sweetly that night, and the next morning he rose early and rode the colt to the palace of the king, taking the golden feather with him. When he arrived at the palace gates, and told the guards he had a valuable gift for the king, he was quickly given a royal audience. The king's face lit up at the sight of the golden feather, and he marveled at its beauty. He asked where it had come from and the lad told him how he had found it while riding on his horse. Then the king accepted the gift, and to show his gratitude he appointed the lad captain of his palace guards.

The young man accepted the appointment happily; the golden feather had given him such an important position that now his brothers could no longer consider him a fool. But the former captain of the palace guards, who had lost his position to the young man, was filled with hatred toward him, and vowed to disgrace him in the eyes of the king. For in such a way he might be restored to his former position. And before long he found an opportunity to present himself to the king, and during their conversation he expressed his admiration for the golden feather. He added, however, that while it was truly wonderful, how much more wonderful must be the bird from which it was taken. And he suggested that the person who presented the feather actually acted with disrespect when he gave the king a single feather, while keeping for himself the golden bird from which it came, whose place should be in the king's palace.

Now these words impressed the king, and he was suddenly taken with a great longing to possess the golden bird itself. He sent for the young man, and said to him: "Hear me, young man. You gave me a fine present, a golden feather, and told me that you found it. I am persuaded otherwise. Surely you kept for yourself the bird from which you took the feather. But such a thing should not be done to a king. Go quickly now and bring me the golden bird! If you disobey, I will have your head! Hasten, for if you do not bring the golden bird within three days, your end will be bitter."

The young man stood mute while the king spoke, and dared not contradict what he had said, for he knew that the king would not believe him. He left the palace in terror, and all day roamed back and forth through the rooms of his home. In the evening he went to the stable, hugged the horse, and gave him feed. Then he combed the colt's mane, and while he stroked its neck a sigh escaped him. That is when the colt spoke up and said: "Why do you sigh?" Then the lad told what had happened, and the colt said: "Did I not warn you not to pick up the golden feather in the first place? But still, do not despair, for I know where the golden bird can be found."

Now the lad was astonished to hear this, and he jumped for joy and said: "Let us waste no time; you will lead me to the golden bird, and I will try to capture it. But let us hurry, for I must be back in three days or I will lose my life." Then the lad ran into the house, taking a net and a few provisions, and he hurried back to the stable, mounted the horse, and set off on the quest.

So it was that they rode a great distance throughout the night, and the colt galloped so fast it seemed as if its hoofs were flying. At last, as day dawned, they arrived at a beautiful garden. There the colt said: "You must dismount and open the gate to this garden, which is the home of the golden bird. In the middle of the garden there are two trees. One of these is the tree of life, and the other is the tree of death. Both trees bear an enticing fruit, and look exactly alike. But you must be very careful that you select the right tree, and once you have found it, you must climb it. For there, in the top of that tree of life, is the nesting place of the golden bird. Wait there, remaining very still, and when the golden bird comes to perch on a branch of that tree, throw the net over it. But take care, for if you let the golden bird escape, you will never have a second chance to capture it."

The lad listened very carefully to all that the colt said. Then he asked: "But how can I distinguish the tree of life from the tree of death?"

"Look at the base of each tree, " said the colt, "and see if you can find there a golden feather, like the one you gave to the king. For it will be resting beneath the tree on which the bird sat when the feather fell, and this will be the tree of life. Still, to be certain, all you need to do is to observe each tree in the mirror of the feather. For it will reflect the tree of life clearly, but the tree of death cannot be seen in any mirror."

The boy thanked the colt and entered the gates of the garden. And in the middle of the garden there were two trees, just as the colt had said, with ripe apples growing from their branches. The lad approached and studied them, and it seemed to him that the two trees were identical in every respect, for each looked like the mirror image of the other. Then he looked at the base of each tree, and beneath one of them he found a single golden feather, glittering in the light, while no feathers were to be found beneath the other. Thus he knew which tree was almost surely the tree of life. But to be certain, he held up the golden feather and saw it reflected that tree clearly. Then he held the feather so as to reflect the other tree, but it did not appear in the mirror of the feather at all. After this he put the golden feather away, and climbed up the tree of life with the net in his hand. When he reached the upper branches he hid himself as best he could, and waited for the golden bird to arrive.

All at once there was a flash of light and the sound of beating wings, and the golden bird landed on its favorite branch in the tree, which was within the reach of the lad. He remained very still, not even breathing, with the net clutched in his hand. Suddenly the bird began to sing, and the song was more beautiful and haunting than any he had ever heard. It filled him with strange feelings, and he felt his determination weakening as the song of the golden bird took root in his soul. Recognizing this, he hesitated no longer, and in a single motion brought the net down on top of the golden bird, which flapped its wings and sought to fly away, but found that it was trapped. Then the lad slowly climbed down the tree of life, the net in his hand, and hurried out of the garden. There he found the colt waiting, mounted it, and rode off, and by that evening they had arrived at the palace of the king.

The boy presented himself to the king and said: "Here, my lord, is the golden bird you requested." And the king was astonished when he saw the magnificence of the golden bird. He pressed the young man's hand warmly and said: "This is indeed a wonderful gift you have given me this time. It is invaluable. But tell me, does the bird sing?" Then the lad replied: "Yes, sire,

I heard it singing just before I captured it." "Good," said the king. "Now how shall I repay you? Let me honor you this day, and appoint you captain over a thousand of my troops."

Now the young man was very pleased to be appointed to such a high position, and his family was also very proud of him, and no longer regarded him as foolish. But the usurped captain of a thousand troops was filled with hatred for the young man, and swore to take his revenge. He waited for an opportune moment, and this soon came. One day the king held a reception for his ministers and the distinguished lords of his kingdom. All the visitors looked with fascination at the vessels of gold and silver, and the art objects and exquisite treasures which decorated the rooms of the palace. But the eyes of all were chiefly directed at the wonderful golden bird, which was displayed in a cage.

The former captain of a thousand troops approached the king and said: "The golden bird is truly a miracle, my lord king, but the cage in which it is kept is poor compared to its worth. Surely somewhere there must be a golden cage which is fitting for it. Perhaps he who brought the gift might know where it is to be found. Perhaps he kept it for himself."

The king was struck by these words, and he was taken with a passion to have a golden cage worthy of his magnificent golden bird. So he called for the young man, and when he arrived, the king said: "All who visit here are filled with admiration for the valuable gift you have given me. But all find the simple cage in which the bird is kept detracts from its worth and beauty. You who gave me the golden bird must surely know where the original cage can be found, and if it is in your home, go quickly and bring it to me! If you do, I will make you general over all my troops. But if you do not return with it in three days, it will cost you your life!"

With a bitter heart the young man left the palace of the king. He did not try to explain that he had captured the golden bird in a tree, and the tree of life at that. Therefore, as far as he knew, the golden cage the king demanded did not exist. And with a heavy heart the young man returned home and lay down on his bed, for he thought that his life was lost. He went to sleep and had terrible nightmares, and when he awoke he went to the stable to feed the colt. As usual, he combed its coat and stroked it with affection. And while he did so a deep sigh escaped him.

"Why do you sigh?" asked the colt. "Is the king still not satisfied?" "No," said the lad, "no, he is still not satisfied. Now he wants me to find a golden cage worthy of the golden bird, but such a cage does not exist." "You need not be afraid," said the colt, "for such a cage does in fact exist, and I can lead you to it. You should know that you must bring the golden feather with you, the one you found beneath the tree of life. But you should also know that this will be a dangerous quest."

"And what could be more dangerous than losing my life?" asked the young man. "Come, let us go now, for I have been given only three days to return with the golden cage." So he packed provisions and took the golden feather with him and they set off on the new quest.

This time the colt again ran all night, and at dawn they reached the garden they had come to the first time, where the lad had captured the golden bird. The colt said: "You must enter the gate once more, and make your way through the garden. Deep within the garden there is a golden palace. Inside that palace are many golden objects, and among them is a golden cage worthy of the golden bird."

"Now listen carefully," the colt continued. "There are one hundred steps that must be climbed to enter that palace. When you reach the door, take out the golden feather, for the palace is very dark, but the golden feather will radiate light, so that you can see where you are going. There you will come upon golden sculptures of every kind, more magnificent than anything you have ever seen. Pay no attention to them, lest you become distracted and touch one, for if you touch any of them, you will be turned into a golden statue yourself!"

The lad shivered when he heard this, for he knew it was very dangerous to go there, but he also knew there was no turning back. The colt continued to speak: "Pass by all of these sculptures until you reach a narrow hall, and follow it to the right. At the end of the corridor you will find a door. Go into that room, and in a closet there you will find an old cage. The room itself will be filled with magnificent golden cages of every kind, but do not touch any of them—only the old one that you find in the closet. But do not even touch it until you first drop the golden feather into the bottom of the cage, and then you will be able to pick up the cage safely. Once you have carried the cage outside the palace and garden, it will no longer possess the power to turn a person into a golden statue, and then you should take out the golden feather and put it away, for who knows, you may need it again someday."

Then the boy thanked the colt and made his way through the garden path to the magnificent golden palace. He climbed the hundred steps and opened the door. Inside it was pitch black, but all at once the golden feather began to radiate light, so that he saw golden sculptures everywhere. He gasped at the wondrous objects—chairs and tables, lamps and mirrors, even windows and doors—all made of the purest gold. But standing alongside these were golden statues that struck terror into the heart of the lad, for they were human in every detail, and in each case the hands of the sculptures were touching one of the golden objects. And the lad knew that these statues were of those who had tried to take the golden treasures from there, but did not have the protection of the golden feather, as he did.

Then the lad hurried away from the golden sculptures, and followed the corridor until it narrowed, and there he turned to the right, as the colt had instructed him. When he arrived at the last door, he entered there, and in that room he saw a multitude of golden cages, of every size and shape, one more magnificent than the next. But he remembered what had happened to the other treasure seekers, who were now frozen as golden statues for eternity, and he was careful not to touch any of those cages. Instead, he opened the closet door, and there he found an old cage, which looked as if it were falling apart. It broke his heart to take this cage when the room was filled with so many magnificent ones, but he remembered the warning of the colt, and did as he had been told, slipping the golden feather into the old cage, and letting it drop to the bottom. Then he stretched out his hand, took the cage, and was relieved to find that he had not become a golden statue. Nor did he linger there after that, but hurried away, and before long he had left the palace and the garden behind him and had returned to the waiting colt. Then he took the golden feather out of the cage, and put it away in his pocket, and as he did so, lo and behold, the cage that had appeared old and broken was transformed into a magnificent golden cage, far more beautiful than any of the others he had left behind. So he rode off, holding the golden cage in his hand, and soon he presented himself before the king and gave the golden cage to him.

Now when the king saw that golden cage, his breath was taken away, for he had never before seen an object its equal. It was laid out entirely in gold, precious gems, and pearls, and by itself it was more valuable than all of the other gold and jewels in the king's treasury. With a beating heart the king took the cage and put the golden bird inside it, and light immediately filled the room. Then the king thanked the young man profusely, and in return for that treasure he appointed him general over his entire army.

Now the young man was proud to be a great general, much respected by the soldiers and the people of that kingdom. But the former general was filled with hatred, and swore revenge. So it was that the next time he had an audience with the king, he praised the valuable gifts the lad had given him, but he also remarked on how it was a pity that the golden bird was mute, and did not sing songs to gladden body and soul.

The king brooded on these words, for he had not forgotten that the lad had told him the golden bird had been singing before its capture. But ever since the bird had been in the palace, it had remained completely silent. Then the king called for the young man and said: "You gave me the gold feather, you brought the golden bird, you bestowed on me the wondrous golden cage—but what good are all of these if the bird remains mute, and does not sing sweet songs? You yourself told me that you heard the bird sing, so we know it is not a silent bird by nature. Yet it has remained as silent as stone since it has been in my presence. This, then, is my last request: If you can make the bird sing, it would complete my happiness, and I would wed you to my daughter, the princess. But if you fail, your end will be bitter." And the king gave him three days in which to succeed in making the bird sing.

Then the lad left the palace weeping and groaning, and his legs would not carry him. For he knew of nothing that could force a captured bird to sing. Oh, if only he had not picked up the golden feather in the first place! And when he came home, he went to the stable to be with his faithful colt, which had consoled him so many times before. The colt recognized at once that he was miserable and asked why, and the boy told him. When he had finished, the colt said: "Fear not, for the golden bird shall sing and you shall wed the princess. Just bring the golden feather and climb on my back, and let us be off!"

So it was that they rode all night once more, until they reached the garden of the golden bird. When they did, the colt said: "Go through the gate and return to the two trees in the center of the garden. When you arrive there, use the golden feather once again to determine which is the tree of life and which the tree of death. Then climb the tree of life once more and this time pick two of its apples and return as quickly as you can."

Now the lad did all that the colt had said, and very soon he returned with the two apples. Then he mounted the colt and they rode to the palace, and when they arrived the colt said: "Take one apple with you, and when you reach the presence of the king, place it inside the cage of the golden bird. And when the bird smells the wonderful scent of the apple, it will be reminded of its nesting place in the tree of life, and will sing for the pleasure of all who are present. Neither should you fear that the apple will ever grow rotten, for an apple from the tree of life remains eternally fresh. As for the other apple, feed it to me."

Now the lad did not know why the faithful colt wanted to eat that apple, but since it had helped him so often, he did not hesitate, and fed it the apple. And no sooner did the colt finish eating the apple than it was transformed into an old man with the appearance of a prophet. The lad was astounded to see this, and asked the old man who he was, and he said that he was a rabbi who had been enchanted by a witch, but that the apple of the tree of life had broken the spell. Then the boy asked him why he did not request to eat one of those apples the other times they had traveled to the garden. And the old man explained that the spell required that he return to the garden three times, and only then could he eat the apple and break the spell.

Then the old man wished the boy good luck, and accompanied him as he brought the apple into the palace.

When they arrived in the presence of the king, the lad opened the door of the golden cage, and placed the apple inside it. And no sooner did the bird catch the divine scent of that apple of the tree of life than it began to sing, and its song was a miracle to all who heard it, echoing to their very souls.

So it was that soon a lavish wedding took place, when the young man and the princess were wed. And before long the lad was called upon to become king himself, and in this way the golden bird was returned to him after all, along with its cage, and its haunting, lovely song. And the new king took for his minister the old rabbi who had once been his loyal colt, and with his help he ruled in wisdom for many years, and it was a time of great peace in that land.

Source: Greece
Oral Tradition

The Mute Princess

n a certain kingdom there was a beautiful princess who never spoke to anyone. She was so silent that many people assumed she was mute, and thus unable to speak. But her father, the king, was certain that she could speak, but that she had chosen, for reasons of her own, to remain silent. Thus when suitors came to ask for her hand in marriage, the king permitted them to meet her on the following condition: "You have one evening to spend with my daughter. If in that time you succeed in getting her to speak, even if it is only one word, then she shall be your bride. But if you fail—you will be hanged on the gallows at dawn." Still, there had been many young men who boasted that they could win the heart of the princess and open her lips, but instead she kept silent in their presence, as verified by a witness who remained with them, and in the end they lost their lives.

Now in another country there lived a prince who was both handsome and wise. One day this prince said to his father: "I wish to set out to wander in the land, to learn the ways of man and to amass wisdom and knowledge." The king replied: "You may set out, if you wish to, my son. For surely you shall be a better ruler once you have become more familiar with the ways of the world. But you must return before the end of a year."

So the prince set out on his travels with his father's blessings. And in his wanderings he learned many things, and became skilled in many tasks. But never did he stay in any one place too long, for he wanted to see as much of the world as possible before it was time for him to return from his travels. In this way he arrived at the kingdom of the mute princess, and when he heard of the king's condition that the princess must speak to her suitor before they could be wed, he desired to seek her hand for himself.

Therefore the prince came before the king, who admired the young man, and tried to warn him against the danger. But the prince accepted the condition, even though his life was at stake. And that evening he joined the princess in her chamber, in the company of a faithful witness. The prince, the princess, and the witness all sat in the room and were silent, for the prince did not even attempt to strike up a conversation with the princess, and this astonished her, for all the previous suitors had kept trying to make her speak.

After an hour's silence, the prince turned to the witness and said: "Let us speak, in order to pass the time, for tomorrow I will be hanged."

The witness replied: "I am not permitted to speak to you or to say anything. I am only a witness whose job it is to listen."

Then the prince said: "And if I were to ask you something, would you reply?"

"Perhaps I would and perhaps I wouldn't," said the witness.

"Well, in that case," said the prince, "listen carefully. Three men—a carpenter, a tailor, and a maggid—were traveling together and came to a desolate wilderness, and when night fell they made a campfire and prepared to sleep. But for safety's sake they decided that each one of them would stand guard for a third of the night. The carpenter would take the first shift, the tailor the second, and the maggid the third.

"So it was that the carpenter stood watch while his companions slept. In order to pass the time, he took a piece of wood from a nearby tree, and carved it into a statue of a girl. And when he had finished the carving his shift was over, and he woke the tailor to take over while he slept.

"The tailor awoke and rubbed his eyes, and when he had wiped the sleep away he saw the lovely statue the carpenter had made. And because he liked it very much, he decided to dress it in suitable garb. And so he did. He took out his work tools and some pieces of cloth, made a dress, and put it on the statue, and the clothes gave the statue the appearance of life. When he had finished his work he saw that it was time to wake the maggid. He woke him and went back to sleep. The maggid arose and saw the statue of the girl and was startled, for it seemed to be alive. But after he touched it he understood it was the workmanship of his two companions. He said: 'The statue is so perfect it is fit for God to breathe the breath of life into it.'

"Then the maggid stood and prayed, and asked the Creator of all to bless the girl with the breath of life. And the Creator of the universe heard his prayer, and turned the statue into a living, life-size figure.

"When morning came the carpenter and tailor awoke and saw a living girl walking among them, and each man said: 'She belongs to me.'

"The carpenter said: 'I made her and molded her and gave her shape, therefore I have the greatest right to her.'

"The tailor said: 'I dressed her, and my contribution to her human appearance is greater than yours.'

"The maggid said: 'I prayed and asked for life to be breathed into her, and that is the main thing; therefore, she belongs to me.' "

Then the prince who had told this story to the witness said: "So, the question is, who do you think has the greatest right to the girl?"

"It is a difficult question, and I can't decide it now," said the witness. "Tomorrow I will put it before our men of judgment, and they will decide."

"You forget," said the prince, "that tomorrow I will no longer be alive. For I will be hanged before I hear the verdict."

Then the princess, who had listened to the tale with great interest, could no longer remain indifferent to this matter of justice. She spoke up and said: "The right of the maggid is the greatest, and therefore the girl should go with him, for it is he who caused her to be given life, and that was decisive in her creation."

"Thank you, princess," said the prince, bowing to her. "I am persuaded that your verdict is the just one."

The next morning the executioner came at dawn and started to drag the prince to the gallows despite his protests, for the executioner assumed that the princess had remained silent, as she always did. It was only when the witness intervened and confirmed that the princess had spoken that the execution was put off, and the young man brought before the king.

"I find it difficult to believe that my daughter has broken her silence after all this time," said the king. "But we'll give you the benefit of the doubt, and allow you to spend another night with her, in the presence of two reliable witnesses, and we'll see what happens."

The second evening, when the four of them sat together, the prince and the princess and the two witnesses, the prince said to the witnesses: "Tell us a tale to while away the time, for tomorrow I shall die."

The witnesses said: "We will not speak, for we are only witnesses, and our job is to listen and remain silent."

"In that case," said the prince, "will you reply if I ask you something?"

"Perhaps . . ." they replied.

Then the prince said: "Three companions climbed together to the top of a mountain. One of them had a magic jewel through which he could see to the ends of the earth. Another had a flying carpet, and the third had a potion with which to revive the dead. The one with the magic jewel looked through it and saw in a faraway land a great multitude following a coffin to a grave-site. And when he told his companions what he saw, the one with the flying carpet said: 'Get on the carpet quickly and we will attend the funeral, for it must have been a great man who has died.'

"The three friends sat down on the magic carpet, and it carried them where they wanted to go in the wink of an eye. And after they joined the procession, they asked the mourners who had died and why there was such sorrow. The mourners told them that the king's fair and lovely daughter had died while still very young. And when the three heard this, they made their way to the king and said: 'We can revive your daughter, sire.' The grieving king replied: 'Whoever can revive my daughter shall have her for a bride.'

"Then the one with the magic potion stood near the girl's body and sprinkled the potion on her, and at once she began to breathe. But when she had been revived, and embraced her father and mother amid great rejoicing, the three men began to argue over her.

"The one with the magic jewel said: 'If it were not for me, the princess would have been buried and not have been revived, for it is I who saw the funeral procession. Since she was saved because of me, she belongs to me.'

"The owner of the flying carpet said: 'If it were not for my magic carpet, which carried us a great distance as fast as lightning, we would not have arrived in time to revive the girl. Therefore she should be my bride.'

"Then the one who had brought the magic potion said: 'If it were not for my potion, the princess would now be in her grave, so I have a greater right to her than either of you.'"

Then the prince who had told this story asked the witnesses for their decison, but they said: "It is a difficult matter which we cannot decide by ourselves. Tomorrow we will ask the judges for their verdict."

"But I am to be hanged at dawn," said the prince, "and I will go to my grave without knowing the answer."

Here the princess intervened and said: "I will reply to your question. I believe that the man who revived the princess with his magic potion should receive her as his bride, for without his potion she could not have been revived."

Then the prince thanked the princess, and agreed that she was correct.

The next day, at dawn, the executioner again arrived and began to drag the prince away, but the witnesses stopped him and said: "The princess spoke to the young man, and he does not deserve to die."

Now when the king heard the witnesses, he did not believe his ears: "It can't be that my daughter has finally spoken after having remained silent for so long. But since I have some doubt about it, let us have a third and final test, this time in the presence of three reliable witnesses."

And on the third evening the prince asked the three witnesses to tell him a tale to pass the time, but they refused. Then he said to them: "And if I ask you something, will you be so kind as to reply?" "Perhaps . . ." they said.

So the prince began another tale: "Three people were walking together—a nobleman, his wife, and a servant. Evening drew near, and the sun went down, and the three were compelled to spend the night in a remote field. During the night they were attacked by highwaymen, who robbed them and beheaded the nobleman and the servant, and his wife alone escaped. She sat down and wept and waited for daylight.

"Meanwhile she heard two owls conversing in the branches of a tree. One said: 'Oh, my, what a terrible thing has happened to the poor nobleman and his servant, and now the nobleman's wife is very miserable.'

'Yes,' said the second owl, 'but if someone were to take some leaves from this tree, pound them, squeeze out their juice, and sprinkle it on the bodies, the dead men would surely be revived.'

"Now when the woman heard this, she hastened to pick some leaves of that tree and crushed and squeezed them, as the owls had said. Then she put the decapitated heads next to the bodies and sprinkled them with the fluid, and they were revived. But when it was daylight, the woman saw that she had made a terrible mistake: she had connected the nobleman's head to the servant's body, and the servant's head to the nobleman's body, and the error could not be corrected.

"The two men began to argue over the woman. The nobleman's head, connected to the servant's body, said: 'She is my wife and I am her husband, as my face reveals.' And the servant's head, connected to the nobleman's body, said: 'She is my wife, as my body clearly shows.'

"The question is this," said the prince to the three witnesses. "To whom does the woman belong, to the nobleman's head connected to the servant's body, or to the servant's head connected to the nobleman's body?"

The witnesses said: "It is too complicated a matter for us to decide. It can be solved only by men of judgment."

At this point the princess broke in, for she could not contain herself any longer, and she said: "The woman belongs to the nobleman's head connected to the servant's body, for the head is the repository of all memory and knowledge, and it can be seen by all, whereas the rest of the body is covered with clothing."

The prince said: "Thank you, your highness, for your excellent reply, which is surely correct. Now, let us sleep and wait for tomorrow."

The next day the three witnesses testified that the princess had indeed spoken to the prince, and no one could still doubt it. Then the king arranged a lavish wedding for the princess and prince, and she returned with the prince to his country with a royal salute. So it was that the prince and princess lived together in love all the days of their lives. And the prince often entertained his wife with tales, and the princess did not hesitate to speak the words of love she felt for him.

Source: Yemen
Oral Tradition

The Princess
on the Glass Mountain

nce upon a time there was a beautiful young princess with a lovely voice, and her name was Sumeitra. Every day the princess went for a walk in the flower garden in the palace courtyard, and as she walked, she sang. Now in the forest next to the garden there lived a wicked witch. And every day, as she sat in her dark hut, she heard the voice of the princess drifting across the garden and into the forest. And because the voice was filled with light, which the miserable witch loathed, she decided to turn the princess into a singing bird.

The next day, when the princess took her walk along the garden path, the witch approached her, and said: "What is your name, pretty maiden?" "Sumeitra," replied the princess, with her characteristic modesty. "How pleasant is your voice and delightful your songs," said the witch, and while speaking she waved her magic wand, and Sumeitra was immediately transformed into a tiny singing bird.

Now when the princess did not return to the palace, the king and his servants searched for her, but before long they realized that she was not to be found, and no one knew what had happened to her. Then they were very sad, for Sumeitra had been the light of their lives.

Seven years passed. The search for the princess had long ago come to an end, but still the little bird continued to hop from tree to tree in the flower garden, singing songs that were both beautiful and sad at the same time. In her songs she told of everything that had befallen her, and although the other birds were aware of her misfortune, no man or woman understood the language of the birds, and thus they did not know the meaning of her songs.

Now in that kingdom there lived a young man who had inherited from his father a leather cap. But since the cap was too large, he did not wear it. Then one day, some years later, he decided to try it on again, and he discovered, to his surprise, that the cap now fit him very well indeed. And since it was a fine-looking cap, he wore it one day when he took a walk in the woods. There he discovered, to his amazement, that when he wore the cap he could understand the language of the birds. But when he took it off, their language was lost to him.

In this way the young man, whose name was Surash, walked through those woods, discovering what the birds had to say. And he heard one bird say to another: "What a shame it is that the princess Sumeitra has been enchanted, for she would have made a wonderful wife for any man." "Yes," said another bird. "If the king and queen only knew that their beloved daughter has been near to them all this time, as an enchanted singing bird in the flower garden." "Perhaps," said a third bird, "they would have found a way to break the spell if they only knew that this had happened."

Now when the young man heard this, he decided to go at once to the palace garden, to see if he could find the singing bird the poor princess had become. And no sooner did he enter the garden gate, wearing his magic cap, than he heard the lovely, yet sad refrain of the enchanted princess. Then the young man approached the bird and said: "I have heard what you have said in your song, and I know that you are the princess Sumeitra, who was enchanted by a wicked witch. My name is Surash, and I would greatly like to help you."

Now the enchanted princess was overjoyed to find someone who could understand her at last, and she said: "O Surash, you have given me hope for the first time in seven years. And if you are able to save me and return me to my human form, I will marry you, and one day you will become king of this kingdom. But you must understand that trying to help me will endanger your life. For the wicked witch will bring harm to you if she discovers you are seeking to set me free from her spell."

"I am willing to take the risk," said Surash. "Tell me, what is it that I must do to break the witch's spell?"

"This much I can tell you," said the enchanted princess, "because I have learned many of the witch's secrets from the other birds of this garden. Go to the forest beyond the garden gate, to the small house that belongs to the witch. Knock on the door, and the witch will invite you inside, and offer you food and drink. But take care—do not eat or drink, for if you do I will remain lost to you even after the spell is broken. Also, refuse to sit near the fire, so that she does not push you into it. Above all, keep your eyes on her magic wand and throw it into the fire. For then the spell will be broken, and I will become the princess Sumeitra again, and you will be safe as well, for without her wand the witch is powerless, and she will flee from you."

Surash listened carefully, and he agreed to do all that the enchanted princess had said. Then he left the garden and entered the forest, where he soon found the house of the witch, exactly as Sumeitra had described it. He knocked once, and the old witch opened the door and invited him in, saying: "Come in, young man, and I'll give you food and drink." He went in, but refused to eat or drink. There he looked around and he saw the fire that burned within, and he also saw the wand that had been placed beside the door. And he said to the witch: "Thank you for inviting me here, old woman. For I have been walking in the forest all day, and I am very grateful for the chance to rest."

"Yes, yes," said the old witch, "but surely you at least want to drink this cup of juice, for you must be thirsty after walking such a long distance."

Then Surash realized that if he did not drink something, the witch might grow suspicious, for a wayfarer would be thirsty after walking for such a long time. And he did not heed Sumeitra's warning, but accepted the cup of juice and drank it. All at once he found himself growing tired, and he realized that the witch had tricked him, and that the juice was causing him to fall asleep. Then, with the last of his strength, he reached for the magic wand next to the door and tossed it into the flames of the fire. The witch screamed when she saw this happen, and she rushed to the fire to try to pull it out. But as she leaned over the fire she fell in, and disappeared in a great puff of ashes. And that was the last thing Surash saw before he closed his eyes and was overcome with sleep.

Now at the very instant the wand finished burning and the witch disappeared in a puff of ashes, Sumeitra was transformed into a princess once again, but she found herself imprisoned in a palace on top of a glass mountain, with iron doors that were locked and bolted. If Surash had refused to drink the juice, she would have found herself back in her own room, in the palace of her parents, the king and queen. But because he drank that one time, the spell of the witch still held power over her, and there on the glass mountain she grieved over her fate, and longed for the life that was still denied to her.

After a long time Surash finally woke up, and found himself in the hut of the witch. Then he hurried back to the garden, hoping that he would find Sumeitra restored to her human form. But when he did not find her, nor the bird that she had been, he remembered that he had accepted the drink offered by the witch, and realized that this must have affected the breaking of the spell.

After this Surash became downcast and pulled his hat down over his eyes and walked through the forest, paying no attention to where he went. At last he sat down at the foot of a tree, and put his head into his hands and wept. And while he was weeping, one bird in that tree said to another: "How sad it is that the young man disobeyed the warning and drank the juice." "Yes," said the other bird, "for otherwise he would have been united with the princess Sumeitra, who has been returned to her human form, and they could have been wed. But instead she is imprisoned in the palace on the glass mountain."

Now since Surash was wearing his magic cap, he understood each and every word the birds spoke, and thus he learned where Sumeitra was imprisoned. He perked up his ears, in case the birds would say anything else. And he heard them say: "It is very far to the glass mountain, across a barren desert. If only Surash knew that there is a magic basket hidden in the cave in this forest that never runs out of food. Then he would have all the food he would need for the long journey." "Yes," said the other bird, "and if he only knew that to reach the glass mountain he must travel directly to the west, for that is where it is to be found."

Surash was delighted when he overheard what the birds had to say, and he began at once to search in the forest for a cave. At last he found the cave's entrance, and when he went inside he found the magic basket the birds had described. Then he took the basket and walked directly to the west. As night fell he came to a large house, and he knocked on the door, hoping that he might be able to spend the night there. But when the door swung open, he found himself confronted by a giant, who towered far above him. The giant gave him a terrible look and said: "You have come just in time, young man. For three days I have not eaten anything, and I am very hungry. Now I will have you to eat."

"If you eat me," said Surash, "there will be nobody to rescue the princess Sumeitra from the top of the glass mountain where she is imprisoned. Here—take this magic basket and keep it. With this you will never go hungry again."

Then the giant took the gift Surash offered him and started to eat. And he discovered, to his joy, that no matter how much food he took out of the basket, it always remained full. Then he turned to Surash and thanked him, and asked how he could repay him for the wonderful gift, for when he was not hungry he was not evil, but good.

"Please help me save Sumeitra," Surash implored the giant.

"Come with me," said the giant, "and I will take you to the glass mountain. It is very far away, across a great desert, but if you get on my back I will carry you there. My legs are long and we will get there quickly."

Then the giant set out with Surash on his back, taking very long strides, and before long they arrived at their destination, and Surash thanked the giant, and parted with him in peace. Now when Surash tried to climb up the sides of the mountain, he found that it was impossible to get a grip on the slippery glass, and he could climb up only a little way before sliding back down. After trying to climb it three times, Surash sat down at the foot of the mountain and put his head in his hands in despair. But while he was sitting there he heard voices from afar: three thieves were shouting and arguing, each trying to prove to the others that the object he had stolen was the most valuable. Surash came up to them and said: "Why are you arguing?"

The first thief said: "I have a magic coat; whoever wears it becomes invisible. I say there is nothing more precious than that."

"I have a magic staff," said the second thief, "that can open an iron door at the slightest touch. Tell me, can there be anything more valuable than that?"

"Yes, there can be," said the third thief. "It is this magic horse of mine that can climb up any mountain, even the glass mountain, without slipping. Surely it is the most valuable of all."

Surash then offered to serve as judge for them. He said: "I will test every object, and then I will decide which is the most precious of all." The three men agreed to this, and Surash put on the magic coat and became invisible. The three thieves tried to find him, but they could not, for he was completely invisible to everyone. Suddenly Surash snatched the staff from the one thief and the horse from the other, jumped on the horse, and started to ride up the side of the glass mountain.

Now the horse climbed up the mountain without losing its grip even once, and at the top Surash saw the palace with iron doors, which were locked and bolted. But he merely tapped the doors with the magic staff, and they opened. All at once a beautiful young woman stood before him—the princess Sumeitra. Surash and Sumeitra got on the horse, rode down the mountain, and returned to their country, where Sumeitra's parents were overjoyed to see her again.

There Surash married Sumeitra and became king. Nor did they forget their friend the giant, whom they invited to their wedding, and afterward the giant came to live in a house next to the palace, where he protected the inhabitants of that kingdom, for with the giant's protection no other king dared to invade them. And they all lived happily and in peace and never knew days of sorrow for the rest of their lives.

Source: Iraqi Kurdistan
Oral Tradition

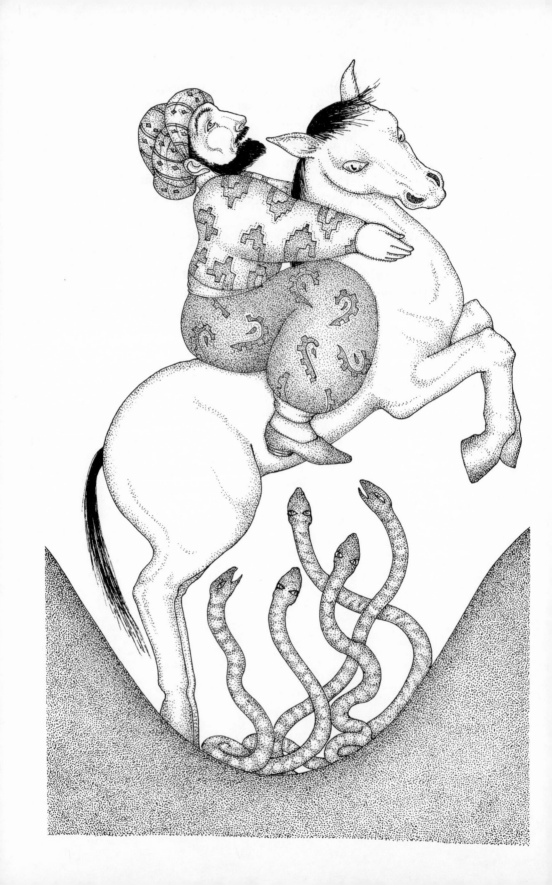

The Wonderful Healing Leaves

king and a queen had three daughters. The king wanted his daughters to marry wealthy princes, and so it was in the case of his first daughter and his second, but the youngest princess fell in love with a poor man, and wanted to marry him. The king and queen opposed the marriage, but the princess went ahead and secretly married her beloved. And when this became known to the king, he was furious, and banished his daughter from the palace. Thereafter she lived happily but in poverty with her husband, whom she loved.

One day it happened that the king awoke and discovered that he had somehow become blind. He summoned doctors from all corners of the kingdom, but none of them could restore his sight. Then a doctor came from a distant city, who said he had heard that there was a special tree in the Land of No Return whose leaves could heal blindness. But, the doctor added, no one who had gone there to obtain those leaves had ever returned.

Even though the way to the tree of the healing leaves appeared to be fraught with danger, it was the king's last hope. So he called on the two princes who were married to his daughters, and asked them to set out on the journey, and promised that if they succeeded they would each receive one third of his kingdom on their return. But he warned them not to come back empty-handed, or it would cost them their lives. Of course, the princes could not refuse to undertake such a journey, so after they had equipped themselves with speedy horses and many provisions, they set out on the quest for the healing leaves.

Meanwhile, when the king's youngest daughter, who was married to the poor man, found out about her father's blindness and the quest for the healing leaves, she asked her mother, the queen, to permit her husband also to join the search, on the same conditions as those set for the two princes. The queen took pity on her, and gave the poor lad a lame horse and meager provisions, and two weeks after the two princes had already departed, he too set out on the quest.

Now after the two princes had ridden for seven days, they reached the province that bordered the Land of No Return. There the princes were told: "Many are those who have tried to reach the area where the healing leaves can be found, but none of them has ever returned, for it is said that the way to the tree on which the leaves grow is guarded by a dragon and a viper, who destroy all those who come within their reach."

When the two princes heard this, they became frightened, and they did not want to continue the quest. But they knew they could not return empty-handed, or it would cost them their lives. Therefore they decided to stay at the place they had reached, and together they opened an inn there.

Two weeks later the lad who was married to the youngest princess arrived at their inn. He recognized the princes at once, but since they did not recognize him, he did not reveal who he was. He stayed there that night, and in the morning he went about asking if anyone knew the way to the Land of No Return. So it was that he spoke to the same people who had warned the two princes. But the young man was not afraid, nor would he abandon the quest. And when the people saw that he was determined to go there, they told him that the only one who knew how to reach the tree of the healing leaves was a giant who lived in the valley below. But that giant himself was very terrible, and ate all those who came within his reach.

Still the lad was not afraid, and he mounted his horse and traveled to the valley that very day, and rode until he reached a house that was as high as a mountain. Another man would have been overcome with terror to see how high was the door of that house, but not the husband of the youngest daughter of the king. Without hesitation he approached the door and knocked on it. Then the wife of the giant opened the door, and when she saw it was a man, she told him to leave at once, for his life was in danger. But the lad insisted that he must talk to the giant, in order to find out how to reach the Land of No Return. And when she saw that he was determined to stay, she allowed him to come in and fed him and then hid him under the bed.

Before long the giant returned home, and as soon as he entered he declared: "Surely my nose does not deceive me—for I can smell the blood of a man even a mile away." The giant's wife tried to convince him that no man was foolish enough to come there, but the giant kept insisting it must be so, and at last she revealed that the lad was hidden under the bed. Then the lad came out, stood before the giant, and said: "Sir giant, you are my host and I am in your power. You can do with me whatever you like. But first let me tell you my story." And the giant was amazed at his bravery and said: "Go on and tell me the tale."

Then the lad told the giant about the blindness of the king, and how he had come in search of the healing leaves. And when the giant saw that he was willing to go to the Land of No Return, even though no one had ever come back from there, he said to him: "Since you do not tremble before me, and are not afraid to risk your life by entering the Land of No Return, I shall not kill you, for you are the first man I have met who is not a coward." Then the giant invited the lad to eat and sleep in his home, and so it was that the lad spent the night there as his guest.

In the morning the lad arose early, and the giant said to him: "When you leave here, you must ride on the road for seven days, until you come to a crossroads. On one of the roads it is written 'A happy journey,' and on the other, 'He who follows this path shall not return.' You must not ponder there, but take the road from which there is no return. Continue to follow this road until it comes to a dead end. This is the first danger. When you come there you must say: 'What a beautiful path! Had I all the horses of the king I would come and dance here!' Then the path will continue, so you can pass.

"The next danger," continued the giant, "is a valley filled with poisonous snakes, through which no man can pass. When you come to it you must say: 'What a beautiful valley filled with honey! If only someone brought some of this honey to the palace of the king, he would gladly eat it!' Then the snakes will disappear, and you will be able to pass.

"The third danger is a valley filled with blood and all kinds of beasts, through which no man can pass. When you come to it you must say: 'What tasty butter! Had I the bread of the king, I would spread this tasty butter on it!' Then the valley will dry up, and you will be able to pass.

"After this," the giant went on, "you will come to a palace, guarded by a dragon and a viper. If their eyes are open, it means they are sleeping; if their eyes are closed, they are fully awake. Wait until their eyes are open, and then you will be able to pass. From there you must enter the palace, and walk down the corridor until you come to the queen's door, which is guarded by four lions. If their eyes are open it means they are sleeping; if their eyes are closed, they are awake. Now, the door to the queen's chamber, which they guard, is made entirely of bells, and when it is opened the sound of the bells wakes the lions. I will give you two packages of cotton with which to muffle the bells. When the eyes of the lions are open, muffle the bells and open the door. There you will find the queen sleeping, for when she sleeps all the beasts sleep with their eyes open, and beside her bed grows the tree with the healing leaves. Fill one bag with the leaves, and also fill your pockets, for they are very precious. Then go to the queen and exchange rings with her. After that, when you return, you must do everything you did before, but in reverse order."

The lad listened closely to what he had to do, and when the

giant had finished telling him, he gratefully thanked him and set off down the road. He acted according to the giant's instructions, so he was able to continue on the path that ended, and to cross the valley filled with snakes and the one filled with blood and beasts. And when he reached the palace he waited until the eyes of the dragon and the viper were open, which meant that they were asleep, and he entered the palace. So too did he wait for the four lions to open their eyes, meaning that they too were asleep, and he entered the chamber of the queen, who was sleeping on her bed. And beside her bed he found the tree with the wonderful healing leaves, its branches reaching to the ceiling, its roots growing beneath the floor. Then the lad filled a big sack with those leaves and his pockets as well, and exchanged his ring with that of the queen. And on the way back he did everything he had done to get there, but in reverse. So it was that two weeks later he returned with the bag full of leaves and the queen's ring on his finger, and came to the inn run by the two princes.

Now when the princes saw the sack, they asked the lad what was inside it, and he told them the whole story, although he forgot to mention that he had exchanged rings with the queen. Then the two princes pretended to be very friendly, and invited him to spend the night, and he agreed.

But while the lad slept, the two princes threw a drug into his eyes to blind him, and put him in a sack and left him in a closet in the inn. They themselves took the bag of the healing leaves and set out to return to the palace of the king. And when they arrived the king's blindness was cured by the healing leaves, and he appointed the two princes to be his ministers, and rewarded each of them with one third of his kingdom.

Meanwhile, when the lad awoke and found himself in a sack, he did not give up hope, but struggled until he had managed to free himself. But when he did, he discovered that he was blind, and he did not know what to do. Then he remembered the healing leaves he had kept in his pockets, and took some of them and rubbed them against his eyes, and his sight was restored. After that he returned to his wife, the king's youngest

daughter, and said to her: "I have brought the healing leaves."
But to his surprise she laughed at him and said: "The two
princes brought them back long before you, and the king has
regained his sight." And the lad understood that his long quest
had all been in vain.

Now it happened that when the queen of the Land of No
Return awoke from her sleep, she saw that her ring had disappeared, replaced by another, and that many leaves were missing
from the tree. She immediately unrolled her flying carpet, and
searched high and low for whoever had taken her ring and the
leaves. After searching in many places, she heard of the king who
had been cured of his blindness, and when she arrived at the
palace she threatened to send the dragon to destroy the city if
she was not told how the cure had come to pass. Then the
princes came forward and showed the leaves to her. She said:
"Tell me where you got them from." And they replied: "We
found a forest and picked the leaves off a tree." "They are lying!"
hissed the queen. "Beat them!"

Just then the lad arrived at the palace and told the queen
how he had obtained the leaves, and showed her the ones he
still had left, which he had carried in his pockets. Then the lad
showed the queen her ring, and she knew that he was telling the
truth. But she wanted to know how the princes had returned
with the leaves before him, and so the lad told her all that had
happened, and all the trouble that they had caused him. After
that the lad gave back the ring to the queen, and she got on her
flying carpet and returned to her kingdom. And the king, who
had heard all that the lad had said, now understood what had
really taken place. He banished the two princes and invited his
youngest daughter and her husband to live in the palace, where
the young man soon became his trusted minister, and they all
lived happily ever after.

*Source: Iraqi Kurdistan
Oral Tradition*

The Princess
with Golden Hair

here was once a pious man who was very wealthy. He had only one son, whose name was Yohanan, and Yohanan had a wife who was both beautiful and righteous. In time the old man took ill, and when he was on his deathbed he called his son to him and exhorted him to follow the commandments of the Lord at all times and always to be generous to those in need. Then he called his son close and whispered in his ear: "My son, when the days of mourning for me are over, go to the market and remain there until you see someone bringing something to sell. Then buy whatever the first man you see offers you, bring it home, and take good care of it, whatever it is." Yohanan vowed to do as his father had asked, and soon after the old man died and was laid to rest. His son mourned for him for thirty days, as is prescribed, and when the period of mourning had ended he remembered his father's last words and went to the market. And there the first thing he saw was a man carrying a very handsome silver goblet. Yohanan went to him and said: "Is that goblet for sale?" And the man said that it was. Then Yohanan

asked: "How much are you asking for it?" And the man answered: "One hundred pieces of gold." This was a very great sum, and Yohanan thought about it and said: "I will give you sixty gold pieces." But the man refused his offer and turned to go.

Then Yohanan remembered his vow to his father, so he followed the man, and when he reached him he said: "I agree to give you one hundred gold pieces after all." But the man said: "If you want it, the price is now two hundred gold pieces." Yohanan was greatly surprised the man had dared to double the price, and he held his ground and said: "I will give you only one hundred, as you first asked." "Then I will be on my way," said the man, and again he left. But when Yohanan thought about it, he decided that he had no choice but to buy the goblet no matter what the price, so he ran after him, and when he reached him he said: "Here, take two hundred gold pieces, as you asked." But the man said: "If you want it, you must give me one thousand gold pieces. And if not, let me take my leave." Yohanan saw that the price kept going up, yet he felt compelled to buy it, since it was his father's will. So he took the man to his home, and there he gave him one thousand gold pieces, and he put the goblet away in a chest.

Now this was not just another silver goblet, for it had a silver cover, and although Yohanan often took it out and tried to open it, he could not. Then Passover came, and Yohanan said to his wife: "Bring me the goblet I bought for my father's sake, and let us put it on the table in honor of the holiday." Then she went and got it, and this time when Yohanan took it and tried to open it, the silver lid lifted at once, and inside it he found a smaller goblet, also silver, and inside it was a small scorpion, asleep. Yohanan and his wife were very surprised to see it, and although his wife was frightened of it, Yohanan said to her: "Not in vain did my father commit me to this thing. We must feed it and raise it and see what comes of it in the end." So they did, and every day the scorpion grew larger, until it could no longer fit into the small goblet, and they had to put it in the larger one. And soon afterward it required an even larger container. Before long it had grown so large it no longer fit inside Yohanan's home, and he had to put it in the courtyard. There it continued to grow until it was as big as a mountain, and Yohanan could no longer afford to feed it, for the scorpion ate so much that his inheritance had decreased almost to nothing. Finally Yohanan's wife said to him: "What shall we do? We can no longer feed the scorpion, for it has cost us everything we owned. Still, sell your prayer shawl today and buy food for it, and tomorrow I will sell my cloak." And this is what they did, but after that they truly had nothing left, and then Yohanan went to the scorpion and fell before it and prayed to God and said: "Lord, you know that I have given everything I had in order to fulfill my father's dying wish. Now I am left with nothing, and I do not know what to do next, for my wife and children are hungry and thirsty. Nourish us, Lord, and tell me what is the nature of this scorpion I have raised, and what will be its end."

And when Yohanan had finished speaking, the scorpion opened its mouth and said: "God has heard your prayer and has given me permission to reply to you. I know that you have done everything you can for me, and you are well deserving of a reward. Tell me what you would like, and I will give it to you." Then Yohanan thought carefully for a long time, and at last he said: "If this is so, teach me all the languages in the world." And the scorpion said: "Your wish shall be fulfilled." And the scorpion took a slip of paper and wrote the Name of God on it and gave it to Yohanan to swallow. In this way Yohanan learned not only all of the seventy languages, but the languages of the birds and the beasts as well.

Now when the scorpion had fulfilled his promise to teach Yohanan all the languages in the world, he said to him: "Your wife was also very good to me, and sacrificed much in my behalf. Now, ask her to name one reward she would like, and I will give it to her." Yohanan asked her, and she came before the scorpion and said: "My lord, give us wealth great enough so that my husband and I and our children will be provided for all the days of our lives." And the scorpion said to her: "Follow me, and bring wagons and horses and donkeys and other animals. And I will load them with gold and silver and precious stones, all that they can carry."

Then Yohanan and his wife did as the scorpion had said, and they followed him until he brought them to a forest called Ilai. And when they were deep in the forest, the scorpion whistled, and one pair of each and every animal in the world came to him, along with snakes and scorpions and birds of every kind. Each pair brought a gift of silver or gold or precious stones, and they gave them to Yohanan and his wife. And after this the scorpion said to them: "Take your bags and fill them, and pile them in the wagons, and be sure that you take enough so that you will never have to depend on any man." And this is what they did.

Now after they had loaded all their wagons and animals with all they could carry, Yohanan said to the scorpion: "How can we ever thank you?" The scorpion said: "Do not thank me, but thank the Lord, for it is at his will that I serve." Then Yohanan said: "Forgive me for asking, but could you tell me who you are and where you come from?" And the scorpion replied: "I am the son of Adam, who begot me by Lilith, who was his first wife, before Eve. For the past thousand years before you released me, I had been growing smaller, and during the next thousand years I will grow larger." When he heard this, Yohanan was greatly surprised, and he said: "If that is so, please bless me." And the scorpion replied: "May God deliver you from the evils which are to come upon you." Yohanan had not expected this blessing, for he felt that his life from then on should be quite secure. And he said to the son of Adam: "What evils are to come upon me?" But the scorpion would not reveal this, and took his leave of them. Then Yohanan and his wife returned home, and there was no one in all of that kingdom whose wealth or wisdom was equal to his own.

Now the kingdom in which Yohanan lived was ruled by a king who was unmarried, and for a long time his counselors had advised him to marry, so that there would be an heir to succeed him. Each time he had turned them down, but at last he agreed to consider this matter seriously, and told them he would reply to them in three days. Then it happened on the second day that as he sat in his courtyard deep in thought a raven flew above him and dropped a beautiful golden hair from its beak that landed at the king's feet. The king picked it up and looked at it, and he was amazed at its beauty. So it was that on the third day he brought the hair with him when he met with his ministers, and he said to them: "If you want me to take a wife, bring me the woman to whom this hair belongs, and I will marry her. But if you fail to bring her to me, I will cut off your heads!"

The ministers were terrified at this ultimatum, and they said: "Give us three days to consult before we decide what to do." The king agreed to give them this time, and at the end of three days they declared that they knew of only one man in the kingdom who could undertake this task, and that was the Jew Yohanan, who was skilled in all languages. The king thereupon sent for him.

Now that same day Yohanan was sitting in his garden and a bird flew over it crying out: "May God deliver you, Yohanan, from the evils about to come upon you." And because Yohanan knew the language of the birds, he understood what this bird had said, and he was very disturbed, for he had not forgotten the warning of the scorpion. Just then the messenger from the king arrived at his gate and said: "Yohanan, come with me at once, for the king has sent for you."

So it was that Yohanan accompanied the messenger to the palace, and when he was taken to the king, the king said: "I have heard that you are very wise, and further that you are well versed in all of the languages of the world. Now it is my wish to be married, so that there will be an heir to succeed me. Therefore I wish you to seek out the woman whose golden hair this is, which a raven brought me, for I know that this woman is destined to be my wife." Now Yohanan could not believe what it was that the king was asking of him, and he said: "My lord king, I am willing to serve you in any way that I can. But what you ask must be reckoned as next to impossible, not unlike asking another to tell you your own dream. Never has a king made a request such as this." But the king did not like this reply, and he said in a cold, cruel voice: "If you do not bring this woman to me, I will have your head and the heads of your people!" "If that is the case," said Yohanan, "then I will undertake this quest. Only grant me three years' time to find your bride-to-be and to bring her back." The king granted him his time, and Yohanan departed from the palace.

When Yohanan reached his home, he told his family of the king's demand, and all of them wept on account of it. Then he packed provisions for the journey, three loaves of bread and ten pieces of gold, and told them he planned to travel first to the forest Ilai, where he had taken leave of the scorpion, for perhaps he could find him there and ask for his assistance. He reached the forest after a week and, shortly after he began to search in it, he came upon a dog of immense size, which was crying and howling. Yohanan asked the dog what was wrong, and the dog told him that because God had created him so large, it was very difficult to satisfy his hunger. To this Yohanan replied: "God did not create you to die of hunger, for his mercy extends to all the creatures He has created. Here, take one of these loaves of mine, and eat." The dog did so, and then it said: "May God deliver you from all the troubles which are about to befall you. And may God grant me the opportunity to reward you for the kindness you have done for me."

Yohanan went farther in that forest, and there he came upon an immense raven, which was crying out in its hunger exactly as had the dog. So Yohanan gave it another of his loaves, and the raven gave him the same blessing as had the dog.

After this Yohanan went on his way until he came to a river. There he sat down at the side and ate the remaining loaf of bread and drank some water. And there on the opposite shore he saw a fisherman, who said: "Would you like to buy the fish I have just caught in my net?" Yohanan replied that he would, and the fisherman said: "The price for it is ten gold pieces." Now Yohanan wondered how it was possible that the fisherman had asked for the exact amount he was carrying, and although he was taking a considerable risk, since neither he nor the fisherman had seen the fish as yet, he agreed to the bargain. So he took out the ten gold pieces and gave them to him, and in turn the fisherman pulled his net out of the water. And when he opened it he discovered that the fish was a very large and beautiful one that was so immense it was worth at least one hundred gold pieces. The fisherman was angry that he had gotten the poor side of the bargain, but the fish now belonged to Yohanan. And when he picked it up, the fish spoke and said: "My lord, you know that I am too large to carry, nor could you eat more than a small part of me. Therefore please do what is right and throw me back into the water, and someday I will reward you for your kindness." And when Yohanan heard this, he tossed the fish back into the river and threw it the last of his bread, much to the amazement of the fisherman, and he went on his way.

Now on the other side of that river there was a town, and two women of that town were sitting together not far from the river bank. One was the princess of that kingdom, who was the most beautiful woman in the entire country, and the other was her handmaid. And the princess said to her handmaid: "Do you see that poor man on the other side of this river? He is searching for a woman with golden hair, for a raven dropped such a hair at the feet of a king, who has sent him on this quest. And who is it that he is seeking? It is I, for the hair he carries with him is my own. But the king he wishes me to marry is an evil one, and I do not care to be his wife. Therefore I will give him three tasks that he must accomplish, difficult tasks, impossible ones. And unless he accomplishes those tasks, he will return empty-handed to the king. But first I must inform him of these tasks. Therefore ask the boatman to cross the river and bring him to me."

The boatman did as he was told, and crossed the river and came to Yohanan and said: "The princess of this country has asked to see you. Please come with me." So Yohanan accompanied him, and thus he reached the princess with the golden hair. And when he met with her he was amazed at her beauty, which far exceeded that of any woman he had ever seen. And the princess said to him: "Where are you coming from, and where are you going?" And Yohanan replied: "I have come from a distant land to seek a woman whose hair this is." And he took out the golden hair he carried, and showed it to the princess. And the princess said: "I, who stand before you, am the very woman you are seeking. Know that I am willing to accompany you to the king and become his bride, but first there are three tasks that you must accomplish for me. If you accomplish these tasks, I will go with you; but if you do not, you will return alone." Then Yohanan saw that the golden hair he carried did indeed belong to the princess, so he asked her what the first task was, and she said: "Here is a pitcher, and I want you to fill it with the waters of Gehenna." And when he heard this, Yohanan began to weep, and he said: "Who is able to do such a thing?" But the princess would not change her mind, and she said: "If you cannot do this, I will not accompany you." "If that is the case," said Yohanan, "give me the pitcher, for I have no other choice." So the princess gave him the pitcher, and he departed on the quest.

The first place Yohanan traveled to was the forest Ilai, across the river. There he sat down beneath a tree and wept bitterly over his fate, and while he was weeping the raven that he had helped came and perched on a branch of that tree and said: "Is there anything I can do for you?" And Yohanan told it of the princess's demand, and the raven instructed him to hang the pitcher around its neck. And when Yohanan had done this, the raven flew off on its journey to the river of Gehenna, which is boiling hot, and filled the pitcher, although the boiling waters burned the bird badly. After this the raven was barely able to return to Yohanan, and when it did, it gave him the pitcher, saying: "Behold, I have done as you asked." And Yohanan took the pitcher and thanked the poor raven from the bottom of his heart, and returned to the princess with the pitcher. And when the princess took it, she recognized that it was truly filled with the waters of Gehenna, for they were still boiling and the odor was very bad. And then the princess knew that Yohanan had indeed fulfilled the first task.

Then the princess said: "Now that you have completed the first task, let me tell you about the second one. Here is another pitcher, and I want you to fill it with the sacred waters of the Garden of Eden." And when Yohanan heard this, he began to weep, and he said: "Is not the way to the Garden of Eden closed to mortals such as myself?" But the princess insisted and said: "If you do not bring me the water, I will not accompany you." "In that case," said Yohanan, "give me the pitcher, and I will try to complete the quest."

So the princess gave Yohanan the pitcher and he returned to the forest Ilai. There he sat down beneath a tree and wept bitterly over his fate, and while he was weeping the raven that had retrieved the waters of Gehenna for him came and perched on a branch of that tree. Then Yohanan told it of the princess's demands, and the raven said: "If only I could fly to the Garden of Eden for you I would gladly do so, but my feathers are so badly singed from the boiling waters of Gehenna that I can scarcely fly." And Yohanan saw that what the bird said was true, and he sat glumly with his head in his hand, for he did not know what to do. But just then the giant dog, whom Yohanan had given one of his loaves of bread, suddenly appeared. The dog said: "Why are you so sad?" So Yohanan told it all that had happened and explained why the raven was unable to undertake the second task. Then the dog said: "Oh, I would gladly assist you in this, for you were kind to me when I was in need. Let the bird climb on my back, and I will carry it to the Garden of Eden, for I know the way there very well." And Yohanan was delighted when he heard this, and he quickly hung the pitcher around the raven's neck, and the bird got on the back of the dog and off they went.

Now because of the dog's great strides, the raven quickly arrived at the gates of the Garden of Eden. There the bird flew over the walls of the Garden to one of the four sacred rivers that flow from beneath the Tree of Life, and it filled the second pitcher with the precious water. And while it was filling the pitcher, a few drops of those wondrous waters splashed upon the raven and immediately healed the burns it had received from the boiling waters of Gehenna, so that it was as good as new.

Before very long the dog and the bird returned to Yohanan, with a pitcher filled with the waters of the Garden of Eden. Yohanan was overjoyed to see it, and he was also very happy that the bird had been healed, and he thanked both of them from the bottom of his heart. Then he returned to the princess with the pitcher, and she found the scent of the waters more wonderful than any perfume. But still to be certain they were truly the waters of the Garden of Eden, she sprinkled them on a bird that had been killed that day, and the bird immediately came to life and flew away. And then the princess knew that Yohanan had indeed fulfilled the second task.

Then the princess said: "Now that you have completed the first two tasks, let me tell you of the third. Twenty-five years ago I inherited my father's ring, which contained a very precious stone, the like of which is not to be found anywhere in the world. One day, while I was walking beside the river, the ring fell from my hand into the waters. We searched for it everywhere and dredged the river, but it was lost. If you can find this ring and bring it to me, I will go with you without delay." But Yohanan said: "How is it possible to find something in a river which has been lost for twenty-five years?" And the princess replied: "If you do not find the ring, I will not go with you."

After this Yohanan returned to the river and sat down on the bank and wept, for it seemed that there was no end to the obstacles that confronted him. And while he was weeping, the immense fish he had thrown back in the river appeared to him and said: "My lord, why are you weeping? Is there some way I can be of help?" And Yohanan told the fish about the ring he was searching for, which was lost in the river. And when the fish heard this, it said: "Yes, I know of that ring, for I saw the fish that swallowed it so long ago. I will seek to retrieve that ring for you, but first I must receive permission from Leviathan, who is the ruler of all the fish." Then the fish went to Leviathan and told him the whole story, and Leviathan gave the fish permission to retrieve the ring for Yohanan, as a reward for the kindness he had done. Soon enough the fish reappeared before Yohanan, and spat out the ring on the shore. And when Yohanan saw it, he was amazed at its beauty and the size of its stone, and he thanked the fish from the bottom of his heart and hurried back to the princess.

Now when the princess saw her long-lost ring, she wept tears of joy, and she said: "I will always be grateful to you for having restored the lost ring of my father. And now I will gladly accompany you to the king, for you have certainly earned the right." And so it was that Yohanan and the princess set out for the palace of the king. And when the king was told that they were coming, he went out to meet them, and led them to the palace. And the king was so overwhelmed with the great beauty of the princess that he desired to wed her at once. But the princess said: "In my country it is not customary to marry at once. Let us wait twelve months' time." This angered the king, but he reluctantly agreed to grant the request.

During that period a war broke out, and there were many civilian casualties, among them the wife of Yohanan. And so it was that Yohanan was among the first of those who set out to drive the enemy from the kingdom. Now it happened that in the course of one battle Yohanan was slain. And when this news was reported to the palace, the princess insisted on going to the place where his body had been taken. The king accompanied her, for he did not want to let her out of his sight. But when the princess reached Yohanan, she sprinkled some of the water of the Garden of Eden on his body. And suddenly Yohanan began to breathe, and his eyes opened. And when the king saw this he was truly amazed and said: "Now that I know you have this miraculous potion, our army will be indestructible." And after that the king was not afraid of fighting on the front line with his troops, for, he assumed, the princess could always revive him.

So it was that during an especially fierce battle the king was cut down, and his body was carried off by the soldiers and brought to the princess, to be revived, but instead of sprinkling the water of the Garden of Eden, she sprinkled the waters of Gehenna, and the body of the king was reduced to ashes, which blew away in the wind. After this the princess and Yohanan were married, and they came to rule the kingdom together. They lived together in peace and tranquillity for many years, and begot sons and daughters; as it is written, *Cast thy bread upon the water, for in time to come thou wilt find it again.*

Source: Palestine
c. Ninth–Twelfth Centuries

The Enchanted Journey

nce it happened that the holy sage Rabbi Adam, who had powers equal to those of the greatest sorcerer, looked into his magic mirror and saw a faraway kingdom where evil ministers were going to pressure its king to sign a wicked decree against the Jews that very day. The decree had already been written, and all that remained was to have the king sign it and affix his royal seal. Then Rabbi Adam, who had at his command many great powers, took down a bottle of ink from the shelf and poured a small amount into the palm of his hand, forming a mirror. After this he unfolded from a prayer book the paper on which he had written the Name of God. And at that moment every shadow and every echo disappeared, and everything became bright. And when he looked into the mirror, he saw the room in which the evil ministers were meeting with the king at that very moment, and with his eyes fixed on that scene, Rabbi Adam pronounced the secret and Ineffable Name.

A moment later Rabbi Adam appeared before the king and his ministers, a most dignified visitor. All were greatly surprised, and could not imagine how he could have entered the palace, especially since the ministers had left strict orders that no one was to be admitted to the king but themselves. So great was their wonderment that they were speechless, and did not think to object when Rabbi Adam said: "I must have a word with the king." Instead, they all moved aside to let him pass, and he accompanied the king outside that room into the palace garden.

Now the king was very curious to know what it was that the old man wanted to see him about, but Rabbi Adam refused to say anything until they reached the well. There he motioned for the king to look down, and when he did, the king saw on the surface of the water an image of a ship standing ready to sail. The king could not understand how such an image was possible in a well, and he raised his eyes to ask Rabbi Adam about this. But when he did, the king found that he was standing on a dock before the very ship he had just seen reflected in the well. The king was dumbstruck, and whirled around to look for the palace, but it was nowhere to be seen. Instead, there was a vast wilderness behind him. The king's heart sank when he saw this, and he grew very afraid. Just then he saw that the ship was about to cast off, and he ran to board it as fast as he could, and reached it only a moment before it set sail.

The king sailed on that ship for several weeks, but he was unable to speak with any of the passengers, for he did not know their language. At last the ship arrived in the port of a beautiful city, and all of the passengers disembarked, and so too did the king. He wandered from street to street, observing the city with fascination, amazed by the beauty of the place. Now and then he would approach a passerby and ask him for the name of the city, but in vain, for no one understood him.

After he had walked for some time, the king reached an inn and realized that he desired to refresh himself. But when he entered the inn and tried to speak to the innkeeper, he found that no one spoke his language. Unable to make himself understood, the king left the inn hungry and disappointed, and wandered around the streets and markets. "What shall I do?" the king thought. "I shall die of hunger if I do not find anyone to whom I can speak." Then he saw a boy in the street, and tried to explain his situation to him, but again they were not able to communicate.

Suddenly the king saw someone he thought he recognized. It was a Jewish musician who had once tutored his daughter, the princess, in the playing of musical instruments. "He will surely help me," the king thought, greatly relieved at having found someone he knew. And the musician did recognize the king at once, although he was amazed to find him there, especially since that country and the king's were at war. He greeted the king, and asked him how he had come to be there. And then, speaking in a rush of words, the king told the musician what had happened to him, and begged him for something to eat. The musician took the king to his home, and saw to it that he received a fine meal. After that he invited the king to stay in his house, for there was nowhere else for him to go. At first the king thought that he would set sail immediately for his own kingdom, but when he discovered that the country he was in was at war with his own, and that no ships were allowed to sail there, he was terrified. For he knew that if his true identity were known to the authorities in this kingdom, his life would be in extreme danger.

Now the king was not a foolish man, and when he realized that the war could last for many years, he understood that he must try to make a new home in this kingdom, and that he must also keep his identity hidden. In order not to attract attention to himself, he decided to dress as a Jew, and to learn Jewish customs and beliefs.

Days passed, and the king was surprised to discover that he greatly enjoyed his study of the Torah and the other sacred texts. He decided eventually that he wanted to become a Jew, and had himself circumcised. The family of the musician was very proud of him, and prepared a festive meal in his honor. So it was that the king continued his diligent studies until he acquired a vast knowledge of the Torah, and before long his great knowledge became recognized, and he was numbered among the finest Jewish scholars. Many important men desired him for a son-in-law, and he finally married the daughter of a wealthy man. He became the father of three sons, whom he raised in the spirit of the Torah and dearly loved.

Seven years passed, and then it happened that the princess of this kingdom became very sick, and none of the doctors in the land were able to cure her. In desperation her father, the king, commanded the Jews to find a way to save her, or else they would all lose their lives. The Jews turned to their wisest men for help, and when they met to discuss what could be done, the exiled king offered to try to heal the princess, although he did not know how.

He left for the palace, and when he arrived he was taken before the king of that kingdom, who warned him again that if he failed to cure her, he and all the rest of the Jews would be doomed. Then he was taken to the room of the princess. There he examined her and found she had an abscess that had formed in her throat, which was slowly choking her to death. And when he saw this, he grew greatly afraid, for he did not know what to do next. But as always, since he had become a Jew, he put his faith in God, and he decided to pray. So he put on his *tallit* and *tefillin,* and stood in a corner and prayed for God's help.

Now the princess had never before seen anyone dressed that way, and she thought it was very funny. She began to laugh, and she laughed so hard that the swelling in her throat broke open and her life was saved. And when her father, the king, found out that this had happened, he was overjoyed, and he told the Jew that he could name his reward. So it was that the exiled king had two requests. First, he asked that the king sign a decree promising the Jews protection during all the rest of his reign; and second, he asked for a ship for himself and his family, stocked with provisions, on which they could set sail. The princess's father gladly agreed to these requests, and signed the decree at once and had it announced in public.

Not long afterward the exiled king and his new family took leave of all their fellow Jews and set sail on a voyage for the kingdom he had left behind. For he had long ago revealed to his family his true identity, and they had agreed to accompany him on the voyage there, so that he could resume his life as king. But after they had sailed for three weeks a great storm arose, and the ship sank. Everyone was drowned except for the king, who swam toward a distant shore. He swam for hours, and finally arrived exhausted at an island. There he threw himself upon the ground and began to weep over the loss of his family.

As he lay there weeping, the king suddenly heard a voice above him. Looking up, he found himself in his palace garden, beside the well. Next to him stood Rabbi Adam, who said: "It is time for you to return to the palace, O king. Your ministers have been waiting for you for more than two hours."

When he heard this and saw where he was, the king was greatly confused, for he could understand neither how he had gotten there, nor what the old man was talking about. He knew that he had not been gone two hours, but more than seven years, and just now he had lost the family that he had so loved.

Then the king stood up and hurried into the palace, where he found his ministers all together, as he had left them so long ago. He began to tell them all that had happened to him, but they stood there dumbfounded, with looks of confusion on their faces. At last one of them found the courage to speak, and said: "But just two hours ago Your Majesty left the palace with the old man, and walked into the garden. What has happened to cause you to lose all sense of time and imagine that seven years have passed?" And the king was at a loss for words, for he did not understand what had occurred.

Then the king looked up and saw that Rabbi Adam was still standing in the garden. He rushed outside and came to him and said: "If you can explain what has happened, please tell me at once, for my life has been turned upside down."

Then Rabbi Adam said: "It is true that you were away from the palace for only two hours. Everything that happened to you was a vision I showed you, so that you would understand the full implications of the wicked decree against the Jews that you were about to sign."

When the king heard this, he was seized with fear and trembling, and he understood that the vision had showed him the true ways of the Jews, which were not at all like what the evil ministers had told him. And although the experiences of the seven years were still vivid in his mind, and his love and admiration of the Jews unchanged, he found that he had forgotten all of his knowledge of the Torah.

Then the king returned to the palace and commanded that the evil ministers all be arrested. And when this was done he signed a decree promising to protect the Jews during all of his reign, and gave it to Rabbi Adam. And after that the king sought out new ministers from among the Jews, and the lives of the Jews of that kingdom flourished, and they lived in peace.

Source: Eastern Europe
c. Sixteenth Century

The Magic Mirror
of Rabbi Adam

ow Rabbi Adam possessed a magic mirror that had once belonged to King David, which permitted him to see things that took place all over the world, and he made it his task to watch over his fellow Jews in that mirror. One day Rabbi Adam looked into this magic mirror and saw that a Jew in a certain city was in mortal danger, although he had done nothing to deserve the fate that awaited him. When he saw this, Rabbi Adam resolved to do something to help this Jew, and he mounted his horse and pronounced a spell, so that the hooves of the horse flew along the ground without touching it, and before an hour had passed Rabbi Adam had arrived in the city of the Jew who was in danger.

As soon as he arrived, Rabbi Adam walked through the city, and saw its streets and markets, and they were crowded with man and beast like sand on the seashore. Rabbi Adam spoke to a man in the marketplace and asked: "Why are so many people all crowded together here?" And the man replied: "Throughout the year the city is quiet and subdued. Only for two weeks of the year does it seethe like a boiling pot, and merchants come here from all corners of the land to sell their wares. These days are the market days, and all the townspeople live for an entire year from the earnings of these two weeks."

Rabbi Adam came to a tavern, and found there many merchants who were eating and drinking, and among them a Jewish merchant from a nearby city. Rabbi Adam sat down beside him and turned to him and said: "Pay heed, for when four hours have passed you will be killed." Now the merchant thought that the old man was mad, so he did not even reply to him. He continued to eat delicacies and drink wine, and then he got up and went over to the men with whom he had traveled to the market, and told them what the old man had said. They laughed and told him not to pay attention to the words of a madman, and not to worry, for what he said was surely nonsense.

An hour later Rabbi Adam returned to the merchant and said: "Know that the hours of life you have left are only three." The merchant laughed at these words, and again told his friends, and they also laughed.

When he left the tavern, the merchant returned to the market and arranged his merchandise, and before long the old man appeared before him again and said: "One hour ago I spoke to you and your mouth was filled with laughter. Now there are only two hours left of your life." And when the merchant heard this, he grew afraid for the first time, and he went to his friends and told them of his fear. They said to him: "Why didn't you stop him before he left you, for perhaps *he* is plotting to kill you." Then the merchant said to them: "When he comes back to me again I will not let him go until he tells me everything, but I am convinced he intends me no harm."

One hour passed, and Rabbi Adam came to the merchant and said: "Know that in one hour you will leave this world." Then the merchant grabbed his arms and shouted: "I will not release you until you tell me who you are, and who it is that is plotting to kill me." The rabbi replied: "You have spoken truly, for there are those who are plotting to kill you. I have discovered this plot, and I have come here to save you from descending into the grave." And this time the merchant recognized that what Rabbi Adam said must be the truth, and he grew afraid for his life. Then he said: "If this is the case, tell me what I should do." And the rabbi said: "Come with me and do everything that I command." The merchant stood there as rigid as a statue, and then he said: "I am ready to follow you."

Rabbi Adam and the merchant walked together until they came to an inn. There Rabbi Adam said to the innkeeper: "How much do you earn a day at the inn?" "Twenty silver shekels a day" was the reply. "If that is so," said Rabbi Adam, "behold I am giving you twenty silver shekels on the condition that you do not allow anyone else to enter your inn for the rest of the day, neither to eat nor to drink. Nor must you allow any wagon drivers to rest in your courtyard."

The innkeeper heeded his words and closed the inn. After this Rabbi Adam turned to the servant of the inn, and requested that a bathtub be brought to the merchant's room, and that it be filled with water. The servant did as Rabbi Adam asked, and then Rabbi Adam commanded the merchant to climb into the tub. The merchant took off his clothes, and climbed in as he was commanded to do. Then Rabbi Adam took out his magic mirror and told the merchant to look within it and to tell him all that he saw. The merchant stretched out his hand and took the mirror and gazed into it, and a great terror descended upon him, and he was silent. Then Rabbi Adam said: "Did I not tell you to reveal to me all that you have seen? Speak!" After this the merchant said: "I see my wife in the company of a man of my town who is known as a sorcerer. They are sitting together, eating and drinking and hugging and kissing, and on the table is a bow and arrow."

Then Rabbi Adam said: "Know that your wife has betrayed you with the evil sorcerer, and even now they are plotting your death. The danger is very great, for the sorcerer has the powers of evil at his command. He is about to shoot an arrow from that bow, and the powers of evil will guide it to you so that it pierces your heart. And after your death the sorcerer and your wife will marry, and will live together without fear of any man. But with the help of God this evil plan will not succeed. Now look again and tell me what you see in the mirror."

The merchant gazed into the mirror again, and said: "Your words are true and correct. Now the sorcerer is making ready to shoot it with his own wicked hands."

Rabbi Adam then said to him: "Do not be afraid or let your heart be faint, for now there is no turning back. Watch carefully what he does, and when you see that he is about to shoot the arrow, then put your head under the water at once. For you must hold your breath and remain submerged until the arrow has passed by you and gone astray. Afterward I will signal for you to lift your head out of the water and sit up." And this is what the merchant did, and a few seconds after he was submerged in the water, a sound was heard in the room like the hissing of an arrow, and when Rabbi Adam signaled him, the merchant lifted his head out of the water. Then Rabbi Adam had him look into the mirror once more, and asked him what he saw, and the merchant replied: "I see my wife and she is in a black mood, and the spirit of the sorcerer is raging within him."

Then Rabbi Adam said: "Good! Now continue to watch closely, and if he sends forth another arrow, do as you did the first time." And when the merchant saw the sorcerer readying the arrow to be shot, he immersed himself fully in the water, and again saved his life.

After this Rabbi Adam said to him: "Look once more into the looking glass, and tell me what you see." And the merchant gazed into the mirror, and saw that his wife was unhappy and that the sorcerer's anger had become like a sea that could not be calmed. He reported this to Rabbi Adam, who said to him: "Look directly at him in the mirror, and if you see that he is going to attempt this evil deed a third time, do as I commanded you at first, but this time while you are submerged extend the little finger of your right hand out of the water."

Once more the merchant looked into the mirror of Rabbi Adam, and once more he saw the sorcerer take up the bow and arrow. Then he immersed himself in the water, but left the tip of his little finger exposed, just as Rabbi Adam had commanded.

And as he was holding his breath under water he felt a sharp pain in his finger, and his hand fell back into the water. After this he lifted up his head, and the rabbi gave him the mirror to look into again. Gazing into the mirror, the merchant said: "Now I see that the sorcerer and my wife are rejoicing." And Rabbi Adam said: "That is because they have been deceived into thinking that they have succeeded in killing you, for your little finger stopped the enchanted arrow, and did not permit it to pass through the inn as it did the first two times. Now you can come out of the tub and put on your clothes. So far you have been saved, but danger still hovers over your head. Still, do not be afraid, just do as I tell you to do and your life will be saved." And the merchant left the tub and got dressed, as the rabbi had directed.

The next day the merchant intended to return to his own city, for the market days had ended. But Rabbi Adam said to him: "You may return to your city, but when you get there do not go to your own house. Go instead to that of relatives, and dwell there in secret. After three weeks have passed go forth from that house and go to the market. Remain there until the sorcerer sees you. Go up to him and greet him and reply truthfully to any questions that he may ask. Do not hesitate to tell him about me, and if he wants to know where I can be found, tell him that I am willing to stand in his presence to test whose powers are stronger. He will surely not decline this challenge, for he is confident of his powers. Then fix a place and time, and I will meet him there."

The merchant did as Rabbi Adam had commanded. He traveled to his home town, but when he arrived there he dwelt in secret in the house of a relative. When three weeks had passed he left the house and walked to the market in the center of town. Before he had been there very long he saw the sorcerer, who turned pale when he saw him, and approached the merchant and said: "It was said in town that you had gone to the grave." The merchant replied: "I was saved from an early grave." "Who saved you?" asked the sorcerer. "A fellow Jew saved me from the hands of those who sought to slay me." Then the sorcerer said: "Who is this man?" "A holy man, whose name is Rabbi Adam," said the merchant. Then the eyes of the sorcerer grew narrow, and he hissed: "If you do not bring this man before me, you are a dead man." And even though the evil sorcerer had revealed himself, the merchant remained calm and said: "Fix a time and a place, and I will send for him. You can be certain that he will meet you there." So it was that a meeting of the sorcerer and Rabbi Adam was set to take place in the sorcerer's home.

Now the evil sorcerer was so confident that he could defeat Rabbi Adam with his powers that he invited all the nobles of that province to witness the contest. And when the appointed hour had arrived, Rabbi Adam came there accompanied by the merchant, and they found many nobles in the house, who were eating and drinking at the sorcerer's table. One drunken noble said to Rabbi Adam: "Perform wonders for us, show us your powers!" And Rabbi Adam said: "I do not perform wonders, but I put my faith and trust in the Lord, whose powers have never failed me."

The nobles, who were not fond of Jews in the first place, did not like this reply. And they urged the sorcerer to begin the contest at once. The sorcerer complied by bringing out an empty bowl, into which he poured water. Then he passed his staff over it, and the water in the bowl vanished. The nobles gasped when they saw this, and the sorcerer passed the bowl around among them, so that they could confirm it was empty. Then, when they gave it back to him, the sorcerer passed his staff over it in the other direction, and the water reappeared, much to the amazement of the nobles.

Then the sorcerer, looking very smug, asked Rabbi Adam to perform the same feat. "Gladly," said Rabbi Adam. He stepped forward and passed his hand over the bowl of water, and again all the water disappeared. Then he passed the bowl around among the nobles, as the sorcerer had done, and when they saw that it was empty and returned it to him, he passed his hand over it in the other direction and it was filled again. But this time it was filled not with water, but with wine! The nobles were even more amazed at this, and the face of the sorcerer was pale with anger.

Then the sorcerer took down a cage in which he kept a dove. He opened the cage and took out the bird. Then he placed it on the table and passed his staff over it. All at once the dove collapsed, and lay there stiff and dead. Then the sorcerer passed his staff over it in the other direction, and the dove came back to life, flapping its wings. The nobles applauded when they saw this, and all were certain that Rabbi Adam could not duplicate this feat.

Then Rabbi Adam took his place before the dove, and passed his hand over it. Immediately the dove dropped to the table with a thump, its feet in the air. The nobles examined it and all agreed that it was surely dead. Then Rabbi Adam passed his hand over it in the other direction, and the wings of the dove began to flap, and it flew around the room. After this it landed on the table and, to the amazement of all, laid an egg. And only a moment later the egg broke open and a small fledgling inside it stretched its wings. And when the evil sorcerer saw this, a look of terrible hatred crossed his face. Then he said: "I am ready to perform one more wonder, which I am quite certain the Jewish magician cannot duplicate. But I must ask that he leave the room as I perform it, so that he does not overhear the spell that I pronounce."

Rabbi Adam departed from the room, and the sorcerer faced the nobles, his staff in his hand. He held his staff upright on the floor and pronounced a spell over it, and lo, the staff began to blossom and branch, and before long it produced green leaves and apples on the ends of the branches, which quickly grew ripe. The nobles were astonished at this wonder, and they applauded the sorcerer's accomplishment. Then the sorcerer bowed to the nobles and called Rabbi Adam into the room. And when he came in there, the sorcerer said: "Observe this tree and its delightful fruit. Now let us see how great is your power, and if you can cause the tree to wither, and become a staff once more." Then Rabbi Adam turned to the nobles and said: "Since the master of the house commanded me to leave the room when he performed this wonder, I request that he also depart the room at this time." The nobles agreed that this was only proper, and they asked the sorcerer to leave the room until they called on him to return.

After the sorcerer left, Rabbi Adam walked around and around the tree, all the time remarking: "How good are these apples and how pleasant this tree!" As he was circling the tree, seven times in all, his eyes were fixed on an apple at the top of the tree which was exceptionally red, a delight to the eyes. He turned to the chief noble among them and said: "Honored sir, would you be so kind as to cut off this very red apple at the top of the tree?" The nobleman agreed to do this, took a knife, and cut off the desired apple and gave it to Rabbi Adam. And no sooner did he do this than the apples left on the tree began to wither, the leaves fell off, the branches withdrew, and the trunk withered until it was the staff that the sorcerer had begun with. All that remained was the apple in Rabbi Adam's hand, which had remained as ripe as ever.

After this Rabbi Adam commanded that the sorcerer be brought back into the room. One of the nobles went out to get him, and behold, he found the body of the sorcerer in one corner of the room, and his head in another. The nobles were greatly shocked at this turn of events, and they asked Rabbi Adam to explain. He said: "Whoever undertakes to perform magic puts his life at risk, for every wonder created contains one weakness, which can be the undoing of the person who has cast the spell. And in this case it was the apple at the top of the tree that was the one weakness."

Then the nobles sat in judgment over Rabbi Adam, to decide if he had sinned in bringing about the death of the sorcerer. They considered this matter for some time, and concluded that Rabbi Adam had only performed his part of the wonder, by returning the flourishing tree to a staff, and that it was the evil sorcerer's fault for putting himself at risk. The Rabbi left the nobles with great honor, and they sent him home in peace.

And the merchant, who had witnessed all that had taken place, rejoiced greatly over the miracle, and thanked Rabbi Adam for saving him from the hands of the powerful sorcerer. But Rabbi Adam told him to give thanks to God, for all great miracles come from Him. After that the merchant went with his wife to a rabbinical court and divorced her. The wife left her husband's house, but in her heart were thoughts of repentance. She began to fast and pray, and eventually she returned to God with her whole heart. And the Lord, who does not desire the death of the wicked but only that they return to the ways of the righteous, accepted her repentance. But the evil sorcerer who sinned and led her to sin was lost and cut off from the earth for all time.

Source: Eastern Europe
c. Sixteenth Century

The King's Dream

here was once a king who oppressed the Jews of his kingdom with harsh decrees. And when the holy Rabbi Adam saw their plight and the cruel deeds of the king, he cast a deep slumber upon him, and caused him to dream. In the dream the king awoke and found that his palace had disappeared, with everyone in it, and that he was lying on his bed at the bottom of a pit. The pit was deep and dark, the smell was rancid, and the light of day was like a roof far above him. The king was overcome with terror, for he did not know what had happened, and he even feared that he might be dead.

Just then the bed on which the king lay began slowly to rise, hoisted up by a rope, until it reached the top of the pit. There the king saw the stern face of a soldier, who pulled the king off the bed and tied his arms and marched him away, without a word of explanation. The king did not understand what was happening to him, and he stumbled along behind the soldier until they reached a castle. There the soldier took him aside, and brought him before the lord of that castle, and told the lord that he had been found trespassing, and was suspected of being a spy. The king tried to explain that he was the ruler of a great kingdom, and that he had been asleep in his own bed, and when he had awakened he had found himself in that deep pit, where the sol-dier had found him.

There was laughter from all of those present. Then the face of the lord of the castle grew solemn, and he said: "It is well known that anyone who is caught trespassing in this kingdom is required to fulfill three demands of the person whose land he has trespassed upon. The penalty for failing to perform any one of these demands is death."

When he heard this, the king bowed his head and was silent. At last he found his voice, and said meekly; "What are the three demands?" "The first," said the lord of the castle, "is for you to empty all of the water out of the well in the garden by the break of day." And he handed the king a dipper, with which to empty the water. But when the king looked at that dipper, he saw that it had a hole in it, and could not hold water. Then he knew that a terrible curse had fallen upon him, and it appeared that his life was as good as lost.

"Take him to the well, to begin his work," said the lord of the castle. And the king was dragged off into the garden, and left alone beside the well. He lay there, stretched out on the ground, weeping over his fate, which he could not understand. He did not even try to draw up any of the water, for he knew it to be hopeless. Just then a figure emerged from the darkness and ap-proached him. The king looked up and saw an old man with a long white beard standing above him. The old man said: "Why are you weeping?" And the king recognized that this man was not evil like the others he had met in that place, and he poured out his heart to him, and told him all that had happened.

After the king had finished telling his tale, the old man said: "How do you expect to empty the well if you do not begin to work?" And the king was confused, and he said: "Did I not tell you that the dipper has a hole in it?" "Is that true?" asked Rabbi Adam, for that is who it was. And he took the dipper in his hand and looked at it, and when he handed it back to the king, it was perfect once more, as if there had never been a hole in it. Then the king put the dipper into the well, and the water came rushing into it, and still it was not full. And even when the water ceased flowing, the dipper was not full, for Rabbi Adam had given it the fullness of the Lord, which is without limits. So it was that the king succeeded in emptying the well that night.

At dawn the lord of the castle arrived with many guards, certain that the king had not succeeded in performing the impossible task. Imagine his surprise when he peered down into the well and saw the muddy bottom, for it was completely empty, and even the spring, which had fed the well, had gone dry. The face of the king turned pale, and he said: "I do not know how you have accomplished this first task, but I doubt very much if you will complete the second."

"And what would that be?" asked the king. "Simply to build a palace of feathers by dawn tomorrow morning," said the lord of the castle. Then he laughed a terrible laugh, and left the desolate king alone in the garden.

Again the king slumped to the ground and cursed his fate. And as he lay there weeping, Rabbi Adam again approached him and said: "Why are you weeping?" The king told him the impossible task that the lord of the castle had given him. But Rabbi Adam told him not to lose hope, and took a whistle out of his pocket. He gave it to the king, and told him to blow on it. The king did so, and all at once there was the beating of a thousand wings all around them, and a flood of feathers began to fall at their feet. Nor did the feathers form uneven piles, but magically arranged themselves into a feather palace, with a fine foundation and many ramps and arches.

Now when dawn arrived, the evil lord of the castle came out to the garden, certain that he would put the king to death that day. But when he saw the magnificent feather palace, he could not believe his eyes. Then he looked for the king, but he could not find him. So he entered the feather palace, and there inside the bedroom chamber, sleeping on a feather bed, he found him. And when the lord of the castle saw this, he was enraged, and he said: "Wake up, my tired man. I see that you have worked hard all night. So I have decided to give you a long rest. Your task is really quite simple. In fact, anyone could do it. All that is required is that you let your fingernails grow, and cut them once in a while. And when you have filled up a snuffbox with your nail clippings, you shall have fulfilled the three tasks. But until then you must remain my prisoner!"

And the king, who had been deep asleep, sat up and listened to his terrible sentence. Then he heard a sound that made his blood run cold, and when he looked up he saw a dark metal box being dragged toward him. As he feared, it was a prison the evil lord had made for him. It had been constructed to the measurements of his body, and when he was inside it he could not move at all. There was only a small opening at the top of the box for the king to receive food and water.

So it was that the poor king was imprisoned in that metal prison, and once a day he was fed stale bread and a little water, and once a month the box was opened long enough for the nails of his hands to be cut, and the clippings were dropped into the snuffbox. In this way six terrible months passed, but even so the snuffbox was not even half full. Then one day, after the guard had departed, Rabbi Adam appeared and spoke to the king through the tiny opening in his metal prison. He said: "Would you like to get out once again into the light of day?"

"With joy and tears if only I could," said the king, who recognized Rabbi Adam's voice.

"And what would be my reward if I freed you?" asked Rabbi Adam. "I would give you half my kingdom," answered the king. "I do not ask for gold or power," said Rabbi Adam. "All I ask is that you sign a decree revoking the harsh decrees against the Jews, and affix your royal seal to it."

"Yes, yes," said the king, "I agree to sign it at once if you can only set me free." Rabbi Adam then touched the lock on the metal prison, and it sprang open, and he released the king. Then, after the king had signed the decree that Rabbi Adam had prepared, and affixed his seal to it, revoking the evil decrees against the Jews, Rabbi Adam gave him a new set of clothing, and led him to safety. Once they were far from the castle grounds, Rabbi Adam took him to an open field, and before long they reached the bed on which the king had been asleep when he had found himself in the pit.

Rabbi Adam directed the king to lie down on the bed, and when he did, Rabbi Adam lowered it into the pit. And the next thing the king knew was that he awoke and found himself in his palace chamber once more. Greatly relieved, he arose and called for his servants. But when they came in, he could not understand why they did not seem surprised to see him. Then he said: "Why don't you ask me how I am? Is there a single faithful servant left among you? Do you not wonder how I escaped after having been held captive for half a year?"

At last one of the servants found the courage to speak and said: "Surely the king must have had a dream, for the king's bodyguards stood guard at his door all night." The king could not understand how the servant could say this, and suddenly he caught sight of the snuffbox sitting on his dresser. He opened it and found that it was half full of nail clippings. This confirmed the events he had just experienced, and he chased the servants from the room. He paced back and forth, and thought of all that had happened to him. And when he remembered how Rabbi Adam had helped him so often, he cried aloud: "Of all the faithful servants in my household, is there not one who can serve me as the holy Jew did?"

Just then a horse-drawn coach approached the palace, and Rabbi Adam stepped out. The king recognized him at once and ran out to greet him. He embraced him and brought him into the palace. When they were both seated, with the servants standing around them, the king said to Rabbi Adam: "How can I explain my captivity to my servants, when they believe I spent the entire night sleeping in my own bed? For you were a witness to all that took place. Indeed, without your help my life would have been lost long ago."

Then Rabbi Adam said: "You have spoken the truth, but your servants are also correct. Listen and I will explain all that has happened to you." Then, amazed and speechless, the king and the servants listened to all that Rabbi Adam said.

"When the king announced his evil decree against the Jews," Rabbi Adam began, "the heavens were in an uproar, and the king was sentenced to death. During the night, when the king fell asleep, his soul departed from his body and was handed over to the evil spirits to be punished. These appeared to him in the form of the lord of the castle and his soldiers. But I came and argued on his behalf, and so I finally saved his soul. His trials in the castle of the evil lord were the journey of his soul through the various stations, until it returned to him at dawn. The snuff-box half full of nail clippings is a sign of the truth of this experience.

"And now," Rabbi Adam continued, "the king surely remembers this decree, which he signed." And Rabbi Adam took out the decree, with the king's signature and seal affixed to it, and when the king saw it, he understood the meaning of his dream, and had it announced that the decrees against the Jews had been abolished. And when the Jews of this kingdom heard of Rabbi Adam's accomplishment, they lifted their voices in prayer, and thanked God for His infinite mercy.

Source: Eastern Europe
c. Sixteenth Century

The Boy Israel
and the Witch

here once was a young man, Israel ben Eliezer, who loved to spend hours alone in the forest. Others wondered why he so enjoyed being alone there, and some even accused him of being lazy, although this was certainly not the case. No, the truth was that one day, while walking in the forest, the boy had discovered a pure spring, and after he drank the water of that spring, he found that he could understand the language of the birds. Now he kept this discovery a secret, for he soon learned that the birds are acquainted with all kinds of mysteries, and he did not want these powers to fall into the wrong hands.

At that time there was a severe drought that had lasted for many months. As a result the plants did not grow, and the harvest was in danger. And although the people often prayed for rain, none was forthcoming. Then one day, while he was sitting in the forest, the boy Israel heard two birds speaking in a tree, and one of them said: "The plants are thirsty, and so are the animals, and so are the people. And all because the evil witch has cast a spell on the rain." "Yes," said the other bird, "it is all the witch's fault.

If only someone knew that the drought was caused by the evil spell that the witch wrote out, and concealed in an amulet, which keeps the clouds from forming, so that it cannot rain. And if only someone knew that the witch hid the amulet in a metal case at the foot of this tree, and that if they found it and burned the spell written inside it until it was ashes, and scattered those ashes on the pure stream that flows in this forest, then the spell would be broken, and the clouds could form again and fill with water, and the rain could fall.''

Now when the boy Israel heard this, he was astounded, for he too had wondered why the terrible drought had descended, and now he knew. And now he knew, as well, what needed to be done in order to break the spell. Then Israel did not hesitate, but stood up and began to dig at the foot of that tree. And lo and behold, before he had dug for very long he struck something hard, and found a small metal case buried there, which was locked. But when Israel struck it against a rock, the case broke open, and an amulet fell out. And inside that amulet was a folded paper on which was written the terrible spell that had prevented the clouds from forming and had thus brought about the drought.

Then Israel wasted no time, but made a fire and burned the spell until it was ashes, and then carried the ashes to the pure spring he had discovered in the forest. And when he scattered the ashes on the water, they burst like bubbles as soon as they touched it. Suddenly the sky was covered by dark clouds, which soon broke open, and a fine rain fell that refreshed all the thirsty plants and animals and people, and everyone was very happy that the drought had come to an end.

Now when the first drops of rain began to fall, the witch was astonished, for she believed her spell was still in effect. And as soon as the rain stopped falling—for she did not want to get wet, since witches are afraid of water—she hurried to the tree where she had buried the amulet with the evil spell, and when she saw that it had been found, she was furious. Then she went back home and pronounced the words of a spell that made a demon appear, to serve as her slave. When the demon stood before her, she said: "Waste no time, demon, but find out for me who it is that has discovered how to break my spell. For I am anxious to take my revenge, and then to cast another evil spell."

So the demon went out into the forest to listen to what the birds had to say. For demons all understand the language of the birds, and know too that they are privy to many secrets. Thus it did not take the demon long to learn that it was the boy Israel who had discovered the secret of how to break the spell, for all the birds were speaking in admiration of him.

Now when the witch learned that it was the boy Israel who had found out her secret, she was even more angry. For she had assumed that a great wizard or sorcerer or holy man had broken her magic spell. But a mere boy! The thought of it made her tremble with fury. Then the witch went directly to the house where the boy Israel lived, and knocked on the door. But Israel was not home then, for he was in town learning Torah at the House of Study. Yet his mother was home, and it was she who opened the door, and when she saw who had knocked she grew afraid, for she knew that the visitor was evil. She told the witch that Israel was not there, and then the witch hissed and said: "Tell your son that I know what he has done, and that if he ever gets in my way again I will cast a spell on him. Then, if he is lucky, I will turn him into a bird, and if he is not, I will make him into a stone, and cast it to the bottom of the deepest well!" And with that the witch turned away and left, and Israel's mother shivered with fear, for she knew that the evil witch had the power to do everything that she had said.

So it was that as soon as Israel came home, his mother told him of the witch's visit and of her warning. Then she asked him what it was that he had done. So Israel told his mother how he had found the amulet buried in the forest, and how he had burned the paper on which the spell had been written, breaking it. When she had heard this, Israel's mother grew even more afraid, and she warned him to stay out of the witch's way, for if he didn't, the witch would not hesitate to cast a spell on him, as she had threatened. But Israel would not promise to avoid the witch no matter how much his mother pleaded, and only said: "I am not afraid of her, for I have trust in God."

Not long afterward a strange thing happened: the Ark of the Covenant in the House of Prayer, where the scroll of the Torah was kept, became locked, and despite the efforts of many men, it could not be opened, and thus the Torah could not be taken out. Now the Jews of that town were very frightened when this happened, for it was a very bad sign. They fasted and prayed and purified themselves, but nothing made any difference, and the doors of the Ark remained closed. Since this had happened during the Days of Awe, the time between Rosh Hashanah, the New Year, and Yom Kippur, the Day of Atonement, the people were especially frightened. But so far no one had succeeded in finding out what had caused this terrible thing to take place.

The boy Israel was also very unhappy that this had happened, and he wondered if he might learn anything about it from the birds. So he went off alone into the forest, and drank from the pure spring, and sat down under a nearby tree. And while he was sitting there, he heard one bird say to another: "The Jews are all so sad because the door to the Ark is closed, and they are cut off from the blessings of the Torah." "Yes," said the other bird, "but if only someone knew that this was caused by the witch, to revenge herself on the boy Israel, because he is Jewish. For she has taken a foul rag that she has dipped in the blood of seven unclean animals, and has hidden it beneath the synagogue, right beneath the Ark. And that is why the doors to the Ark have remained closed—to protect the Torah from that terrible impurity. And all that someone has to do is to take that rag and burn it in a fire, and scatter its ashes on the pure spring, and the doors of the Ark will swing open."

Now when Israel heard this, he did not hesitate, but ran back to town and crawled beneath the floor of the synagogue and there, directly beneath the place of the Ark, he found the foul rag, exactly where the bird had described it. Then he picked it up and wrapped it in some clean rags, so that he would not have to touch it again, and burned it in a fire, and carried the ashes into the forest, where he scattered them on the pure spring, and once again they burst like bubbles.

After this Israel returned to town, and when he arrived he found that the people were all dancing and singing in the streets, for the doors of the Ark had opened, and the terrible danger had passed. Israel too was very happy, although he did not reveal his role in breaking the evil spell, for he was very modest, and did not want to draw attention to himself.

But when the witch found out that the spell had been broken, and that the doors of the Ark had opened, she fell into a fury. Then she invoked the demon slave again, and sent him to find out what had happened. It did not take him very long to learn that the boy Israel was responsible, for although the people of the town did not know it, the secret was well known among the birds. And when the witch learned that it was Israel who had foiled her evil plans again, her wrath was terrible to behold, and she decided that she would punish him once and for all.

Now the boy Israel was no fool, and he knew very well that the witch might try to harm him, and that he had to be especially careful. He decided to go into the forest and to drink from the pure stream and to listen to what the birds had to say, so that he might have a warning if the witch tried to revenge herself in some way. So it was that he drank from the stream and sat down at the base of a tree, and no sooner did he do this than he heard one bird say to another: "My, how the witch has fallen into a terrible fury. And now she has sent a demon after the boy Israel, to touch him. And when that happens he will turn into a stone, which the demon will deliver to the witch, and the witch will drop to the bottom of the deepest well." "Yes," said the other bird, "but what a shame if this should happen—then there would be no one to struggle against the evil witch. Oh, if only Israel knew that he could protect himself against the demon by lighting a torch and carrying it with him, for demons are afraid of fire. Any demon who is touched with fire is condemned to serve as a slave in Gehenna for a thousand years, where fire burns everywhere day and night. So too could Israel protect himself with water, and especially the water of the pure spring. For if a demon is splashed with the water of the pure spring, he will become a small fish that will surely be swallowed by a larger one, and cease to exist." "Yes," said the first bird, "that is all true. And it is also true that the water of the pure spring could destroy the wicked witch as well, for if she were to be splashed with it, that would be the end of her."

Now Israel did not hesitate when he heard what the birds had said, and he hurried to make himself a torch, and made a fire and lit the torch in it. He finished making the torch just in time, for a moment later he heard something approaching him in the forest, and saw that it was the demon. Then Israel took the torch and hid behind a large rock, and waited until the demon had passed him. Then he jumped out, with the torch stretched out toward the demon, who found himself trapped between the fire of the torch and the pure stream. Then Israel said: "If you take one step toward me, demon, I will throw this torch at you, and you can spend the next thousand years in Gehenna. And if you do not do as I say, I will push you into the stream, and you can become a fish that will serve as food for a bigger fish, and that will be the end of you." And the demon saw that he had fallen into Israel's trap, so he agreed to do whatever Israel told him to do.

Then Israel told the demon to create a long chain that not even a demon could break, and to shackle it to his own right hand. This the demon did, and Israel took the other end in his hand. After this he told the demon to create a bucket, which he also did, and Israel filled the bucket with the water from the pure spring. Then Israel picked up a stone and tossed it to the demon, and told him to take it to the house of the witch, and to give it to her there. And he warned the demon that if he disobeyed, he would not hesitate to splash him with the water, for he would be close behind.

So it was that the demon approached the house of the witch and knocked on the door. And when the witch answered it, the demon handed her the stone, and said it was the stone that the boy Israel had become. Then the witch let out a terrible, shrill laugh, and while she was laughing, Israel ran up with the bucket of water in his hand, and threw most of the water at her. Suddenly her laugh turned to a horrible scream, and all at once she disappeared, and all that remained of her was a puddle of water. And when the demon saw the witch vanish, he panicked and started to run away, but slipped on the puddle, and suddenly there was a little fish flipping around where the demon had been.

Then Israel picked up the little fish and put it in the bucket, and carried it into the witch's house. He filled a jug he found there with the fish and water, and closed it tightly with a cork. Then he carried the jug into the forest, and hid it there in the hollow trunk of a tree.

Years later, when the boy Israel grew up and became famous as the Baal Shem Tov, he was traveling with his disciples through that same forest. Then he walked off alone and came to the hollow tree and looked inside and saw that the jug was still standing there, with the little fish still swimming around inside it. When he came back he was laughing, and when his disciples asked him why, he told them this story.

Source: Eastern Europe
Eighteenth Century

The Lost Princess

nce there was a king who had six sons and one daughter. His daughter was very dear to him, but one day when he was with her he became angry for a moment, and an evil word escaped his lips. That night the princess went to her chamber, as usual, to sleep, but in the morning she was not anywhere to be found. And when her father, the king, realized she was missing, he was filled with sorrow and remorse, and he began to search for her everywhere. Then the king's minister, seeing that the king was in sorrow, asked to be given a servant and a horse and enough silver for expenses, in order that he might undertake the search.

So it was that the minister traveled through all of the realm in search of the lost princess, across deserts and mountains, through forests and fields. He searched for her for many years. One day, as he was traveling in a desert, he glimpsed a path he had never seen, and he said to himself: "Since I have been searching for the princess in this desert such a long time, perhaps I shall follow this path and come to a city." After following the path for a great distance, he finally arrived at a splendid palace, guarded by many soldiers. Now the minister was afraid the guards would not let him enter, but still he dismounted and walked toward the palace, and to his surprise the gatekeeper opened the gate for him at once, without asking any questions. From there he passed from the courtyard into the palace, and after that he entered the chamber of the king who commanded all the troops. Nor did anyone try to stop him from entering into the presence of the king. There many musicians played their instruments, conducted by the king, and the minister stood off in a corner of the royal chamber, and waited to see what would happen. After a while the king commanded his servants to bring in the queen. They left with great rejoicing, and the musicians sang and played as she entered the room. And when they led her to the throne, the minister saw that she was the lost daughter of the king.

Before long the queen looked up and saw the minister in the corner of the chamber and recognized him at once. She rose from her throne and said: "Do you recognize me?" And he replied: "Yes, you are the lost princess. But how did you come to be here?" And she answered: "Because of that evil word that escaped from the mouth of my father. For this is the palace of the Evil One." Then the minister told her that her father, the king, was very sad in her absence, and that he had sent the minister to find her, and that he had been searching for many years. After this he asked her: "How can I take you away from here?" And she replied: "It is not possible to free me until you dwell in one place for a year, and throughout the year yearn to set me free. And on the last day of that year you must fast and not sleep for a full day and night."

Then the minister left that palace and did as she said. He went to a forest, and made his home there. And at the end of the year, on the last day, he fasted and did not sleep. But that day he saw for the first time a tree on which very beautiful apples were growing. He desired them very much, and finally arose and ate of the tree. But as soon as he ate, he fell down and sleep snatched him away. He slept for a very long time, and although his servant shook him, he could not wake him up.

When at last the minister woke from his sleep, he asked his

servant: "Where am I?" And the servant told him: "You are in a forest, where you have been sleeping a very long time, and all the time I sustained myself with nuts and fruits." The minister despaired, but found his way back to the palace of the lost princess, and there he met her again in the chamber of the king. And when she saw him she was filled with sadness and said: "Had you come on that day, you could have taken me away from here, but because of that one day all has been lost. Still, I understand that fasting is very difficult, especially on the last day, for then the Evil Inclination becomes most powerful. Therefore return and dwell again for another year, but on the last day you are permitted to eat. However, do not sleep, and do not drink any wine lest you sleep, for it is important above all to remain awake."

Then he went and did as she said. And on the last day of the long year he saw for the first time a spring whose waters were reddish, and whose smell was that of wine. The minister pointed out the spring to his servant, then went and tasted of its waters, only to fall asleep again, and this time he slept for many years. Near the end of that time many soldiers passed by, and the servant of the minister concealed himself. And after the troops had passed, a carriage came by, in which sat the daughter of the king. As soon as she recognized the minister she left the carriage and approached him. And although she shook him very strongly, he did not wake up, and she began to lament, saying that he had made such a long effort, and suffered for so many years to free her, and because of one error on that last day, he had lost everything. She wept greatly over this, and then took the kerchief from her head and wrote a message on it with her tears. Then she returned to her carriage and drove away.

Not long afterward the minister awoke and asked his servant: "Where am I?" The servant told him all that had happened, about the troops that had passed by there and the carriage that had stopped, and how the lost princess had tried so hard to wake him up. Then the minister saw the kerchief and asked: "From whence did this come?" And the servant told him that the lost princess had written on it with her tears. So the minister took it and lifted it up toward the sun. There it was written that she was no longer to be found in the first palace, but from then on would make her home in a palace of pearls upon a golden mountain, and that it was there that he would find her.

So the minister left his servant, and went off alone to search for her. He searched for many years. Finally he decided that such a palace of pearls could not be found in any inhabited place, for by then he knew well the map of the world. Therefore he decided to search for her in the desert, and after searching for many years he encountered a giant in that place, who carried a tree for a staff. Then the minister told him the whole story of the princess, and how he was searching for a palace of pearls upon a golden mountain. The giant said that surely such a thing did not exist. But the minister began to weep, and he insisted that it must surely exist *somewhere.* And at last the giant said: "Since you are so certain, I shall call all the animals which are in my charge, for they run about the whole world. Perhaps one of them will know about a palace of pearls." Then he called all the animals, from the smallest to the largest, of every kind, and asked them all what they might know, but not one of them had seen any such thing. Then the giant said: "You see, they have confirmed that your quest is nonsense. Listen to me and turn back, for surely you cannot find what does not exist." But the man insisted that it must. So the giant said to him: "Behold, farther in the desert lives my brother, who is in charge of all the birds. Perhaps they will know where to find it, since they fly high in the air. Go to him and tell him that I have sent you. And since you are so determined to carry on with your quest, let me assist you, so that at least you will not be hindered by a lack of gold." And he gave him a pouch, and said: "Dip your hand into this pouch whenever you need golden coins, for there you will always find as many as you will ever need." And the minister thanked the giant many times for his valuable gift, and for all of his help, and left to search for the giant's brother, who was in charge of all the birds.

So it was that the man walked for many years, seeking the second giant. At last he encountered him, also carrying a great tree for a staff, and he told him about his quest. But this giant also put him off, insisting that such a thing could not be. But when the man refused to give up, the giant said: "Behold, I am in charge of all the birds. I shall call them together, and perhaps they will know." So all the birds were called, each and every one, from the smallest to the largest, and they all replied that they did not know of any such palace of pearls. Then the giant said to him: "Now you must surely see that your quest is folly. Listen to me and turn back, for surely such a palace is not to be found in this world." But the minister would not abandon his quest, and at last the giant said to him: "Still farther in the desert lives my brother, who is in charge of the winds, and they cross the world back and forth every day. Perhaps they will know. I hope so, for never have I seen anyone so determined to complete a quest, even though you are beset with difficulty after difficulty. Therefore let me give you this gift, and perhaps it will be of use to you someday." And he reached into his pocket and pulled out a golden key and gave it to him. And he said: "This key can open any lock in the world. If there is a door that you must enter, simply insert this key into the lock, and when you turn it, the door will open." The minister thanked the giant many times for this priceless gift, and for his help, and set off to search for the giant in charge of the winds.

The man walked for many years, searching for the giant. At last he encountered him carrying a tree, and told him the whole story. And although this giant also tried to put him off, the minister at last convinced him to call all the winds together for his sake, so that he could ask them what they might know. The giant called all the winds to come there, but none of them knew about a palace of pearls on a golden mountain. Then the giant turned to him and said: "You see, you have been searching for something that does not exist." And the man began to weep and said: "I am still certain it can be found in this world." Meanwhile, one last wind arrived, and the giant was angry with it and said: "Why did you come so late? Did I not command that all the winds in the world should come here? Why did you not come with the others?" And the wind answered that it had been held up, because it had to bear the daughter of a king to a palace of pearls on a golden mountain. And when he heard this the minister rejoiced. Then the giant in charge of the winds said to the minister: "You have been searching for such a long time, my poor man, and you have had so many difficulties. Therefore let me give you this gift, which may someday be of use to you." And he reached into his pocket and pulled out a whistle, which he gave to the man. The giant said: "If you are ever in danger or in need of help, just blow on this whistle, and one of the winds will come to your assistance, and will do whatever is in its power to do." The minister thanked the giant many times for such a wonderful gift, and for all of his help. Then the giant commanded the wind to bring him to that palace. And the wind carried him there, and brought him to the gates of the city at the base of the golden mountain, on top of which the palace of pearls was to be found.

Now few strangers had ever entered this city, and once they had been admitted, they were never permitted to leave again, nor could any of the other inhabitants depart. For this was the hidden and secret palace of the Evil One, from which he cast his spells, like the spell that gave him power over the lost princess. And he had kept the existence of that city and palace secret for many centuries, since none had left the city to tell the tale. So it was that when the wind set the minister down before the gates of the city, the guards refused to let him enter. But he dipped his hand into the magic pouch the first giant had given him, and took the gold and bribed them, and thus he managed to enter the city after all. Then he went to the market to buy himself food, for he had to tarry there, since it required much thought and wisdom to set the princess free.

Now when the minister came to the market, he saw a servant who bought all of the fruits of a vendor. And after the servant left with them, the minister approached the vendor and said: "Surely all of those fruits cannot be for a single family." And the vendor replied: "Of course not. They are for those who live in the palace of pearls on the top of this mountain, for the king sees to it that the finest foods are selected for those who live there. And today the king's servants judged my fruits the finest, and that is why he purchased them all."

"Tell me," said the minister, "who is it that lives in the palace of pearls? For I am a stranger here, and I do not know."

The vendor replied: "Only the king and his servants, as far as I know. Although it is rumored that a princess also makes her home there, for not long ago the king selected twelve ladies-in-waiting from among our daughters, and took them to live in the palace, where they are said to serve her."

Now when the minister heard this, he decided to disguise himself as a merchant, and to present himself at the palace of pearls. First he went and bought the clothes of a wayfaring merchant and a fur hat. After this he asked to know who was the finest seamstress in the city, and he was shown to her house. When he came there, he asked her how much it would cost to sew the finest dress of silk and lace. And when the seamstress told him, he said: "Therefore sew twelve of these dresses." And he put his hand into the magic pouch given to him by the first giant, and he paid her in full. Then he asked her how long it would take to sew all twelve dresses, and the seamstress told him to come back in twelve days.

So it was that the minister stayed at an inn in that city until the dresses were ready. In the meantime he found out what he could about the king who ruled that kingdom and about his prisoner, the lost princess. In this way he learned that the palace of pearls was the hidden abode of the Evil One himself. So too did he learn that the princess was locked in a room that had seven locks, and that in the next chamber lived the twelve ladies-in-waiting.

When twelve days had passed, the minister returned to the seamstress, and found that the dresses were finished. Then he put the dresses in his merchant's pack, and climbed the golden mountain until he reached the palace of pearls. When he reached the gates of the palace, he showed the guard his merchandise and was admitted with ease, for new merchants were few and far between in that city, and the ladies-in-waiting were always happy to examine their wares, since they had little else to do.

So it was that the merchant was shown to the chamber of the twelve ladies-in-waiting, who were delighted to see him. He took out one dress for each of them, and when they saw how beautiful they were, they all rushed off to try the dresses on, and to study themselves in the mirror, and thus they left the merchant alone in that room. He looked around and saw that one door had seven locks on it, and he knew that must be the chamber of the lost princess. He hurried to that door and took out the golden key that the second giant had given him. With the key he quickly opened all seven locks, and went into the room. There he saw the lost princess, sitting at the window and sobbing over her fate. She was very surprised to see anyone at all, for she was kept apart even from her ladies-in-waiting. And when the minister saw that she did not recognize him in his disguise, he took out of his pocket the kerchief she had left with him, on which she had written with her tears. And when the lost princess saw this, she knew that the minister had found her at last, and she embraced him and wept tears of joy.

Then the minister said: "Come, let us hurry and depart the palace before the ladies-in-waiting return." "Alas," said the princess, "we cannot escape that way. For the Evil One has cast his spell so that it cannot be broken as long as my feet or those of my rescuer touch the ground. And it is this spell that is keeping me captive here even more than the seven locks on the door, which you have somehow opened."

At first the minister despaired over this unexpected obstacle, but then he remembered the whistle he had received from the third giant. He took it out of his pocket and blew on it, and in an instant a wind blew into the room through the open window and said: "How can I be of help to you?" Then the minister told the wind about the spell, and asked if it could carry them away from there with neither the feet of the princess nor his own touching the ground. "Of course I can do that!" said the wind. "But where is it that you want to go?" And the minister told the wind to take them back to the palace of the king who was the father of the princess, and the next thing they knew they found themselves soaring through the heavens, and before long the wind set them down in the kingdom from which they had been gone for so long. So it was that the loyal minister at last succeeded in his quest, and when the king and his daughter, who was no longer lost, were reunited, their sadness changed to a joy so great it cannot be described. May everyone know such great joy at least once in a lifetime!

Source: Eastern Europe
A Tale of Rabbi Nachman of Bratslav
Nineteenth Century

The Prince Who Was Made
of Precious Gems

here once was a great king who ruled over a vast kingdom. This king possessed unlimited wealth and power, and had everything a man can have, except that he had no children, and thus had no one to inherit his throne. Now the king longed to have an heir, for the thought that his kingdom would one day fall into the hands of strangers haunted him. So it was that he spent much of his time consulting with doctors and wise men, as well as with every kind of sorcerer and soothsayer. But none of these was able to help him, and the king and queen despaired of ever having a child of their own.

Then one day, when the king was very desperate, he turned to his ministers and asked them if they could think of anything else that he might do. An evil minister among them spoke up and said: "If I may be permitted to speak, my king, I have a proposal which might possibly provide the solution to your dilemma." The king replied: "Yes, yes, speak up." And the evil minister said: "It is rumored, my lord, that there are secret sorcerers among the Jews of our kingdom who possess great powers. They are said to have learned the secrets of King Solomon, who was familiar with the language of the birds and many other mysteries. I propose, O king, that we demand of the Jews that they bring forth one of these sorcerers, and let him beg their God to provide you with an heir, or else let them pay with their lives!''

Now the truth is that the evil minister did not believe the rumors he had heard about the powers of the secret sorcerers among the Jews, but he hoped to draw disaster upon their heads, as well as to put himself into a position where he might one day inherit the throne. The king was deceived by his proposal, and ordered that the Jews bring forth a wise man, who would intercede on his behalf. He added that if he was not blessed with a child by the end of one year, the Jews of his kingdom would pay with their lives! So it was that the frightened Jews turned to their rabbis, and begged for their help. And the rabbis met with each other, and agreed that they must search for one of the hidden saints among them, one of the *Lamed Vav*, or thirty-six Just Men, who are the pillars that support the world. For the prayers of such a man would surely be heard. But since these holy men are hidden among the people, no one knows for certain who they are, and therefore no one knew where such a Just Man might be found.

Time passed and the people grew more frightened, and still no hidden saint was identified. Then it happened that on the same night three rabbis in three different cities in that kingdom had an identical dream. In their dream they met with one of the Just Men, who lived in a cave deep in the forest, from which the sound of a nearby waterfall could be heard. And when the dream of these rabbis became known, it was recognized as a miracle, and many of the men organized search parties, and set out to find the hidden saint who lived in a cave somewhere in the forest. So too did the three rabbis who dreamed the same dream join this search, and traveled together, in hope that they would recognize some detail from their dream. So it was that when they recognized the sound of a waterfall, they remembered the sound of the falling water they had heard inside the cave of the hidden saint. Then they searched very carefully in that area, and at last they discovered a cave.

When the three rabbis entered the cave, they saw it was familiar. There they found the same old man with a white beard, whom they had met for the first time in their dream. He was seated on a stone ledge, and was intently studying an ancient text, which he read in the light cast by the flames of a fire burning within. When he saw the three rabbis the old man stood up and said: "Come in. I have been expecting you, for I met each of you in a dream. I do not know why I have been called upon to perform this task, for I have spent my life alone, in the study of the sacred texts. But I recognize the danger that threatens us, and that there is no other choice. Therefore I will agree to come with you, and to meet with the king, if you will vow never to reveal where this cave is hidden." The rabbis did so, and the old man was brought to the palace of the king, where he was given an audience at once. The king was very surprised by his ragged appearance, for all of the other sorcerers with whom he had consulted were wealthy men. But he accepted that the ways of the Jews might be foreign, and besides, he had no better hope. Then the king told the Just Man that he and his wife, the queen, greatly longed for a child. It was for this that they had sought his assistance. The Just Man assured the king and queen that they would be parents, and he promised them that before the year was out they would indeed be blessed with a child.

And within the year the queen gave birth to a beautiful daughter, who was the apple of everyone's eye. She was exceptionally beautiful, and when she was four years old she already knew how to read and write, as well as how to play the violin. She also had a great gift for languages, and had already mastered six. Kings traveled to that kingdom to see her, and from a young age the king began to receive marriage offers for her from the rulers of many kingdoms, who wanted to match her with their sons. It was then that the king realized that his daughter was destined to serve as a queen in a foreign realm, while his own kingdom might fall into the hands of strangers. Once more he began to brood. And when the evil minister saw that he still was not satisfied, he again proposed forcing the Jews to come to the king's assistance, for he still hoped to bring down disaster upon them. And the king agreed that this would be done. So it was that the Jews were forced once more to seek out the hidden saint. Again they turned to the three rabbis who alone knew where his cave was hidden, since they had never broken their vow about its location. But when they came to his cave they found that the Just Man had taken leave of this world, to claim his portion in Paradise. When they discovered this, the three rabbis at first despaired, for where were they to find another hidden saint? But then they said among themselves: "Surely such a holy man must have known that one day we might need his assistance again. Come, then, let us search in this cave for any clues he might have left us as to where his successor might be found." For they knew that whenever a Just Man leaves this life, there is always another who takes his place, so that the number of them remains at thirty-six at all times.

Then the rabbis carefully searched through the cave where the hidden saint had made his home. There they found that he had few possessions except for his sacred texts, which were all well worn. But then one of the rabbis noticed a crevice that they had all overlooked, and inside that crevice he found a small, finely crafted silver mirror, engraved with intricate designs and secret symbols. When he looked into that mirror he saw reflected there a man he did not recognize, yet he knew at once who that man must be—the Just Man they were seeking, the one who had taken the place of the hidden saint who had made his home in that cave. He showed the mirror to the other rabbis, who agreed that they must seek out the man reflected there. Together they set out, wandering from village to village, and showing the mirror to whomever they met, until at last they found someone who recognized the man they sought, and directed them to the village in which he made his home. When at last they found him, they told him of the king's order and of their quest. At first he did not seem to believe that he had inherited the mantle of one of the *Lamed Vav*, but when the rabbis showed him the mirror that reflected his face at all times, and told him how they had found it, he accepted all that they had to say, and agreed to serve as best he could. After that the Just Man prayed for guidance, and his prayers were answered, and he learned in a dream what it was that he should do to bring about the birth of a son for the king.

So it was that this Just Man soon found himself in the presence of the king, as had the hidden saint who had served before him. This time the king was careful to specify his desire for a son, who would serve as the heir to his throne. Then the Just Man agreed that he would strive to fulfill the king's wish, if the king would agree to supply him with one of every kind of precious gem. Nor did the king hesitate, for he said: "I would give up half of my kingdom for a son." Then the king ordered that one of every kind of precious gem be gathered, and delivered to the hidden saint. This was done, and then the Just Man crushed each gem, ground it to dust, and mixed it with wine, for that is what he had been told to do in his dream. This wine he poured into the cups of the king and queen, half into one and half into the other. Then the king and queen each drank the potion, and before the Just Man took his leave he said: "Before a year is out you will have a son who will be made entirely of precious gems. He will have the charms and qualities of each of the gems that was mixed into your wine, for each gem has its own special charm."

Once more the prophecy proved true, and before the year was out the queen gave birth to a son, and the king was exceedingly pleased, even though the child was not made of gems, but was flesh and blood, like every other child. And just as his sister was, this child was very beautiful and very wise. Before the age of four he could read and write, play many musical instruments, and speak a dozen languages. Kings came from every corner of the earth to see him, and to propose that their daughters might one day be his queen. So it was that the young prince became the center of attention, and his sister became jealous, and her love for him turned to hate. Her one consolation was that he was not made of precious gems, as the Just Man had predicted. Then one day the prince was chopping wood and cut his finger, and when the princess came over to bandage it, she saw a gem gleaming on the inside. Then she was overcome with jealousy, and decided to pretend to be ill, that she too might receive some attention. So she went into her room, and refused to come out of it, even to eat.

Now the king and queen were very concerned about their daughter, and they summoned doctors from all over the kingdom, but they were all unable to cure her mysterious illness. Then the king called in his sorcerers, and among these there was a wicked one, who had made an alliance with the evil minister. This sorcerer saw that the princess was only pretending to be ill, and when he confronted her with this fact she confessed that it was true, and revealed her hatred for her brother, the prince. Then the princess asked the wicked sorcerer if there was any way to cause a person to become ill. And he said that he knew of a way to cause a person to be covered with scabs. Then she asked if another sorcerer could cure this disease, and the sorcerer replied that if the talisman that had caused the disease was concealed in water, the spell could not be broken.

So it was that the princess fell into the trap set for her by the evil minister and the wicked sorcerer. For they had long wanted to find a way to be rid of the young prince, so that the evil minister might fulfill his dream of one day becoming king. Until then they had been afraid to act on their own, but now that the princess could be blamed, they became bolder, and the wicked sorcerer cast a spell on the prince, and caused him to be covered with scabs all over his face and body. Then he gave the talisman that had cast the spell to the princess, who hid it under a rock in a pool outside of the palace. Of course the king sent for all of his doctors, but none of them was able to cure the prince. Then he summoned his sorcerers, but none of their spells had any effect. Finally the king decreed that the Jews must assist him once more, and find a cure for the prince, or else they would pay with their lives.

So it was that the people turned once again to the Just Man who had already interceded with the Holy One in their behalf.

Now the Just Man believed, like the rest of the world, that the prince was merely flesh and blood. For this reason he began to doubt the dream in which he had learned that the prince would be made of precious gems, and was afraid that he would be unable to bring about a cure. Still, because of the danger to the Jews, he went before the king, and sought to undertake a cure. And through his prayers it was revealed to him that the disease of the prince had been caused by witchcraft. This the Just Man reported to the king, and told him that nothing could be done unless the talisman containing the spell was recovered, and the one who bewitched the prince was cast into the sea. When the king heard this he said: "I will give you all of the sorcerers in my kingdom. You can cast them all into the sea. I would do anything to save my son."

Now the young princess was present when the king said this, and she became very frightened that her role was about to be revealed. Then she hurried away to be certain that the talisman was safely hidden. And when the Just Man saw her hurry off, he became suspicious, and told the king to have her followed. So it was that a guard followed her to the pool outside the palace. But when the princess bent over to lift up the stone under which the talisman was hidden, she fell in the water, and began to cry out. This caused a great commotion, and the King and the Just Man hurried outside to see what had happened. But the Just Man told the king not to worry, for the princess would surely be saved by the guard who had followed her, and now the prince would recover. And as soon as the guard pulled the princess to safety, she confessed that she had asked the wicked sorcerer to cast the spell, and revealed where the talisman was hidden. And when the king heard this, he understood that the princess was not to blame, but that she had been led astray, and he forgave her. Then the king had the wicked sorcerer brought before him, and forced him to confess, and the sorcerer also admitted that the evil minister had put him up to the plan.

So it was that the wicked sorcerer and the evil minister were cast into the sea, and the prince began to recover the same day.

The scabs that had afflicted him began to drop away, and as they did it was revealed to the world that he consisted entirely of precious gems. And all those who came to know him found that he possessed the charms and qualities of those very gems.

Source: Eastern Europe
A Tale of Rabbi Nachman of Bratslav
Nineteenth Century

The Water Palace

n a faraway land there was a king who conquered many kingdoms, and whose wealth was so great there was nothing he desired that he was not able to obtain. His palace was filled with treasures of every kind— there were golden objects encrusted with precious jewels, rare rugs from every corner of the world, and mirrors made of silver so highly polished that they reflected better than any mirror of glass. There was nothing this great king lacked, but nonetheless he was not happy, and always searched for something more precious than what he already possessed.

Then one year it happened that this king received the king of a faraway kingdom, who had embarked on the long journey to see with his own eyes the most precious treasure in all that realm. This was the mysterious water palace, which was to be found on the southern shores of that kingdom, and which had existed there as long as anyone could remember. Now this water palace was truly one of the greatest wonders of the world, for it consisted entirely of water. The floors and walls of the palace were made of water, the grounds and gardens that surrounded it were made of water, and the fruit trees that grew there—all were

made of water. And this palace was surrounded by ten walls, one inside the other, and all ten walls were made of water. And because the palace and walls consisted of water, it was impossible to enter there, for whoever tried to do so would surely drown. Still, travelers came from all over the world to marvel at the wonder of that palace, which remained unchanged amidst the waves, not that far from the shore of the sea.

Now it happened that when the king who ruled that kingdom met the king from the distant kingdom, he also met the visiting king's daughter, the princess, who had traveled with him, along with their guards and servants. And the extraordinary beauty of that princess struck the wealthy king with amazement, and from the first he knew that he would not rest until he had made her his own, for to him it was she, and not the water palace, that appeared to be the most precious treasure in all the world.

Therefore the wealthy king offered to accompany the visiting king and the princess on the journey to the water palace, and put at their disposal all of his resources. Before long their caravan departed for the journey south. The procession was led by the two kings and the princess, dressed in the silks and diamonds of a court celebration. Behind them came their countless servants, walking together in twos and threes. The caravan was watched by the subjects of the kingdom as it passed through the forests and fields; it proceeded in a stately manner, not so fast as to frighten the horses or cause the carriages to shake, while the two kings and the princess held the diamond-studded reins in their hands. During the journey the wealthy king took every opportunity to speak to the princess who rode beside him, for he felt a longing for her which was unlike anything he had ever known, so sharp was his craving that she might be his wife.

Now at first the princess paid little attention to this king, and resisted his approaches, but when the caravan arrived at the cove facing the water palace, the princess, like everyone else, was awed at the marvel of it. And the more the princess looked at its enchanted beauty, the more certain she became that she had somehow seen it before, perhaps in a dream. Nor did she want to depart from that place when the sun began to set, but insisted on staying there as night fell, for she had heard that the water palace was somehow illumined from within, so that its every ramp and arch could be seen even on the darkest night. And the wealthy king, out of his longing for the princess, chose to remain with her in that place, and when he observed how much she was drawn to the palace, an idea entered his mind of how he might convince her to become his bride. Late that night he told her that if she would marry him and become his queen, he would agree to build an ivory palace on the very shore where she stood, facing the water palace, and that he would make that ivory palace their home. And when the princess understood that in this way she would never have to leave the pristine beauty of the water palace, she accepted, although she did not truly love him, and agreed that she would become his queen.

The king was enthralled at the prospect of spending his life with this beautiful princess, and for the first time he thought he understood what was truly meant by love. Soon preparations were made for their wedding, which was declared a holiday for all, and at the same time construction of the ivory palace was begun. And because the king put all of his vast resources into building it, the palace was completed by the day of their wedding. At the king's command the architect had sought to model it after the water palace in every respect that could be seen—for neither he nor anyone else had seen it from within. And the bridal chamber of the king and the princess had been built to face directly the inaccessible palace surrounded by and constructed of water.

Then it happened on the very night the king and princess were wed, as the king slept beside his bride for the first time, that he had a vivid dream in which the princess approached the bed on which he lay, with a bow and arrow, and both arrow and bow were made of gold. And before he could speak, she took aim and shot the golden arrow into his heart. Now when the king awoke from this dream he was deeply disturbed and afraid for his life. He took his leave of the sleeping princess, and ordered a servant to stand guard outside that chamber, to prevent her from leaving it until the king had consulted with his advisers.

The next morning, when the princess awoke and discovered that the king was not to be found beside her, she was surprised, but she did not attach any importance to it. She simply assumed that he had returned to his duties as king. And since her food was brought to her, she did not question the matter, but instead hurried to the window from which the water palace could be seen, and filled her eyes with its unearthly beauty.

Meanwhile, the king had gathered all of his dream interpreters together, and he told them his dream. Then he called on his oldest interpreter, and bid him to speak. He said that the king need not fear, for the arrow that the princess had shot into the king's heart was surely the arrow of love, and the dream had come because he was so filled with love for her. Then the king called on another interpreter, and the second confirmed what the first had said, adding that the king had been "slain," so to speak, by the great beauty of his bride. But the third to speak disputed this interpretation, and insisted that the dream posed grave danger to the king, since it prophesied that the princess would bring about his death. After this every other dream interpreter agreed with this interpretation, for they saw in it a way to rid themselves of the princess, who had already caused them to lose much of their influence over the king. And when they had all spoken, the king returned to the first two interpreters and, out of fear, they too agreed that the interpretation of the others was correct, and withdrew their own.

After this the king asked them what he should do with the princess, who posed such a danger to his life. Those two who had understood the dream as a sign of his love suggested that he banish her. But the king refused this idea from the first, for the thought that she might ever belong to another tormented him, since he had made such an effort to make her his own. And those who had interpreted the dream as a warning told the king to put her to death. But the king refused this advice as well, for he was afraid that his grief at her death would be unbearable. Therefore he decided to delay his decision and meanwhile he continued to live with his bride, although he kept a guard near them at all times, close enough to call on a moment's notice. And every day he had the palace searched for the golden bow and arrow, but never was any hidden weapon to be found.

Yet, even with these precautions the king could not forget his dream. He thought of it whenever he was in the presence of the princess, and it came to haunt him day and night, until his love for her became spoiled. As for the princess, she saw how her husband had become remote and sensed that he did not trust her, although she could not imagine why. Thus, little by little, her trust in him also faded. Then there was nothing that kept her in that place except for the enchanted vision of the water palace, which possessed her even when she slept, so that she dreamed of it every night. So it was that the princess spent more and more time sitting at her window, letting the watery ramps and arches of the palace beckon to her, for while she could not bear to live with the king any longer, she also knew that she could not bear to abandon the mysterious palace.

One night, in her desperation, the princess slipped away from the king while he was sleeping, and climbed out of the window that faced the water palace, and made her way from the ivory palace to the palace in the sea. But before long the king awoke and found the princess missing, and became enraged. He assumed that she had left to get the golden bow, and that she intended to kill him that very night. He shouted for his guards, and they came running, and word was quickly spread to search for the princess wherever she could be found, and it was soon reported that she had been seen running along the shore, in the direction of the water palace. Before long the princess heard the clamor of the guards behind her, and knew that they were already in pursuit. Therefore she walked directly into the water, for she preferred to drown rather than to be captured by the king. And when the king, who had accompanied his guards, saw this, he shouted to the guards to shoot their arrows at her, and to kill her, as he thought she had intended to kill him.

Now there were ten guards with the king, and each of those guards carried a bow and arrow, and each of those arrows had been dipped in a poison, and each of the poisons was more deadly than the next. The guards took aim as they saw the princess running into the sea, and shot their ten arrows at the same time. And each of those arrows pierced the princess, and she was gravely wounded and fell into the water. But the instant she touched the water a wave rose up and carried her out into the sea, through every one of the gates of the ten walls that surrounded the water palace. For there was a gate in every wall, and each of those gates opened when the wave carried her close to it, and closed again the instant she had passed through. At last the wave brought her into the innermost chamber of the water palace, and set her down on a circular bed, where she fainted and fell into a deep sleep, and not even the waves that washed against the wall of the palace caused her to waken.

Meanwhile the king and his guards had become so obsessed with capturing her that they did not stop when they reached the sea, but continued to pursue her into the water as if they were still on land. Then a great wave came and carried them far off from the shore, where they struggled and soon sank. Every one of them, including the king, was drowned.

Now when the people of this kingdom learned that the king had drowned, and that the princess had also very likely lost her life, they sent a messenger to her father, who had not yet left the kingdom, and invited him to become their king, for they had recognized that he was a wise and good man, and would not lead them astray. The father of the princess agreed to remain in their kingdom and serve as their king until another king could be found, for he still hoped that his daughter might be alive, having somehow reached safety in the water palace.

After the new king had been installed, he made a proclamation that whoever succeeded in reaching the water palace and discovering the fate of the princess would receive a great reward, and if she was alive, whoever brought her back from there would become her husband, and would succeed him as king. Then brave princes and many other daring young men came from all over the world and sought to reach the water palace in various ways. Some tried to swim out to it, and some tried to travel in rafts, and others in boats. But one and all, they failed to pass through the ten walls that surrounded it, and many were drowned making the effort. And among those who survived, all insisted that it was surely impossible that the princess could have reached the water palace, and that even if she had, she could not have passed through the ten walls, and must surely have drowned in the strong currents there. But even as the months passed and nothing was heard of the princess, the king refused to give up the hope that his daughter might still be alive.

Now in a nearby kingdom there lived a young prince whose family had ruled that realm for many generations until their army had met defeat at the hands of the wealthy king. The prince's father had died defending their kingdom, and the prince, who had barely escaped with his life, had gone into hiding. But in his heart he was determined that someday he would defeat the king who had brought about his father's death and had taken their kingdom by force. And so it was that this prince disguised himself as a wandering beggar, and traveled to the kingdom of the water palace. Like all the others who entered that land, he was told the tale of how the king had lost his life pursuing the princess, and of the reward that awaited whoever could reach the water palace and discover her fate. The prince was exhilarated when he heard this news, and he decided at once to present himself, still as a beggar, to the new king, in the hope that he could somehow win back his father's kingdom.

That night the prince dreamed that birds flew to the seashore from every corner of the world. And in the dream he heard them singing melodies, ten in all. As they reached the shore each dropped a single feather, until at last the feathers had formed into a swan-shaped boat of feathers. And no sooner was it complete than a wave arose and picked up the swanboat, and carried it on top of the waves. When the prince awoke he remembered this dream, and even recalled each of the ten melodies. And he realized that such a boat of feathers might well suit his purpose in rescuing the princess.

Later that day the beggar prince was given an audience with the king, during which he offered to seek to accomplish what so many others had already failed to do—to penetrate the ten walls of the water palace. And because a considerable time had passed since anyone else had been prepared to undertake the risk, the king welcomed his offer, even though it came from a beggar. The beggar prince told the king that it would be necessary to gather one feather from every kind of bird in that kingdom, from the most glorious to the most common, for with those feathers he intended to build a boat of feathers with which he might confront the waves. For, he said, only a boat of feathers could pass over the ten walls, since any other would be too heavy. And the king ordered that the feathers be gathered, and the prince built a fine swan-shaped boat with them, exactly like the one he had seen in his dream.

On the morning that the beggar prince was to set off in the boat of feathers to try to make his way to the water palace, the king accompanied him to the shore, followed by a great many of his subjects. And when the beggar prince placed the boat in the water, all were amazed at how lightly it floated. Then he climbed into the boat of feathers, and the first wave that came carried it off so that it seemed to fly, so lightly did it travel on the waters. With those who watched as witnesses, the boat sailed above the ten walls with room to spare, and in this way the beggar prince soon reached the water palace, and made his way inside. Now why he did not sink is a mystery which has remained unknown to this day. But there, in the innermost chamber, he found the princess, still deeply asleep. For she had not awakened since she had been carried into that chamber, nor could she be awakened until the ten arrows were removed, and she was cured of the ten poisons.

It was there, behind those walls of water, with the winds raising up the billows of the sea, that the beggar prince removed the ten different arrows from the princess. And with each of his ten fingers he felt one of the ten pulses, and set about to cure her, using the ten different melodies he had learned in his dream. And when he had felt the tenth pulse and sung the tenth melody, the eyes of the princess opened, and she sat up on the bed. And she knew from the first glance that the one who stood before her was her true love, as the suspicious king had never been. So the beggar prince took the princess out of the water palace, and returned with her in the boat of feathers to the shore. There she was reunited with her father, the king, who wept long and hard when he saw his beloved daughter was still alive. Then the beggar revealed his true identity as a prince, and it was announced that they would be wed. So it was that in this way the prince came to rule both his own kingdom, and that of the king who had usurped it. And it is said that once a year, on the anniversary of the day the beggar prince took the princess out of the water palace, they would return there together in that boat of feathers, and spend the day in the innermost chamber, where she had slept for so long, although what they did or spoke of in that place has never been revealed.

Source: Eastern Europe
A Tale of Rabbi Nachman of Bratslav
Nineteenth Century

The Pirate Princess

nce upon a time there were two kings, each of whom was childless. And each one set out on a journey to discover a remedy that would make it possible for a child to be born to him. Now fate led both kings to the cave of an old sorcerer on the same day, and the sorcerer met with them at the same time. And after each had explained what it was that he sought, the two kings were amazed to discover that they both were on the same quest—each searching for a remedy so that he might be blessed with a child of his own.

After they had spoken, the sorcerer said to them: "I have read in the stars that each of you is destined to have a child, one a boy and one a girl. And I have also read there that these two are destined to marry. If you permit their marriage to take place, you and your descendants will share a great blessing. But if you keep them apart, for any reason, many will suffer before they are reunited." Then the sorcerer stood up, and the kings left the cave. But before they parted they each vowed that if one had a boy and the other a girl, the children would be betrothed.

It happened that before a year had passed the two kings had each become fathers, one to a beautiful boy, and the other to a lovely girl. But the demands of their kingdoms were very great and the distractions endless, and so it happened that they both forgot about their vows concerning their son and daughter. And when their children came of age, they sent them off to study in a foreign land. And fate caused them both to study under a famous scholar, who was, in fact, the sorcerer who had predicted their birth.

In this way the prince and princess met, and knew from the first that they loved each other, and wanted to be wed. Yet even though the sorcerer saw this, he did not reveal their destiny to them, for he wanted them to stay together solely by the power of their love. So it was that the prince and the princess were together every day for several years. When the studies came to an end, he returned to his kingdom and she to hers. But when they were apart each became dejected, and soon it became plain for all to see that they were unhappy, but no one knew why it was.

At last the king who was the father of the prince asked him what was wrong, and why he had become so sad. Then the prince revealed his love for the foreign princess, and when the king heard this, and learned who she was, he recognized the father of the princess to be the king with whom he had made a vow to betroth their children. Therefore he wrote a letter to the other king, and reminded him of the vow, and suggested that their children should now be wed. And he gave the letter to the prince, and sent him to deliver it in person to the king.

Now when the king who was the father of the princess had received the prince and read the letter, he grew afraid, for he had forgotten about the vow he had made with the prince's father. And he had since made an engagement between the princess and a prince whose father ruled a rich and powerful kingdom. So it was that the king decided to delay the prince for as long as possible, until the princess had been wed to another. He then invited the prince to remain with him in the palace, so that he might observe him, and see if he had been properly prepared to be a ruler. But the king also left orders that the prince was not to be permitted to see the princess, nor was she to be told of his presence there.

In this way the prince and princess remained apart, although they were both living in the same palace. But one day the princess overheard two of the servants whispering about the prince, and learned in which chamber he was staying. Then she made a point of passing in front of that chamber as often as possible. Before long the prince caught a glimpse of her in his mirror, and soon they managed to meet in secret. Then the princess told the prince how her father had betrothed her to another, and they decided to run away together that very night.

So it was that the prince and the princess climbed out of their windows at midnight, and ran together until they reached the ship of the prince. They set sail in the middle of the night, and by the time it was discovered that they were missing, they were already far away. They continued to sail together for a long time, until they were in need of fresh food and water. Soon afterward they spied an island on which fruit trees could be seen growing, and they sailed there, docked the ship, and walked together in the forest. There the princess climbed a fruit tree and tossed the fruit that she picked down to the prince, who filled up a sack with it. But it happened that a wealthy merchant's son was passing near that island in a ship, and he was observing the island with his telescope. In this way he happened to see the princess in the tree, and was astonished at her beauty. He had his ship brought to shore, and he set out with several sailors, armed with weapons, to capture the lovely girl in the tree, and to make her come with him whether she wanted to or not.

Now when the princess, from the vantage point in the tree, saw the men coming in their direction, and saw the long swords they carried, she told the prince to hide and not to reveal himself, no matter what happened. Then she tossed her ring to him, which he caught, and she vowed that even if they were separated, they would still one day be reunited. The prince hid himself in the dense woods, and saw the merchant's son and his men arrive at the foot of the tree, but there was nothing he could do about it, for he was unarmed.

At first the merchant's son spoke sweetly to the princess, but when she refused to reply he ordered his men to cut the tree down. And then, when she saw that she could not escape, the princess descended from the tree and returned with the merchant's son to the ship. But before she climbed on the ship, the princess made the merchant's son vow not to touch her until they were married in his land. And even though she was his prisoner, he agreed to this vow, for he was smitten with love for her, and hoped to win her love as well. Nor would the princess tell him who she was, but she promised him that once they were wed she would reveal the secret, but until then he must not ask to know. And this condition, too, the merchant's son agreed to honor. So it was that the princess entertained him on that voyage by playing various musical instruments, and the time quickly passed.

When the day came that the ship approached the land of the merchant's son, filled with much valuable merchandise, the princess told the merchant that the proper thing to do would be for him to go to his home and inform his family that he was bringing with him the one who would become his bride. The merchant agreed to this, and also to the request of the princess that all of the sailors on the ship should be given wine to drink, so that they would share in their celebration.

In this way the merchant's son left the ship to inform his family, and the sailors began to drink. Before long they were all drunken, and they decided to leave the ship to look around the town. And when she had the ship to herself, the princess untied it from its moorings and unfurled the sails and set sail by herself.

Meanwhile the family of the merchant's son all came down to the harbor to greet his bride-to-be. But when they found the ship gone, including all the merchandise it had carried, the merchant was furious with his son, and asked him what had happened. All the merchant's son could say was "Ask the sailors," and when they searched for the sailors they found them sprawled drunken on the ground, and neither then, nor later, when they were sober again, did they have any idea at all of what had happened to the ship. So it was that the merchant, in a great rage, drove his son out of his house, to become a wanderer in the world.

Meanwhile the princess continued to sail the ship, intent on searching for her lost love. As it happened, she sailed by the kingdom of a king who had built his palace on the shore of the sea. And that king liked to watch the passing ships with his telescope. So it was that he noticed a ship sailing by that seemed to be empty, and sailing without any guidance. Then he sent his sailors to catch up with it, to bring it into port. This they did, and in this way the princess was again captured, and became a prisoner of the king.

But when the king met his lovely prisoner, who had been sailing the ship by herself, he was greatly struck with her beauty and royal bearing, and he desired to marry her. This she agreed to do on three conditions: that the king not touch her until after their wedding; that her ship not be unloaded until the same time, so that all might see how much she had brought the king, and so that none would say that she had come empty-handed; and, finally, she asked that she be given eleven ladies-in-waiting, to remain with her in her palace chamber. The king agreed to these conditions, and made plans for a lavish wedding. So too did he sent to her the daughters of eleven lords of his kingdom, to serve as her ladies-in-waiting. And before long they had all become good friends, and they all played musical instruments together to amuse themselves.

One day before the wedding the princess invited her ladies-in-waiting to go with her onto the deck of the ship, to see what a ship was like. They all were glad to join her there, for they had never before been on a ship, and greatly enjoyed themselves. Then the princess offered them the good wine that she had found stored there, and they drank the wine and soon became intoxicated and fell asleep. Then the princess went and untied the moorings and raised the sails and once again escaped with the ship.

Now when the king was told that the ship was no longer docked, he became afraid that the princess would be distressed to hear it was missing, for he did not know that it was she who had taken it. But when they looked for her in her chamber, they did not find her there, nor did they find her ladies-in-waiting.

Finally they realized that the princess and her ladies had disappeared along with the ship, and the lords who were the fathers of the ladies were enraged, and forced the king to give up his throne, and afterward drove him from the land, so that he too became a wanderer in the world.

Now the princess and the eleven ladies were already far away at sea when the ladies awoke. And when they saw that they had sailed far beyond the shore, they were afraid and wanted to turn back, for they had never sailed in a ship. But the princess said to them: "Let us tarry here awhile." So they did, but when the ladies asked her why she had left the harbor, the princess said that a storm had arisen, and she had been afraid that the ship might have been broken in the harbor—therefore she had set out to sea. And soon afterward a storm did arise, and the ladies saw that they could not turn back, but were at the mercy of the currents. And when the storm subsided, they found themselves alone at sea, with no idea of how to seek out the land they had left, so they agreed to sail with the princess until they should reach land somewhere.

So they continued to journey at sea, the princess and the eleven ladies. At last they came to an island, and landed there, hoping to find fresh food and water. But it turned out that this was an island of bloodthirsty pirates, and when their sentries saw the ladies on the island, they approached them with their weapons drawn, and brought them to the chief pirate among them, asking if they might kill them right then and there.

Now when they stood before the pirate chief, the princess spoke for the others and said: "We too are pirates, but while you are pirates who use force, we are pirates who use wisdom. If you were wise the twelve of you"—for there were twelve pirates in all—"would each take one of us for a wife, and make use of our wisdom, which will surely help you to become far richer. And for our part we will each contribute a twelfth of the merchandise we have captured as pirates, which you will find on our ship."

Now the chief among the pirates was taken with the great beauty of the princess, and thought to himself how nice it would be to take her for a wife. So too did he think that what she had said made sense, and when the pirates saw all the wealth in the ship, which the princess had taken from the merchant's son, they agreed that they were indeed fine pirates. Therefore the pirates agreed among themselves that they would each, according to his rank, choose a lady to take for a wife. And after the chief of the pirates had chosen the princess, and the other pirates had made their choices among the ladies, the princess invited them to share the fine wine that they had on their ship.

So the princess poured out twelve goblets of wine for them, and the pirates drank until they all became drunk and fell asleep. Then she spoke to the ladies and said: "Now let us go and each kill her man," and they went and slaughtered them all. And there, on that island, they found such great wealth as is not possessed by any king. There was such an abundance that they resolved to take only the gold and precious gems, and unloaded all the merchandise from the ship, to make room for it. In this way they filled the whole ship with treasures, and prepared to set sail. But before they did, the princess had each of them sew a uniform to wear, so that they would all look like sailors, and then they set out to sea.

Once again they sailed for a long time, until they reached a distant port. There they docked the ship and descended into the city, wearing the sailors' uniforms that they had sewn. They roamed about the city, looking very much like men, and in this way they reached the center of the town, where they heard a great commotion and saw many people all running in one direction. One of the ladies inquired as to what was the matter, and she learned that the king of that country had just died childless, and that in such a case it was the custom of the country to have the queen go up to the roof of the palace and from there to throw down the dead king's crown. And on whomever's head it fell, that person became king.

Now the princess had hardly heard of this custom when she was struck with a heavy object, which landed on her head. She cried out, "Oh, my head!" But immediately she was surrounded by the viziers and wise men of the kingdom, who raised her onto their shoulders and cried out: "Long live our king!" The crown had indeed fallen on her head, and since she was wearing men's clothing, no one knew that she was a woman.

When the funeral of the former king was over, the wedding between the new king and the old king's widow was to take place. But the viziers, seeing that the new king was very young, preferred to marry the new king to the daughter of the chief vizier. The old queen agreed that this could be done, for she no longer wished to rule, and the wedding was set for the very next day.

Now the princess, disguised as a man, was afraid of what would happen when the truth came out, and she did not know what to do. Finally she called in the daughter of the vizier, and after pledging her to secrecy, she confessed that she was a woman, and told her the story of how she had been traveling with the other ladies, and how they had just come into port in that city and reached the center of town when the crown had landed on her head. The girl promised to help her, and together they worked out an excuse for postponing the wedding.

Meanwhile the disguised princess had the sculptors of the city brought into the palace, and ordered them to make many sculptures of the new king's head, and to put these up at every crossroad and at every road leading to and from the city. Soldiers were to be stationed at every spot where a sculpture was placed, and they were commanded to arrest anyone who stopped and showed great emotion at the sight of it.

It happened that three such people came along, and were arrested. The first was the prince who was the true bridegroom of the princess. The second was the son of the merchant whose ship the princess had seized, and who had afterward been banished by his father. And the third to be arrested was the king who had been driven out of his kingdom because the princess had sailed off with the eleven daughters of the high lords. For each had recognized the features of the princess, even though the sculpture represented a man.

Then, on the day of the wedding, the princess had these three brought into her presence, and she asked them what had happened to them since she had last seen them, and they told her their stories. The prince who was her true love had journeyed all over the world in search of her. He had come to the kingdom where she had escaped with the merchant's boat, and had passed through the kingdom where the king had been driven out because the princess had escaped with the eleven ladies. And he had also found the island of the pirates, and found their bodies there, along with the clothes of the princess and the ladies. So it was that he had sailed after them and reached that kingdom, which was the closest to the island of the pirates, and he had been searching for her there when he had come upon the sculpture of the king who was about to be crowned, and had recognized her face. So too had the merchant's son and the deposed king traveled around the world, seeking only their daily bread, and wondering why such disaster had befallen them.

And when the princess had heard what they had to say, she turned first to the king who had lost his kingdom and said: "You, king, were driven out because of the eleven ladies who were lost. Take back your ladies. Return to your country and your kingdom, where you will surely be welcomed." And to the merchant's son she said: "Your father drove you out because of a ship filled with merchandise that was lost. Now you can take back your ship, which is filled with much more valuable treasures, whose worth is many times that which you had in it before." Finally she turned to the prince who was her true bridegroom: "It is you to whom I was betrothed before any other. Come, let us be married to each other."

Then the princess called in all the viziers and ministers, and revealed that she was not a man, but a beautiful woman. And she showed them the ring the prince carried with him, which she had given him in the forest before she had been captured by the merchant's son, which proved that it was he to whom she was truly betrothed. And the viziers were so impressed with the character of the prince and princess that they asked them to remain among them as their king and queen, and this they agreed to do. That day the prince and princess were married in a great celebration, and afterward they ruled with an evenhanded mercy that all admired, and they lived happily ever after.

Source: Eastern Europe
A Tale of Rabbi Nachman of Bratslav
Nineteenth Century

The Golden Bird

ow it was the custom of Rabbi Nachman of Bratslav to take long walks in the forest alone, as did his great-grandfather, the Baal Shem Tov. One day Rabbi Nachman was walking among the majestic trees, deep in thought, when he heard the trill of a bird in the distance. And that melody was so sweet and resonant that Rabbi Nachman hurried farther into the forest, in the hope that he might catch a glimpse of the bird that had such a beautiful song. He traveled an untold distance, ignoring the way as he went, so great was his curiosity. But although his ears sought out the slightest sound, the forest was strangely silent, and Rabbi Nachman did not hear as much as a rustling leaf, for even the wind seemed to be holding its breath.

At last Rabbi Nachman concluded that he had set off in the wrong direction, and in despair he sat down at the base of one of those towering trees, whose upper branches seemed to reach into heaven. Perhaps because he was leaning there, a verse from the Psalms suddenly came into his mind: *The Torah is a Tree of Life to those who cling to it,* and at that moment a feather fluttered down through the branches of that tree, and fell beside Rabbi Nachman where he sat, and at the same instant he heard clearly the haunting trill of the bird that had lured him to that place. Then Rabbi Nachman jumped up and searched in the branches, in the certainty that the bird must be in that tree, but nothing was to be seen. He continued to look long after it was apparent that the bird had eluded him once more, then he sat down and picked up the feather, and was amazed to discover it was golden, and that it shone in the sun like a mirror. And when he saw that golden feather he knew it must have come from the bird with the enchanting song, and once again he was over-whelmed with longing to seek it out. But then Rabbi Nachman noticed that the rays of the sun were slanted through the trees and realized that the afternoon was coming to an end. He knew very well how dangerous it would be to be caught in the forest after dark, and with great reluctance he left that place and made his way back. Then, to his amazement, he seemed led as if by an unseen guide, for he flew through the forest as if he had made his home there all of his days, and before the sun reached the horizon he emerged from it, with the golden feather in his hand. And with one look backward, he returned to his home in Brats-lav. Nor did he reveal the events of that day to anyone. And that night, before he went to sleep, he placed the golden feather be-neath his pillow.

So it was that no sooner did Rabbi Nachman fall asleep than he found himself in the forest once again, the golden feather still in his possession. In the distance he saw a circular pool and real-ized he was very thirsty. He went to the pool, bent down, and drank from the clear water, which satisfied him to his soul, and when he stood up he saw in the water the reflection of the gold-en bird, flying overhead, more wonderful than anything he had ever imagined. But when he raised his eyes, it had already disap-peared. And once again Rabbi Nachman knew he could not rest until he had seen that bird with his own eyes. And then he woke up.

All the next day Rabbi Nachman wondered if he would be permitted to continue that night the quest for the golden bird that had so far evaded him. For he sensed that nothing would be served by searching for it in the forest outside Bratslav, but that it was his destiny to seek out that bird in the kingdom of dreams. And that night, as he slept, it did happen that he found himself walking in the forest once more. This time he reached a place where he glimpsed a garden in the distance. But no matter whence he tried to approach it, it would vanish before he was able to find an entrance. And each time the garden reappeared, Rabbi Nachman heard the haunting song of the golden bird, which pierced him to his soul. And he knew that if he could only find a way to enter that garden, he might well find the golden bird, for no other could have such an unearthly song. Yet although he continued to glimpse the garden from time to time, he was never able to find any entrance, no matter how many times he circled the area in which it appeared.

It was then Rabbi Nachman remembered the golden feather, and how it had shone like a mirror in the sun. He took it out, holding it so that it faced the direction in which he had glimpsed the garden, and saw at once that in the mirror of the golden feather the garden did not disappear from his sight, but remained clearly in his view. Then he circled the garden once more, this time viewing it from the mirror of the feather, and in this way he was able to discern the gate, previously invisible. And he saw how that gate opened and closed in the blink of an eyelash. So he made his way there, and stood before the gate and closed his eyes, and when he opened them he found, to his dismay, that he had awakened. Once more the dream had ended before he had achieved his goal. But this time he was confident that the quest had not come to its end, and that he might still find his way into the garden of the golden bird.

So it was that when Rabbi Nachman closed his eyes to sleep on the third night, he opened them to find himself standing inside that glorious garden, where he heard the haunting song of the golden bird clearly once more. And in the distance he saw a tree so wide he estimated it would take a five hundred years' journey to travel around it. Beneath the tree flowed four streams, which spread throughout the garden, one in each direction. And high in that tree Rabbi Nachman saw the golden bird, glowing in the branches like a golden star. And when the bird started to sing, its song carried his soul to the heights.

It was then Rabbi Nachman saw a man walking in the garden. The man's face was glowing, and his eyes cast such a great light that they seemed to illumine the path on which he walked. This man approached Rabbi Nachman, who cast down his eyes, knowing he was in the presence of a holy man. And the man said: "Welcome to this garden, Rabbi Nachman. I have been waiting for you to arrive ever since you found the golden feather, for I knew you would not rest until you found the bird from which it came. As for me, I am the gardener here; it is my blessing to tend the sacred fruits and flowers and to see that they grow ripe."

And Rabbi Nachman said: "Peace be with you. I had longed to find one who could guide me in this enchanted place, and who knows the ways of the garden better than the gardener? But tell me, what is your name, and how is it that you have come to tend this garden?"

The man said: "I am the Ari. Just as I was a gardener of the Torah, and found the hidden meanings buried beneath the surface, and understood how scattered sparks can take root and bring forth a harvest of abundance, so it is that I have been rewarded by being made gardener of this garden, in which the golden bird makes its home."

Rabbi Nachman was overwhelmed to find himself in the presence of the Ari, as Rabbi Isaac Luria, of blessed memory, was known. At first Rabbi Nachman was silent, but then he found the courage to speak, for at last he had the opportunity to discover the secret of the golden bird, whose golden feathers reflected in the sunlight like the facets of a jewel, and whose melody had lured him the way a flame attracts a moth. And he asked if the Ari could share this secret, and the Ari said in reply: "That golden bird, Rabbi Nachman, is the beloved bird of the Messiah. For the song of that bird translates the prayers of Israel into a haunting music that fills the heavens."

It was then that Rabbi Nachman suddenly remembered something that had completely slipped his mind until that moment. It was a tale about his great-grandfather, the Baal Shem

Tov, who once was praying with his Hasidim when he prolonged the Eighteen Benedictions for such a long time that his Hasidim grew impatient, and one by one departed from the House of Prayer. Later the Baal Shem told them that by leaving they had brought about a great separation. For while the Baal Shem he had prayed he had ascended the ladder of their prayers to reach a place where he had seen a vision of a golden bird, whose song could not but bring peace of mind to all who heard it. And he was certain that if such a song were brought to the world of men, it would surely bring peace everywhere it was heard. And the Baal Shem told them that by stretching forth his hand he had come within reach of taking the bird from that tree. But just then the ladder of their prayers had broken, and he had fallen back to this world as the bird flew away.

Then the Ari, who could read Rabbi Nachman's thoughts, spoke and said: "Yes, this is the same golden bird that the Baal Shem saw. Nor was it any accident that his Hasidim grew impatient, for heaven made certain of this, so that the Baal Shem would not succeed in taking the bird before the time had come for the Messiah to be born among men. For it is in this garden that the Messiah makes his home, and that is why his palace is known as the Bird's Nest, for it is the song of that bird that sustains the worlds above and below. The Messiah enters that hidden abode on New Moons and holy days and on the Sabbath, for that is when the bird leaves this enchanted tree and returns to its nest. And all the while the bird sits in its nest it sings, and the Messiah glories in its song, which contains the essence of a hundred thousand prayers. Had the Baal Shem succeeded in bringing back even one golden feather, peace would have followed for many generations. And had he brought back the golden bird, the Messiah would surely have followed, so little can he bear being separated from its song."

Now Rabbi Nachman was startled when he heard this and became very solemn, for like the Baal Shem he longed for nothing more than that the Messiah should usher in the End of Days. At last he said to the Ari: "What if I should attempt to bring the golden bird out of this garden?" But no sooner had he spoken

i a sudden wind arose, and plucked the golden
hand, and carried it off, so that Rabbi Nachman
s gone. Nor was that warning lost on him, for he
might be expelled from the garden as swiftly as
the wind. Then the Ari replied: "You, Rabbi Nach-
tered this kingdom as a dreamer, while the Baal
ᴑᴨᴇ. ᴧere as one awake. Therefore that path is closed to
you, for even if you succeeded in capturing the golden bird, you
could not carry it beyond the gate of the kingdom of dreams. At
the very instant you touched its feathers, you would find yourself
alone and empty-handed in the world of men, and all that has
transpired so far would be lost to you, like a dream lost between
sleeping and waking."

Now Rabbi Nachman was not surprised to hear these words,
for he had not forgotten that he had entered the kingdom of
dreams. And the last thing he wanted was to be expelled from
it. Then he said to the Ari: "But tell me, if I am permitted to
know—how may I make my way back to this garden in order to
hear the sacred song of the golden bird as it translates the prayers that ascend from the world below? Nor does it matter if I
come here as a dreamer or as one awake, as long as I am permitted to be in its presence and to hear that haunting melody."

The Ari smiled and said: "For you that will be very simple,
Reb Nachman. You need only turn to the verse in which it is
written that *The Torah is a Tree of Life,* and it will serve as your
key to this kingdom. For on that night you will travel to this
world in a dream, and share in the presence of the golden bird
and the song that transforms the prayers of men, which as you
see, are themselves the keys of heaven."

And no sooner did the Ari finish speaking than Rabbi Nachman awoke and found himself in the world of men once more.
But this time he did not feel the quest was incomplete; on the
contrary, he understood that his roots among the living were just
as deep as those that drew him to the world above, where the
song of the golden bird filled the heavens. And from that time on
his Hasidim noticed that Rabbi Nachman left the Holy Scriptures
by his bed every night, opened to the Psalms. And from that time

on they also noticed a divine smile that could be seen on his lips and in his eyes when he awoke. And all who knew him marveled at how peaceful he was every morning, as if he had returned from a journey to a faraway kingdom of peace.

Source: Eastern Europe
Nineteenth Century

The Imprisoned Princess

nce there were a king and queen who had no children. After having tried many remedies for barrenness, all of which had failed, they made an announcement that anyone who could assist them in having a child would be greatly rewarded.

Now many were those who offered an amulet or potion to the king and queen, but none of these remedies had any effect. At last, when the king and queen had begun to despair of ever having a child of their own, a merchant arrived from a faraway kingdom bringing with him three things which gave them hope again. The first of these was a round mirror, small enough to fit into the palm of a hand, which was enclosed within a golden frame. The second was a ball of yarn. The third was a golden box. And when the queen took that mirror from the merchant and looked into it, she saw herself holding in her arms a beautiful child, who was surely a lovely girl. Then the amazed queen handed the mirror to the king, who saw himself in that mirror looking considerably older, and standing beside him was a beautiful young lady, whose features left no doubt that he was her father and the queen, his wife, her mother.

Now the king and queen gasped when they saw this bright

vision of the future, which revealed that they would receive that which they wanted most in the world—a child of their own. The king then said to the merchant: "This mirror you have shown us has given us hope that the future holds the happiness of the child we both long for. Tell me, how can we go about making our dream come true?"

Then the merchant said: "Here, O king and queen, is a ball of yarn that you must follow as it unravels. For if you cast it into the road it will begin to roll, and it will continue to unravel until you have reached the place it is destined to lead you to. Simply keep the ball in your sight, and let it lead you wherever it might." Then the merchant handed the ball of yarn to the king, who held it tightly in his hand, for it was precious in his sight.

"Finally," the merchant continued, "I am entrusting to you, my queen, this golden box. It is required that you deliver it to whomever the ball leads you to. But take heed of what I am telling you now—do not open the box, for if you do your quest for a child may be harmed." And the merchant handed the small box to the queen. And when she examined it, she saw that all kinds of signs and symbols had been engraved on it, whose meaning she did not comprehend.

Then the king said: "We will certainly do as you have directed. We will cast the ball and set out to follow wherever it leads us, and my wife will guard the golden box and see to it that it remains closed. For we would do nothing to jeopardize having a child of our own. But tell me, merchant, what is it that you wish as a reward for having revealed this remedy to us?"

Then the merchant said, "Until the remedy takes effect, and you have the child you long for, there is nothing that I expect. And when this blessed event has taken place, you will repay me by permitting me to serve as godfather to your child, for that would reward me more than all the gold in your treasury."

The king and queen were amazed that the merchant did not ask to be paid in gold or silver or precious gems. And it was then that they recognized they were in the presence of a holy man. Then the king asked the merchant to tell him who he was, and the merchant replied: "My name is not important. All that matters is that you follow carefully the directions I have given you, so that the future shown in the mirror of destiny may come true. For even though we each have a fate, it is for us to seek it out, and to let it lead us, like the ball of yarn that you are soon to follow. If we let it out of our sight, it is lost to us—who knows for how long?" Then the holy man who had disguised himself as a merchant took the mirror of destiny and put it away in his pocket, and took his leave of the king and queen. And no sooner was he gone from their sight than the king ordered that their bags be packed and a carriage be made ready for their departure the next morning.

So it was that at dawn the king took his place beside the driver of the coach, while the queen sat inside. The king cast the ball of yarn before him, so that it started to roll, and while the king kept his gaze firmly fixed on the ball of yarn, the driver followed his every direction, sometimes slowing down when the ball rolled uphill, and speeding up when it rolled downhill.

Now it happened that all the time the king and driver followed the ball of yarn with that coach, the queen sat alone inside, the golden box held in her hands. She became caught up in its beauty, and in the mystery of the signs and symbols that adorned it. And she turned it over and over and shook it next to her ear, and wondered what it could possibly contain. At last she could not bear the mystery any longer, and forgot the warning of the holy man, and opened the lid of the box only a little, and peeked inside. For she said to herself: "What harm could there be if I open the box for a moment and look inside? Who will ever know that this has happened?" And there she saw that the box was filled with a fine powder, which seemed to glow as if it were illumined from within. But in that instant a small breeze passed through the carriage, and plucked twelve grains of that precious powder, and carried them out of the window. Now the queen did notice this small loss, but she thought it was of no consequence, for the box was still filled with the powder, and the little that had been lost seemed unimportant.

Meanwhile the coach arrived at a forest, where the path ended, yet the ball of yarn continued to roll, although it seemed to slow down, as if to wait for them. Then the king did not hesitate, but leaped from the coach, opened the door and helped the queen down, and after ordering the coachman to wait for them until they returned, they followed the ball on foot.

So it was that the ball of yarn unraveled before them, although it never seemed to grow any smaller. And they followed it through the dense forest, managing to keep it in their sight. At last it approached a cave and rolled inside, and the king and queen followed after it. Inside the cave they saw a large bonfire burning, and beside it, facing the fire, sat an old woman, with long, white hair. She had picked up the ball of yarn that had rolled to her feet, and she began at once to knit with it.

Then the king spoke and said: "Greetings, old woman. We have followed that ball of yarn with which you are knitting, and it has led us to this cave. We bring with us a golden box which we were instructed to deliver to you. Please tell us who you are, and what is expected of us so that we may be blessed with a child." Then the old woman said: "I am an old woman who has made my home in this cave for many years. Some call me a witch, while others know that is not the case, for it is my duty to knit with the yarn of fate. Now, give me the golden box." Then the queen gave the golden box to the old woman, who examined it closely. She was silent for a long time, and at last she said: "The seal of this box has been broken." The king was stunned to hear this, and turned to the queen, who confessed, with tears flowing, that she had opened the box for an instant. "Then tell me," said the old woman, "were any grains of this magical powder lost?" "I will not lie to you," said the remorseful queen. "A few grains were carried away by a small breeze, but I did not think it mattered."

Then the old woman took down an old scale she kept in that cave, and carefully poured out the powder and weighed it. At last she said: "Twelve grains are missing. That will mean that the princess, your daughter, will have to remain within a cave for twelve years. And if she sees the light of day before that time, she will be lost to you—who knows for how long? Then from the ages twelve to fifteen you may take her outside every day, but she must be escorted, and never left there alone."

Now on the one hand the king and queen were greatly relieved to learn that they would still have a child of their own, but on the other they were grieved to know that such a danger would hang over their child's head, for they knew they could never bear to lose her. And they knew as well that they could not argue with the one who knitted with the yarn of fate. Therefore they bowed their heads and swore that they would keep their daughter from the daylight for a full twelve years, and escort her whenever she walked outside for three years after that, and they asked to know what else was required of them.

Then the old woman took down an old bottle of wine and broke the seal and poured it into two golden goblets. After this she divided the powder into two parts, and poured half into one goblet and half into the other. Then she handed one goblet to the king and the other to the queen, and told them to drink it to the last drop. This they did, until not a single drop remained. And when they had done this the old woman said: "Now you can go back to your palace, and in nine months you will be blessed with a child of your own. Take with you the shawl I have knitted from the ball of yarn that led you here, and wrap your infant in it when she is born, for as long as this shawl is wrapped around her shoulders, she will be safe. But do not fail to heed my warning and keep her concealed from the daylight for the first twelve years, and watch her closely for three years after that, or else you will live to regret the day that your child was lost." Then the old woman gave them the shawl, and the king and queen took their leave. Nor did they lose their way in that forest, for when they departed the moon had risen, and illumined the way. So it was that in a short time they reached the coachman who still waited at the edge of the forest, and they returned to their palace. And in nine months' time the queen gave birth, and they were blessed with a beautiful daughter, who was their joy and delight. And from the first they wrapped her in the shawl knitted by the old woman, and had living quarters built for her in a cave, which did not admit the light of day, but was lighted instead by the fireplace within. They took great care that the princess remained there, for they did not doubt the consequences if they disobeyed the warning of the old woman. So too did they name the holy man her godfather, as he had requested.

When the princess was somewhat older, the king and queen hired a tutor for her and saw to it that she was well educated, learning many languages and being instructed in many musical instruments. But whenever she read of the sky, or of trees or water, she wondered what these were. Everything was a wonder to her, and all her tutor could tell her was "When you are older you will know everything."

Twelve years passed, and at last the king and queen were able to hold a great ball for the princess, and afterward the king took her out walking for the first time. She marveled the most when they arrived at the shore of the sea, and she saw the waves rising and falling, and smelled the salt in the air. After that the princess begged her father to take her to the seashore every day. But one day he was unable to do so, and the princess, who had a great longing for the sea, slipped away by herself and went there alone. And when it was discovered that she was missing, there was a great fear, for her shawl had been found on the shore. A search began, dispatches were sent everywhere, but the princess was not to be found. The despair of the king and queen was terrible to behold, for she was the light of their lives, and they blamed themselves for not having watched her more closely.

Eventually, when no more was heard of the princess, and it was greatly feared that she had drowned, the king announced that he would reward whoever found his daughter with half his kingdom, and the princess would become his wife. Among those who undertook this quest there was one prince who had become enchanted with the portrait of the princess, and searched for her not for the reward, but in the hope of winning her love. This prince presented himself to the king, who was so taken with the youth's sincerity and determination that he bestowed on him his own signet ring, as a sign to his daughter that he had been sent by her father, for she would recognize the ring at once.

Now when the prince was leaving the palace he was met by

the same holy man who had once disguised himself as a merchant for the king and queen, and this time he had disguised himself as a beggar. He approached the prince and said: "Perhaps you would like to see a mirror that reveals the future?" Now the prince was a patient man, so he did not ignore the beggar, but stopped and spoke with him, and asked to see the enchanted mirror. The beggar held out the mirror of destiny, into which the king and queen had once peered. And when the prince looked into it he saw himself standing beside a beautiful bride, and that bride was the lost princess, who was even more beautiful in that mirror than she was in the splendid portrait that had fascinated him in the first place.

Then the prince grew solemn and said to the beggar: "At first, I must confess, I spoke to you in jest, for who could imagine that such a marvelous mirror truly exists? Now tell me, I beg you, how I might find the princess, so that this prophecy can be fulfilled."

Then the beggar gave the prince a ball of yarn, and told him that when he set out on his voyage he should tie one end of the yarn to the mast of the ship, and then throw the ball of yarn into the sea. And he should follow the ball wherever it floated, and never let it out of his sight. Then the beggar took off the hat he was wearing, which had been knitted by the same woman who knitted with the yarn of fate, and offered it to the prince, and said:"When the right time comes, put on this hat, and you will become invisible." The prince took the hat, and thanked the beggar, saying to him: "Tell me, how can I reward you for your assistance?" And the beggar said: "Just invite me to your wedding, for I would like to dance with the bride." The prince assured him that he dearly longed for that day, and he and the beggar took their leave. Then the prince took the hat and the ball of yarn with him and went to the ship, which was being made ready for the voyage.

At dawn the next day the ship cast off, and the prince did as the beggar had said, tying one end of the ball of yarn to the mast, and casting the ball itself into the sea. And he followed the ball wherever it floated in the currents, and let it lead him. In this

way the ship sailed for many months until it came into view of an
island, on which there had been built a great palace. There the
prince brought the ship to anchor, for the ball of yarn had rolled
up to the shore, and rolled down the path leading to the gates of
that palace, and the prince followed after it.

Standing at those gates were many guards, with spears in
their hands. Then the prince put on the hat the beggar had given
him, and at once became invisible. In this way it was easy for
him to slip inside during a changing of the guard. He passed
through the rooms of the immense palace, every one of which
was built of gold and silver. He searched for the princess everywhere, but he did not find her in any of the rooms. Finally he
came to the last room at the far end of the palace, which was
locked. He knocked on the door and from the other side a voice
called out: "Who is there?"

"A man," the prince replied.

"If you are a man," said the princess—for that is who it
was—"then flee for your life. There is no hope for me, but you
can still escape. This is the palace of a terrible giant, Niemar,
who will not hesitate to kill you if he finds you here."

"Who are you?" asked the prince.

"I am a king's daughter," the voice replied. "One day I was
walking at the shore of the sea when a ship appeared, and Niemar came out of the ship and captured me and took me with him
as his prisoner. And here he has kept me imprisoned ever since,
so that I never see the light of day."

"Do not fear," the prince said. "I will help you escape from
here."

Suddenly the prince heard footsteps, and Niemar himself approached. As soon as the prince saw him, his heart failed, for the
giant was so large the prince could not even see his face. But
then the prince remembered he was still wearing the hat of the
beggar, which made him invisible, and his confidence was restored.

"Who is it that you are talking to?" bellowed Niemar
through the door. And when he said this, the princess realized
that the giant had not yet seen the prince. Then she said: "Alas, it

was only me, talking to myself, so lonely have I become." "And that is how you will remain for the rest of your life!" said the giant. "For you are my prisoner, and I will never let you go."

Then Niemar took out his key and opened the door of the princess's room, and went inside. And once inside, he locked the door again. After that he took a handkerchief from his pocket, waved it over the table, and instantly it was set with all the finest food and drink one could wish for. Then Niemar said: "Today it is one year since I captured you. Let us celebrate!" And he poured himself a giant glass of wine, and drank it down in a single gulp. And while he was drinking the invisible prince came up to the princess—for he had slipped into the room when Niemar had opened the door—and he whispered in her ear that he was there, and that she should not be afraid. Meanwhile Niemar kept drinking more and more wine. And when at last the giant was dead drunk and had fallen asleep, the prince took off his hat, and revealed himself to the princess. Then he unsheathed his sword and cut off Niemar's head, and took the keys from the giant's pocket. After that he unlocked the door and let the princess out of the room, saying to her: "You see, I have killed him, and now we need fear no one." And the prince was right, for when the guards and servants of Niemar discovered that he was dead, they all threw up their arms in celebration, for he had been a terrible tyrant, and they, too, had been his prisoners.

Then the prince and princess packed all the treasures of the palace, and loaded several ships full of gold and silver, and set out for home. When they returned, there was great rejoicing, and the king held a magnificent wedding for the prince and princess, during which the holy man danced with the bride. And the prince and princess lived together in love for the rest of their lives, and became the parents of three beautiful children, who loved to play outside every day, and were the source of great joy and satisfaction to their grandparents, the king and queen.

Source: Eastern Europe
Oral Tradition

The Exiled Princess

ong ago there were a king and queen who had only one child, a daughter. They were very wealthy, as befits royalty, and lived in a great palace. The king concerned himself with the details of ruling his kingdom, and the queen, who was very kindhearted, concerned herself with charity, to which she gave generously. And she impressed upon her daughter, the princess, the importance of being generous.

Time passed and the queen died. Eventually the king remarried, and the stepmother disliked the princess, and especially did not like her generosity, for the new queen was very selfish, and wanted to keep her riches for herself. But when the princess continued to be kind to poor people, the stepmother went to the king and complained that if the girl did not stop, they would end up impoverished. Now the king did not really mind that his daughter was so generous, but he could not bear the nagging of his wife. So he told the princess to give less to others. But the princess could not bear to see poverty, and she ended up giving more rather than less. The stepmother was quick to notice this, and she threatened to leave the king unless he put a halt to it. The king again warned the princess, and told her that if she disobeyed him, she would be expelled from the palace. Still, the girl insisted on giving even more to charity than before.

When the king learned this, he grew very angry and called in his servants and told them to take the princess, to blindfold her and tie her hands, and to lead her into the forest, and return without her. So it was that the reluctant servants, who loved the kind princess but were afraid to disobey the king, packed up all her dearest belongings, including her crown and the bridal gown of her mother, the dead queen, and led her into the forest, blindfolded and with her hands tied. But before they left her alone, they loosened the ropes that held her hands and hurried off, believing that in any case she would lose her life to the beasts that roamed there.

When the servants had gone, the princess freed her hands from her bonds, loosened her blindfold, and began to weep bitterly. She remained standing throughout the night, terrified at every noise she heard. But at dawn, when she was still weeping, she saw an old man who was walking through the forest. The old man approached her and said: "Why do you weep so bitterly, my child?"

Then the princess told him everything that had happened, and he said: "Come with me, child, and I will lead you out of this forest to a road. Take your belongings and follow this road and you will come to a town. When you arrive, ask for the way to the almshouse, and you will have a place to stay."

So it was that the old man led the princess out of that forest, to the road. There he took his leave of her and returned to the forest, where he lived, and the princess followed the road until she came to a town. When she arrived there it was already Friday evening, and the night was beginning to grow dark. Then she noticed a light in the distance, and followed its beams until she reached a small house. She was very hungry and thirsty, and sat down on the steps of that house and wept. Now in that house lived a rabbi and his wife, who had an only son. And when the wife had finished saying the prayer over the Sabbath candles, and had called out "Amen," she heard the sound of crying from outside the window. Then she went to the window and called out:

"Who is there? If it is a demon, go away; if it is a human being, come in and be welcomed." Then she opened the door and found a girl sitting on the steps and asked her: "Why are you crying, my child?" And the girl replied that she was an orphan with no one in the world, and that she had been traveling alone when she had met an old man who had told her there was an almshouse in that town where she could find a place to stay.

When the rabbi's wife heard this, she said: "Where will you go on Friday night after the candles have already been lit? Come, spend the Sabbath with us, and I will take you to the almshouse at the end of the Sabbath." And so it was—the girl spent the Sabbath in the rabbi's house. But when it was time for her to be taken to the almshouse, she pleaded with the rabbi's wife: "Please let me stay here and let me be your servant. I ask only for food and drink." The wife replied: "I would not mind if you were here, but I have nowhere to keep you." Then the girl continued to plead: "Let me stay here. I can sleep on the floor next to the stove, it is good enough for me. Please, just not the almshouse." The rabbi's wife considered the matter, and decided that it might be worthwhile, after all, to have a servant for the mere price of food and drink, and she agreed to let the girl stay. So it was that the princess remained there, and served them well. And even though her portion was small, the girl always saved a part of it for the beggars who wandered through the town.

Now this rabbi was highly respected in that town, and when the wealthy landowners held a wedding for one of their children, or some other celebration, they invited him to attend with his family. And before long a wealthy man held a wedding for his daughter. The rabbi and his wife and son were invited and they all went, and the girl remained alone in the house. But she too wanted to attend, for she had never been to a Jewish wedding. So she took out the parcel of her belongings, which the king's servants had packed for her, and chose one of her finest gowns, put it on, and went to the wedding.

When she got there, everyone stared at her, for she was very beautiful in her royal gown. But no one knew where she came from, and if she belonged to the guests of the groom or those of the bride. She was soon asked to dance, and she danced with everyone. And the rabbi's son also noticed her, and asked her to dance with him many times, without recognizing her at all; nor did she reveal who she was. Finally she noticed that it was getting late, and she pulled herself away from him and ran home. There she quickly put away her fine gown, donned her rags, and crawled back beside the stove, just as the rabbi and his wife and son returned.

Time passed, but the rabbi's son could not stop thinking of the beautiful girl with whom he had danced, although he did not even know who she was. Then there was another wedding, and again the rabbi and his wife and son were invited. When they had all left for the wedding, the girl again decided to go, and she put on an even more beautiful dress. This time the rabbi's son saw her at once, and again asked her to dance. They danced and danced all evening, until she saw that it was getting late. Then she tore herself away from him and ran home. But this time, because of her great haste, she broke an earring, and part of it fell into the wash basin and lay there, although she did not notice it. Then she put on her rags and pretended to be sleeping by the stove.

Now when the rabbi's son returned home with his parents, he was still under the spell of the beautiful girl who had danced with him all night. And when he took the wash basin, he recognized the earring he found in it, and he wondered from where it had come. Then he first became suspicious that it might belong to the servant girl who lived in their house, for he knew that the mysterious girl with whom he had danced at the wedding must live somewhere. And he could not stop thinking of her, for he was in love with her.

Sometime later there was again a celebration held by one of the town's landowners, and again the rabbi's family was invited. But as they were about to leave the house, the rabbi's son told his parents that he did not feel well, and would join them later. Meanwhile he waited in his room, although the servant girl thought that he had left with his parents. Then she dressed in an even more beautiful gown, and left for the celebration. And when the rabbi's son came out of his room and saw that she had gone, he too went to the celebration, and spent the evening dancing with the beautiful girl. And while dancing with her he noticed that she was wearing only one earring, and he knew that the part of the earring he had found in the basin belonged to her. Then he whispered to her that he had learned her secret, and when she saw it was true, she tore herself away from him and ran back to the house. There she quickly changed her clothes and crawled back beside the stove.

So it was that the rabbi and his wife soon learned that their son wanted to marry the servant girl. But such a match did not suit them. They said: "A rabbi's son should not marry a servant. No, we will not permit it!" The son was heartbroken, and so was the girl. But he dared not disobey his parents.

Then one night, while the family slept, a fire started in the chimney of their house. The servant girl was awakened by the smoke and hurried to wake all the others. And because she was so alert, they were able to bring the fire under control, and the house was saved, as well as their lives. Then the rabbi and his wife were very grateful to the girl, and they realized that even though she was poor she was a fine, trustworthy person, and so they agreed to let their son marry her after all. A wedding was planned, and the rabbi's wife told the girl that she would sew a wedding dress for her, but the girl told her that she already had a dress of her own to wear. Then she took out her mother's bridal gown, and a crown, which the king's servants had packed for her, and she put them on, and the gown was embroidered with precious stones, which were also set in the crown, and the rabbi and his wife and son were amazed when they saw them. Then she told them the whole story of how she had been cast out by her father, the king, because she had insisted on giving charity. And it was then that the rabbi and his wife fully recognized what a pure soul she was, and they were also very proud to learn that their son was marrying a princess.

Now after the king had sent his daughter, the princess, into exile, he greatly regretted what he had done. And his terrible mistake haunted him day and night, until his remorse became so great that he decided to go off in search of her, and vowed that he would not return to the throne until she had been found. And before he departed he divorced the evil wife who had insisted he expel his daughter, and banished her from the kingdom so that she would know the fate that she had brought upon the exiled princess.

So it was that the king searched for the princess for more than a year, but he did not succeed in finding her. Meanwhile, she had married the rabbi's son, and they knew great happiness together, for their love was very strong. Soon the princess found that she was with child, much to her delight and that of her husband. And shortly before she gave birth she had a dream in which she saw the old man who had led her out of the forest. He told her that her father had set out alone to search for her throughout the world, and that he was in the vicinity of that town. Her father had put aside his royal garments and had dressed himself as a beggar in order not to draw attention to himself. So too did the old man tell her to invite all the poor people in that town to the circumcision, and in this way her father would also come. And when she saw him, she should give him all the kinds of food found at the ceremony, but it should be left unsalted. For as a king, he would be too accustomed to the taste of salt to do without it. And so it was as the old man said: the princess gave birth to a handsome son, and a circumcision was held on the eighth day, to which all of the town's poor people were invited. And among them the princess recognized one of the men as her father, but he did not recognize her.

Then the princess called in a servant and told him to seat the beggar who was her father at a separate table, and to give him a fine variety of food, but all without salt. And so it was that her father was served soup and fish and fine meat, which had a wonderful smell, but after he had tasted only a morsel from each dish, he did not touch them anymore.

After the dinner each of the poor guests went to congratulate the princess and received a nice gift from her of half a silver ruble. At last the old beggar also went to her to thank her, and she asked him how he had liked the food. He replied: "The food was very good, but I couldn't eat any of it." And then the princess looked into his eyes and said: "Know then that I felt an even bitterer taste when you ordered me taken to the forest and left there alone!" Now the old king could not believe his ears, and he suddenly realized that the young mother who stood before him was none other than his lost daughter, the princess. And he fell down at her feet and begged her to forgive him for the great wrong he had done her. And when she saw his tears, the princess too began to cry, and she embraced her father, and they were reunited at last.

So it was that the king was able to return to the capital and resume his life on the throne. And he brought with him not only his daughter, whom he now realized that he loved more than life itself, and her newborn son, but also her husband, the rabbi's son, and the rabbi and his wife as well. And the king appointed the rabbi and his son to be his ministers, and he came to value their advice more than any other, for they spent their time immersed in the study of the Torah, and were steeped in its wisdom. As for the princess, she saw to it that the needs of the poor of that kingdom were amply met, and that charity was the rule and not the exception. And so they all lived happily in the palace for the rest of their lives.

Source: Eastern Europe
Oral Tradition

The Underground Palace

nce, long ago, a king and his entire family went walking together. While they were walking a great storm arose, and everyone started to run back to the palace. But when they arrived there, they discovered that the queen was missing, for she apparently had become lost in the storm. Soldiers and servants were immediately sent out to search for her, but she was nowhere to be found.

Now the king had two sons, who thought that they were very clever, and they had a young Jewish lad who served as their servant. The king sent out his two sons and their servant to search for the queen, since all of the others had been unable to find her. They sought her for many months, but had no success, and the two princes were ready to turn back, but their servant reminded them that the king might be angry if they returned without the queen, and they decided to continue their quest.

Then it happened one night that while they were sleeping the servant had a dream in which an old man came to him and told him a riddle:

> Not wasteland
> But an underground palace

With all its treasures underground—
That is where the queen can be found.

When the servant awoke he remembered the dream and the riddle, and at once told the two princes. Now they did not put any
faith in dreams or riddles, but because they had no other clues to
go by, they agreed to follow the servant if he could figure out the
riddle's meaning. The young man brooded on it for a long time,
and at last he said: "I think we must search for a palace that lies
underground, beneath a wasteland. But first we must find out
what wasteland is meant. Now in our kingdom the only wasteland is to be found in the North, not far from where we are. This
is an area in which we have not yet searched, so let us go there."
And the two princes agreed that this was as good an interpretation of the riddle as any other, so they agreed to search there.

They made their way into the vast wilderness of the North,
in which nothing was to be found, except for the wild brush that
grew up everywhere, and a multitude of birds. And the first night
they slept in that wasteland the servant again dreamed that an
old man came to him, and this time he told him another riddle:

Not a dead end
But an entrance is what you will find
If you follow the flock
And do not linger behind.

Once again the servant recalled the dream and the riddle, and
shared it with the two princes. But they said that they had had
enough of riddles—after all, the first one had taken them to that
desolate place, where nothing had been found. Still, the servant
pleaded with them to consider the riddle, for it was the only clue
that they had. So the two princes agreed that they would let the
servant figure it out, since he was so good at riddles, and if what
he said made sense they would follow him.

The servant did not sleep any more that night, but contemplated that riddle until dawn, and at last he decided that it was
telling them to follow a flock of birds to a place that would not
be a dead end but an entrance—perhaps an entrance to an underground palace. He shared this interpretation with the two

princes in the morning, and while they were discussing it a great flock of birds passed above them in the sky, so many that the sky was covered with birds and grew dark. The servant noticed the great flock at once, and jumped up, telling the two princes to hurry, for surely this was the flock they should follow. But the two princes were too tired to follow it, and besides they had not yet eaten that day, so they told the servant to go ahead and follow the flock, and they would catch up with him later. And when he arrived at wherever it was that he was going, he should build a fire and when they saw the smoke they would seek him out.

So the servant packed up his belongings and hurried after the great flock of birds, always keeping it in sight. He ran after it all that morning and into the afternoon, and just before dusk the great flock came to rest in a circle of trees. The young servant also came to that place, and when he arrived there he discovered in the center of that circle a large stone, flat and round, which lay upon the ground. He tried to lift up the stone, but it was much too heavy for him. Then he built a fire, and lay down to await the dawn, when, he hoped, the two princes would catch up with him.

Meanwhile the two princes had laughed when the servant ran off, for they did not have faith in dreams or riddles, and besides, they did not care to continue the quest. Instead they decided to turn back, and perhaps to wait for the servant in an inn near the border where the wilderness began. And if he did not show up in a few days, well, they would return without him.

So it was that the servant waited all the next day, keeping his fire going, hoping that the two princes would soon arrive, so that they could help him lift up that stone. But when dusk came and they still had not arrived, he began to lose hope, and became discouraged. For he had traveled that far, and felt that he might have reached the source of the secret, since it was possible after all that something might be found there, and that it might not turn out to be a dead end but an entrance to an underground palace. And that night the servant dreamed for the third time that the old man came to him and told him a riddle:

Not scattered sparks
But magic seeds
That take root in the ground
Wherever they touch down.

Now when the servant awoke from this dream, he began to consider this riddle at once, for he hoped that it would reveal how to raise the heavy rock. It was then that he noticed how the fire he had built sometimes threw out scattered sparks, and that wherever these landed they took root, and a new plant sprang up in that place. Then the lad built a new fire, right beside the rock, using the same wood as before. And lo and behold, as the fire began to scatter sparks, and these landed around the rock, plants began to sprout up with a great many roots, and these roots burrowed beneath the rock on all sides, and before the fire burned out these roots cast off the heavy rock as if it were a feather. Then the lad bent down and peered inside, and saw that the rock had covered a deep pit, although he could not see what was at the bottom. But when he listened he thought he could hear distant voices, and he decided that he must descend into that pit, in the hope that he might find the lost queen there.

Then the lad tied one end of a rope around the heavy stone that lay beside the entrance, and lowered himself inside. As he reached the bottom he found himself in a palace chamber, decorated with paintings, illumined with lamps that cast flickering shadows on the walls. The room was empty, and the lad went to look at the paintings.

In the first painting he saw a lovely princess, seated in an elaborately decorated chamber. In the second was the portrait of another princess, even more beautiful than the first. In the third painting there was yet another princess, the most beautiful of all. And in the fourth he saw the lost queen, whom he had been seeking for so long. And then he knew that he had interpreted each of the riddles correctly, and that they had led him to the right place.

The lad began to search through all the rooms of that enormous underground palace, which extended in every direction. All of the rooms were empty of people, but filled with objects. One was filled entirely with golden coins, not in sacks, but piled loose up to the ceiling. Another was filled with silver, also piled in a great heap. But other rooms were not filled with treasures, but with bones, great heaps of them. And when he saw those bones, the boy became afraid, for he knew he was in the presence of something evil, but he did not know what it was.

Now every room that he had come to so far had been open, but then it happened that he came to a door that was locked. Then he knocked softly at the door and heard a voice say: "Who is there?" And he replied: "The servant of a king, who seeks to set you free." And without further ado, the door opened and the lad found himself face to face with the first princess, whose portrait he had seen in the room he had descended into from above. She was very glad to see him, and told him that she was a princess who had been wandering in the woods outside the palace when a great whirlwind had suddenly snatched her away and carried her to that place. There she had been forced to marry a terrible giant who was invincible because he had a magic flask of oil, which, when he spread it on his body, made it impossible for anyone to harm him. The lad begged the princess to steal the flask of oil for him, and so she did, hoping that he would save her from her cruel fate. Then the boy spread the oil over his body and hid the flask of oil in a pouch. Suddenly he felt himself grow strong as ten lions. Just then the giant rushed into the room, and when he saw the lad he said: "So, you have come to save your queen, have you? You may know that you will never see her, for I am about to kill you and eat you! For I not only collect gold, but also bones, and I want to add yours to my collection!" But the boy felt himself bursting with strength, and without hesitating he strode up to the giant, raised his fist, and gave him such a mighty blow that the giant fell dead at his feet.

After this the lad went farther into the underground palace, taking the princess with him, and soon they came to a second locked room. The lad knocked and when the second princess heard it was the servant of a king, she opened the door at once. There the lad found that this princess was even more beautiful and charming than the first, and looked exactly as she was portrayed in the painting in the room he had reached from above. The lad asked her how she had gotten there, and she told him that she had been walking in the palace garden when a great bird had swooped out of the sky and carried her off to that terrible place, where she had been forced to marry a giant even more ferocious than the first. This one got his strength from eating the apples of a certain tree that grew near her room. The lad asked her to steal one of the apples for him, and she did so. He ate the apple, and finished it just in time, for all at once the giant confronted him and said: "So, you have come to rescue the queen, have you? But you shall not see her, for I shall first eat you, and add your bones to the pile I am collecting, which is already larger than that of my brother!" Then the giant noticed the princess, and he said: "And how is it that you are here, my pretty princess? Why are you not with my brother?" And the giant reached for the princess, but before he touched her the lad drew back his arm and gave him a mighty blow that left him dead before his body hit the floor.

The boy then traveled farther into the underground palace, taking the two princesses with him. When he reached a third door that was locked, he knocked again, and soon found himself face to face with a third princess, the most beautiful and charming of all, even lovelier than she appeared in her portrait, which he had seen in the first chamber. And when the young man saw that beautiful princess, he fell in love with her at first sight. Then he asked her how she had come to be there, and she told him that she had been sleeping in her bed, when a giant had crept up to the palace and had reached inside and carried her off in the dead of night, so that no one knew that she was missing until the next day, and then it was too late. That terrible giant had forced her to marry him, and no one could save her; he was stronger than any man on earth, for he got his strength from a magic pool inside the palace, in which he bathed every day. The lad asked her to tell him where the pool was, and the princess pointed down the corridor to a large oak door. Then the lad went and bathed in the pool, and when he emerged from it he felt even stronger than he had after he had covered his body with the magic oil and eaten the magic apple. For now the strength of all three magic potions made him feel as if he were a whirlwind of strength. When he was returning to the room of the third princess, the giant saw him, and rushed toward him waving his arms in anger. But before the giant had a chance to do anything, the lad took a mighty swing and killed him with a single blow.

Then the boy went on through the palace, followed closely by the three princesses. At last they came to a very large room that was locked. But when the lad knocked at the door and identified himself, the queen opened it at once, and embraced him, so happy was she that she had been found. Then she grew sad again, and began to weep, and while she wept she told how the giant had created a great storm and in the confusion had carried her off as his prisoner. And now he was forcing her to marry him, although she was already married to the king, and the marriage was planned for the very next day. Then she begged the servant and the other princesses to hide themselves, for he was a terrible monster who would stop at nothing. She said that his strength came from a staff he carried, which gave him enough power to overthrow an entire city. The servant begged her to steal the staff, and later that day, while they were hidden, she managed to take it from him. But no sooner did the boy have the staff in his hand than the giant saw what the queen had done. He rushed at the boy while thunder and lightning rent the air, and the room became filled with smoke. But as the giant was about to grab the staff away from the lad's grasp, the boy raised it and struck a great blow, and the giant collapsed on the floor, dead.

Now when the queen saw this, she was overjoyed. Then she and the lad and the three princesses returned to the entrance, taking with them all the gold that they could carry. They climbed out of the pit, and afterward used the lad's rope to pull up the gold that they had brought with them. Then they followed the lad, who led them through the wilderness, and when they had emerged from it, they decided to take their rest in the inn near the border where the wilderness began. It was there, in that inn, that they found the two princes, who had been drinking day and night since they had left the servant. They were delighted to see the queen, and greatly impressed with the beauty of the princesses. But most of all they were fascinated to see all the gold, and refused to return to the palace until the servant had shown them where it could be found. So the lad left the queen and the princesses at the inn, and he led the two princes to the underground palace. There he descended with them, and showed them all the treasures to be found there, as well as all of the bones. Then the princes filled their pouches with gold, and climbed out, ahead of the servant. But when they got to the top they hurried and pulled the great rock over the entrance, trapping the servant inside. Then they left him and returned to the inn. There they frightened the queen and the princesses, and made them vow never to tell the king the truth about what had happened, but to say instead that the two clever princes had saved them all.

When they returned to the palace, the king was overjoyed to see the queen, and gave each of the princes great rewards. And when the king asked where the servant was, they said that he had become lost somewhere in the wilderness, for he was a fool and could never find his way anywhere. Soon afterward a wedding was arranged for the two princes and the first two princesses, and a great celebration was planned. It was to be the finest wedding that had ever been seen in that country.

Meanwhile the servant had been trapped in the underground palace, and did not know what to do. Suddenly he remembered the staff of the third giant, and took it in his hand, and as soon as he did so a powerful demon appeared and asked the lad what it was that he wanted him to do. The boy then told him to throw off the heavy rock from the entrance, and this the demon did in the wink of an eye. After this the lad told the demon to carry him to the king's palace, along with all of the gold to be found in that underground palace. This too presented no difficulties to the demon, and in a flash the lad found himself standing outside the gates of the king's palace, and beside him was a pile of gold as tall as the palace itself.

While he was standing there the lad heard the sound of music inside, and he noticed that there were lights in all the windows, and that many people had gathered there. He went inside, and asked the people what was taking place, and they told him that on that day the two princes were to marry the princesses they had saved from the underground palace. This made the lad terribly angry, and he decided to get even with the princes. So he disguised himself as a merchant, and went to that part of the palace where the third princess was living. When the princess heard that a merchant was there, she came out and asked him what he had for sale. He showed her some of the very same treasures that the giant had kept in her room, and when she saw them she grew frightened, and asked where he had gotten them. With that the lad revealed who he was, and the princess recognized him as the one who had saved her from the giant. Then she ran through the palace until she came to the king, and for the first time revealed the true story of how they all had been saved. The king asked the queen if the story was true, and she confirmed it in every detail, and also told how she and the princesses had been threatened by the two princes not to reveal the truth.

The king grew very angry when he heard of the cowardly and treacherous conduct of his sons, and wasted no time in expelling them from his realm and sent the princesses they were planning to marry back to their own kingdoms. Then he adopted the brave Jewish boy as his own son, and made him the heir to the throne. The lad soon married the third and most beautiful of the princesses, whom he had loved from the first, and they lived happily ever after.

Source: Eastern Europe
Oral Tradition

The City of Luz

ong ago there was a kingdom that had been ruled by the same dynasty for more than ten centuries. And it was the custom in this kingdom, each time a new ruler was crowned, to bring forth the royal mantle— the very mantle which had been used when the first king was crowned. Now this mantle had been woven of the finest silk, and had been dyed a shade of blue that was unique, for nowhere else was that color to be found. And when it was wrapped around the shoulders of each new king, the people clapped and cheered for their new ruler.

It came to pass that the old king decided to step down from the throne to allow his son, the prince, to be crowned in his place. Preparations for the lavish ceremony were begun a year in advance, and it was then that a servant was sent to fetch the royal mantle from the golden chest where it had lain for forty years. But when the chest was unlocked, the servant discovered to his horror that the royal mantle had been devoured by moths, and that all that remained of it were rags.

When the old king heard about this, he began to tremble with fear, for the mantle was the symbol of the dynasty, and if another were used, the seal of authority of the king could be

endangered. Therefore the king called in his ministers, and asked for their advice. They all agreed it was a very serious matter, and warned the king that if the people found out, his enemies might proclaim it as a sign that after ten centuries the dynasty was coming to an end. The ministers told the king that he must find a way to have another mantle made, of the same color. For the people would not accept any other.

Then the king gathered together all of the royal soothsayers, and asked for their advice. But none of them knew of a way to duplicate the shade of the color, and they were silent. Then at last the oldest soothsayer among them spoke and said: "I remember hearing as a child, O king, that the royal mantle was a gift of the Jews. If that is true, then they must know how to prepare the dye and duplicate the color."

Now when the king heard this, he wasted no time, but ordered that the leaders of the Jews be brought to the palace the very next morning. And when they stood before him, the king showed them what was left of the royal mantle, and he said: "It was your people, the Jews, who gave this mantle to the first king of this dynasty. Somehow a moth must have entered the golden chest in which it was stored, and during the past forty years the moths multiplied and destroyed the royal mantle. This is all that remains. In one year the coronation of my son is to take place. Plans have already been made, a palace is being built for the occasion, and many great kings have been invited to attend. It cannot be delayed. I want you to take one of these rags with you, and before nine months have passed, I want you to deliver the dye that produces this exact color. If you do not, all of the Jews in this kingdom will be doomed. So too must you keep this mission a secret, for if you do not, there will be a bitter end."

The Jewish leaders were terribly frightened when they heard the harsh edict of the king, for they too were familiar with the legend that the royal mantle had been a gift of the Jews. And they also knew that the blue dye that had been used was the same dye that the Torah commands be used in the corner fringes of the prayer shawl worn by the men, known as the *tallit*. But the secret of how to produce that dye, known as *tekhelet*, had been lost for centuries, and since then a white thread had been used in its place. One of the leaders tried to explain this to the king, but he grew flushed with anger, and sent them from his presence, reminding them that the edict was still in effect.

In great fear the Jewish leaders met in the synagogue and discussed the matter. They knew that they could not reveal the edict to the rest of the community, since the king had commanded it be kept secret on penalty of death, and besides, they did not want the others to become terrified as well. Therefore they vowed to keep the matter a secret among themselves, and not to reveal it even to their wives.

After this they began to discuss the problem of how to obtain the dye, the secret of which had been lost for so many centuries. For no one knew for certain the shellfish or snail from which it came, and therefore it could not be produced. Long ago the rabbis had decided that it would be better to leave the corner of the prayer shawl white rather than to err in trying to fulfill the commandment, and this is what had been done. Now, though, they were forced to seek out the dye once again.

Then one old rabbi among them, whose name was Rabbi Abraham, spoke and said: "There can be no doubt that we must find a way to satisfy the demand of the king, otherwise he will carry out the threat he has made, and we will all be doomed. Let us concentrate, then, on fulfilling this task, which appears to be so impossible."

The others recognized that what the old rabbi had said made sense. Then Rabbi Isaac, who was highly respected, spoke and said: "The question is, where can this dye be found? I recall it is said in the Talmud that the secret of how to prepare the dye was known in the city of Luz. This is the city in the Holy Land that was built at the place where Jacob dreamed of the ladder that reached from earth into heaven, with angels ascending and descending upon it."

"Yes, that is true," said Rabbi Abraham, "and according to the Talmud the natives of the city of Luz are spared the fate that is inescapable for all other men—the inevitability of death. For when God decreed that man must die, he left one place on earth where the Angel of Death never held sway, and that is the city of Luz. Not even the armies of Nebuchadnezzar could disturb the city."

"But, with all respect," said the youngest among them, whose name was Rabbi Jacob, "what good does it do for us to think of the city of Luz, for it is to be found in the Holy Land. The journey there could take a year in itself, as well as a year to return, and the king has commanded that we deliver the dye to him within nine months. Even if it were possible to reach the city of Luz, and even if the secret of how to prepare the dye is still known there, how could this be accomplished in the time remaining?"

After Rabbi Jacob had spoken there was silence for a long time, for what he said was all too true—the journey to the Holy Land and its return could not take place in the time remaining to them. All of their faces were fixed in a frown, but suddenly the face of the old rabbi lit up and he said: "Fear not, for all hope is not yet lost!" And all of the others turned to him with wonder in their eyes, for they could not imagine what he had to say. Then Rabbi Abraham said: "All my life I have kept the secret that I am about to reveal to you, which I learned from my father, and he from his father before him, for this secret has remained within my family for many centuries. My father made me vow to keep it unless a day should come when all the lives in the community hang in the balance, and only this secret can save them."

All of the others held their breaths in anticipation of a secret that had been kept for so long, but was about to be revealed. Then the old rabbi said: "This, then, is the secret: When the End of Days has come and the era of the Messiah is upon us, all souls will travel to Jerusalem for the resurrection. And how will they get there? Through underground caves. And the secret that I know is the location of one of these caves, which leads directly to the Holy Land itself, to a place that is not far from the city of Luz! And the entire journey to the Holy Land through this cave will not take longer than a week!"

When the others heard this, they could not believe their ears, and for the first time a ray of hope entered their hearts.

Then Rabbi Abraham continued: "This, then, is what we should do: Let us choose two among us to undertake this mission. I would go myself, for I have always longed to enter that cave, but I know that it is too long a journey for an old man, and there must be no delay. I will take the two who are chosen to the mouth of the cave, which is hidden, and reveal it to them. I am afraid that no others may accompany us, for the location of the cave must be kept secret."

Things had developed so quickly that all of the leaders were in a state of awe, and they wondered who among them should be chosen to go. At last one of them spoke and said: "The important decision that now lies before us is who we shall send on this quest, on which all of our lives and those of our families depend. In such a case we must choose those in whose hands we can safely entrust our lives." All of the others nodded in agreement, and then Rabbi Abraham spoke again: "When I was a child, there was once a situation of life or death such as this, in which it was essential to choose the right one to represent us before the king, who had just signed an evil decree against the Jews. Then the elders gathered outside this very synagogue at midnight on the night of a full moon and the decision was made there. I know this because I concealed myself behind a tree and observed all that took place. If you will accompany me outside, we may be able to reach our decision, for it is almost midnight, and tonight there is a full moon."

Then all of the others followed Rabbi Abraham out of the synagogue. He led them to a tree that stood a short distance from it, above which the full moon could be seen. "Let each of you stand before this tree," said Rabbi Abraham, "as did the elders in my childhood. And let us see if anyone's shadow, cast by the moon, is long enough to reach the door of the synagogue. For the elders believed that he whosever shadow reached the door was the one who was destined to represent them. That night when I was a child there was only one among them—and it was my own father—whose shadow reached the door. And it was he who went before the king, and convinced him to cancel the evil decree against us."

The others nodded, and one by one they stood by the tree, but one after another they discovered that their shadows fell short of the door of the synagogue. Soon there were only two of them left who had not yet taken the test, Rabbi Isaac and Rabbi Jacob. But when Rabbi Isaac took his place by the tree, his shadow seemed to grow longer before their very eyes, until the edge of it touched the base of the door. The rabbis cheered, for at last one of them had been found worthy of the quest. Then it was Rabbi Jacob's turn, and when he stood before the tree, his shadow grew so long that it reached not only to the door of the synagogue, but climbed up to the very handle. All of the others gasped when they saw this, and they understood that in this way the Holy One had identified those who should undertake this essential mission.

That night Rabbi Isaac and Rabbi Jacob packed their belongings for the journey, and took leave of their wives and families, although they did not tell them where they were going. At dawn they met Rabbi Abraham at the synagogue, and he gave them a letter of introduction to take with them, and then led them to the forest that surrounded their town. They walked through the forest until the sun was high in the sky, and at last they reached a small spring. The old rabbi followed this stream until they reached a carob tree of great beauty, which was filled with fruit, behind which the stream seemed to disappear. Then Rabbi Abraham said to them: "Behind this tree lies the mouth of the cave that leads to the Holy Land. Know that not any man can enter this cave, but only those who possess pure souls will be permitted to pass. All others will be stopped by the flaming sword inside the entrance, which guards the way. If the sword stops spinning and permits you to pass, then you will know that the test of the shadows chose well. And if the sword does not stop spinning, then you must turn back, for it is not destined that you go on."

Then Rabbi Abraham pointed to the unlit torches that the two younger rabbis carried, and he said: "If you do succeed in passing the flaming sword, you should hold your torches near it, and light them with that fire. It will sustain you for all of your journey through the cave, for that is the same fire that Moses saw when he beheld the burning bush, which burned but was not consumed. You should also know that the water of the stream that runs through this cave is pure, and will sustain you. Know too that the carobs that grow on this tree will be your only food for the seven days that you journey through the cave. For while you are in this cave it will be your spirit that requires sustenance, and not your body, and that is why you will eat carobs, for in no other food is such a pure essence of the spirit contained. There-fore fill your pockets with them." This is what the two rabbis did, and then they stepped behind the tree and found before them the mouth of the cave, just as Rabbi Abraham had said.

Rabbi Isaac, who was the elder of the two, entered first, and when he had passed beyond the first turn in the cave, he found himself confronted with a flaming circle that whirled before him, and he knew that this was the flaming sword of which Rabbi Abraham had spoken. As Rabbi Isaac stood there, the whirling sword slowed down, so that he could see the blade, but it did not stop. A moment later Rabbi Jacob joined him, and as soon as he stood beside him, the flaming sword came to a halt. Then the two rabbis did not hesitate, but hurried past it into the cave. And no sooner had they gone beyond it than the sword started spin-ning again. Then the two rabbis held out their torches near the flaming sword until each torch caught fire. And the fire burned with a purity unlike anything they had ever seen, and illumined the cave for a great distance. So it was that at last they were on their way to the city of Luz, and there was no turning back.

As Rabbi Isaac and Rabbi Jacob made their way through the long cave, following the stream in its twists and turns, they saw that the walls of the cave were lined with beautiful stone that seemed precious in itself. And the farther they went, the more the air was pervaded with a perfume, like the scent of balsam, and the rabbis were intoxicated with that scent.

After they had traveled for six days they reached a large cav-ern which was like a room built of well-hewn stones. At the far end of that room they saw a wooden tabernacle which had been set up there in a crevice in the wall of the cavern. And before the Ark there was a stone which seemed to resemble a pulpit. Then the two rabbis did not hesitate, but together they approached the pulpit, and although they did not have prayer books with which to pray, when they opened their mouths and sang, the words rose up by themselves and were carried upward as if on wings. And the echo of their voices filled the cavern so that it sounded as if a chorus of many voices had joined them in prayer, although no one else was to be seen.

Afterward the two rabbis spent all of the seventh day in that cavern, for they knew it was the Sabbath, and they did not want to continue traveling on the day of rest. All that day their spirits were high, and they were at peace. And the next morning, when they had gone only a short distance, they saw a golden glow, and knew that they were about to reach the other end of the cave. And when they came there, they found another carob tree, even more beautiful than the first. And as they stepped from the cave they fell to the earth and kissed the ground of the Holy Land, and gave thanks for their good fortune in reaching that sacred place. Then they left their torches burning in the entrance of the cave and replenished their supply of carobs, which they had grown to love, and set off to find their way to the city of Luz.

Not far from the entrance of the cave they saw a hut in the woods, and hurried to it. There they met an old man who lived alone. They asked him about the way to the city of Luz, and he pointed out the path to them, but warned them that they would have to cross woods and swamps and heavy underbrush along the way. So it was that they walked and walked until they could hardly move their feet any longer. Their garments were torn by brambles, and their shoes were worn out by the time they reached Luz.

Once they arrived in the city, the two rabbis asked at once to be brought to the rabbi of Luz. When they met him they showed him the letter of introduction written by Rabbi Abraham, and they revealed the purpose of their quest and asked for his advice. Imagine their astonishment when the rabbi said: "My friends, you have come to the city of Luz, but this is the modern city of Luz, and the place you are seeking is the ancient city of Luz. It is to be found many miles from here, in the wilderness, but only

God can say whether or not you will be permitted to enter it. In any case, when you reach the city, keep these words in mind: 'The nut has no mouth.'"

The two rabbis almost wept when they learned that they still had not reached their destination. They were so weary and the wilderness looked so terrifying that they almost fainted in despair. But then they remembered the grave danger facing their people, who had put all of their trust in them, and their courage was renewed. They went back into the wilderness, walking rapidly through the thick underbrush and black forests and on through great stretches of fields. They walked for days, and it seemed as if they had walked to the ends of the earth. At last they reached a clearing, and within it they saw a city encircled by a high wall—the ancient city of Luz. The two rabbis threw up their hands in joy that they had reached it at last. Then they ran from the forest to the clearing, despite their exhaustion, and reached the wall of the city. From where they stood they saw no entrance, so they decided to walk around the wall until they reached the gate.

The two rabbis began their walk beside a giant almond tree that stood outside the wall of the city. The wall itself, built in a circle, was several miles in diameter, and it took them three hours to circle the entire city and to return to the tree whence they had started. But when they reached it, they were appalled, for they realized that there was no gate to the city at all. Never had they heard of such a thing, and their eyes filled with tears, for they had not expected that there would be still more obstacles to overcome. Still, they were determined not to give up now that they had traveled so far.

It was then that Rabbi Isaac remembered the words of the rabbi of the modern city of Luz, and he said to Rabbi Jacob: "What could the old rabbi have meant when he said that 'The nut has no mouth'?" And Rabbi Jacob replied: "Perhaps it is a riddle in which we may discover the secret of how to enter the city." Then the two rabbis sat down beneath the almond tree, and contemplated the riddle. Suddenly an idea occurred to Rabbi Jacob, and he said: "Let us remember that the word for nut is 'luz,' and that this is also the name of the city. Perhaps this almond tree we are sitting beneath, which stands outside the city, somehow bears on the mystery."

Then the two rabbis went closer to the tree and examined it, and to their amazement they discovered that its trunk was hollow, and that the opening was large enough to admit a man. Then Rabbi Isaac said: "Perhaps by saying that 'The nut has no mouth,' the old rabbi was telling us that no man could discover the entrance to the city, for perhaps it has no gate but this almond tree." "Yes," said Rabbi Jacob, "let us step into the hollow trunk and see if it leads anywhere." This they did, and to their amazement they found that the hollow trunk led to the entrance of a cave. Then they entered the cave, which led beneath the wall of the city. "Surely we have discovered the entrance," said Rabbi Jacob, and Rabbi Isaac agreed that indeed this must be so, for no other entrance was to be seen. And behold, before they had traveled very far, they saw the faint light which signified they had reached the other end of the cave. And when they emerged from the cave, they found themselves in the city of Luz.

Now at first the rabbis thought that the city was a city like every other, and the people seemed like those seen everywhere else. Children played in the streets, and men and women went about their business. But soon they saw strange sights. They saw very, very old men walking in the streets. Some had beards so long they tripped over them. Finally, the two rabbis approached one of these old men, who seemed downcast. Rabbi Isaac said to him: "Tell us, what is the matter?" And the old man replied: "Alas, my father has punished me because I fell asleep by the bed of my grandfather, and did not hear him ask me for a glass of water." The two rabbis were amazed to hear this, and they asked the old man how old he was. "I am three hundred years old," said the old man. "And how old is your father?" they both asked at the same time. "He is five hundred years old," came the reply. "And your grandfather?" "He is eight hundred." "And is his father still living?" "Yes, he is," said the old man, "and may all Jews be saved from such a fate. He is one thousand years old, and sleeps all week in his bed and only wakes on the Sabbath."

The two rabbis were astonished to hear what the old man said, and they were especially surprised that he did not consider living to such an age a great blessing. Rabbi Jacob asked him about this, and the old man said: "It is a terrible thing to have to live forever. For God has cursed us with eternal life." Now the two rabbis had not forgotten that Rabbi Abraham had told them that the inhabitants of the city were immortal, but it was amazing to hear it firsthand.

Then Rabbi Isaac said: "And it is impossible, then, for any inhabitant of this city to depart from this life?" "Yes, unless they first depart from the city," said the old man. And Rabbi Jacob said: "But why would anyone, young or old, choose to take leave of this city?" And the old man said: "Because sometimes we grow tired of living."

The two rabbis looked at each other and realized that the old man had been talking about himself. Then Rabbi Isaac said to him: "Tell us, old man, what is it that you do for a living?" "It is my work to produce the blue dye that is used in prayer shawls," said the old man. The two rabbis were overjoyed to hear this, and Rabbi Jacob said: "Surely Providence has sent you to us as we were sent to you." Then he revealed the purpose of their mission to him, and when he had learned it, the eyes of the old man came alive, and he said to the two rabbis: "Come with me to the home of our rabbi, and repeat to him what you have told me, and then perhaps he will realize how important is my work in the eyes of the Lord."

So the two rabbis accompanied the old man to the home of the rabbi of Luz. However, when they arrived they were told that the rabbi was very ill. When they asked what was wrong, the rabbi's disciples told them that the rabbi had once tasted a carob when he was a child, eight hundred years ago, which a stranger had brought into the city. And since that had been the last stranger who had entered the city, the rabbi had never been able to taste another carob, since carob trees did not grow in that city. Lately he had been taken with a terrible longing to taste the fruit of the carob once again, but it was impossible to obtain it for him, for no inhabitant who left the city was ever able to return.

Then Rabbi Jacob smiled and put his hand in his pocket and pulled out a handful of carobs. And he said: "We are strangers who have just entered the city from the outside; here are the carobs that the rabbi has been longing for." And when the disciples saw the carobs, they hurried to bring the two rabbis into the presence of the old rabbi.

At first the old rabbi of Luz was angry to be disturbed, but when he saw that they had brought him the carobs he so longed for, tears of joy filled his eyes. And no sooner did he take the first bite of the carob than his strength returned, and his pale color became ruddy again. Then he found the strength to sit up in bed, and asked the two rabbis to tell him who they were, and why they had come to that city. So it was that they told their tale and explained the reason for their quest. And as soon as the old rabbi learned of the vital mission, he commanded the dyemaker to hurry home to get a bottle of the dye that the two rabbis needed.

While he was gone, Rabbi Jacob turned to the old rabbi and said: "Why is it that the Holy One, Blessed be He, permits the inhabitants of the city of Luz to be immortal?" And the old rabbi replied: "No one knows for certain why this is so. There are those who say that after the sin of Adam and Eve, God wanted to preserve one boundary in the world that the Angel of Death could not cross. Others say that when God decreed that man would live from dust to dust, he left one small bone that the grave does not consume. This bone is called the luz, and it will be from this bone that man will be resurrected at the End of Days. And in the same way that God left one bone in the back which is not destroyed, so he also left one place on earth where the Angel of Death cannot enter, and that is this city. Still others, those who feel that our eternal lives are a blessing, say that the Holy One made Luz immortal because it was here that Jacob dreamed of the ladder reaching from earth to heaven, since this is one of the Gates of Heaven. But those who despise our eternal lives say that this city has been cursed by God because when Jacob ran away from Esau, the people refused to let him rest here, and he had to sleep in the wilderness. Therefore, God cursed us with eternal life."

"Tell me," said Rabbi Isaac, "why would anyone choose to abandon such a city? And why can these wanderers never come back?" The old rabbi replied, "Why do they leave? Some may have grown tired of living, others are said to have been called by an angel to another place. No one knows what they found once they left the city. Perhaps they lost the way and spent their lives trying to find the road that would lead them back. Or perhaps the Angel of Death took them as they turned to go, and buried them in the fields beyond the wall."

"In any case," the old rabbi continued, "whatever the reason, the histories of this city, reaching back for centuries, do not record a single war, a single flood or fire, nor the death of a single man, for all who are born here have their name inscribed in the Book of Life, and there it remains unless they depart from the city."

Just as the old rabbi finished this explanation, the old dyemaker returned with a bottle of the unique blue dye in his hand, and gave it to Rabbi Jacob. Then Rabbi Jacob, who had carried with him the rag that had been part of the royal mantle, took it out and compared it to the dye in the bottle, and the color was identical. Then he gave the bottle to Rabbi Isaac for safekeeping, and Rabbi Isaac put it in a pouch and tied the pouch to his belt. And now that they had completed the quest, they knew they had to hurry, for they had no time to waste, but Rabbi Jacob had one last question before they departed. He said to the dyemaker: "Tell me, does this dye come from a shellfish or from a snail, for this is a question that our rabbis still debate." "It comes from a snail that is found only in this city," said the dyemaker, "and for every bottle the size of that I have given you, twelve thousand snails are required." The two rabbis were amazed when they heard this, and they realized that the bottle of dye they had obtained was even more precious than they had thought. Then they took their leave from the old rabbi and the dyemaker with many thanks, and set out on their journey home. They made their way to the cave that ran beneath the city, and returned the same way they had entered.

Somehow the distance did not seem as far this time, and the

hours flew, and before long they reached the carob tree that guarded the way to the cave, where their torches were still burning, and a week later they arrived back in their own kingdom. And when they came to the synagogue, they found all of the leaders assembled together, praying for their safe return. And when they showed them the dye that perfectly matched what was left of the old mantle, there was great rejoicing, for their lives had been saved. Then they revealed all that had happened to them, and the others marveled at the tale. Now not only could they satisfy the king, but there was also enough of the dye for the fringes of every prayer shawl as well, making it possible to fulfill the commandment once more, and this is what they did. Now only three months had passed since the departure of the two rabbis, and when they showed the dye to the king, he was overjoyed to see that it was exactly that which was needed, and ordered that a new royal mantle be made up at once, identical to the first. And as a gift to the Jews who had caused the precious mantle to be restored to his dynasty, the king signed a decree freeing the Jews from all taxes and harsh decrees for as long as the dynasty should last, and had it announced everywhere. And thus began a period in which the lives of the Jews blossomed as never before, for the Holy One had seen to it that they were blessed with great abundance.

Source: Eastern Europe
c. Fifteenth–Seventeenth Centuries

Sources

The most important recent development in Jewish folklore is, as might be expected, taking place in Israel, where oral tales are being collected from Jews representing virtually every Jewish ethnic community. This good work is being accomplished by the Israel Folktale Archives, which was founded twenty-five years ago by Professor Dov Noy of Hebrew University. The collectors of the archives work under the considerable pressure of the likely extinction of most of the oral traditions that still survive, because of the rapid transition from languages such as Yiddish and Arabic to Hebrew among the Jewish immigrants to Israel. Thus the tales which are known only in the old languages are dying out. Faced with this situation, the Israel Folktale Archives has rushed to collect as much material as possible before it is too late. So far the collectors have admirably succeeded in their task, and among the tales they have collected are many fairy tales, including those here from Egypt, Morocco, Greece, India, Yemen, Kurdistan, Persia (Iran), and Libya.

All of the fairy tales in this collection are based on either Hebrew, Aramaic, Yiddish, or Judeo-Spanish sources. These are listed following this note. Those tales selected from the Israel Folktale Archives are identified by their IFA number, as well as by the names of the teller and the collector of the tale, if these were available. The tales have been linked to a particular country either by the nationality of the teller or, in the case of the Talmudic and medieval tales, by the country from which the manuscript derives.

Following each fairy tale in the text the country of origin is noted, along with the approximate date it was originally recorded. Naturally such dating must be regarded as approximate, since the dating of ancient manuscripts is a difficult matter in any case, and it is likely that the tales existed orally for a long period before they were written down. Thus it is not possible to set a date prior to this century for those tales which have been collected orally by the Israel Folktale Archives and other modern collectors. The phrase "Oral Tradition" at the end of a tale is meant to indicate that it has been recorded only in this century, and that it is not possible to suggest a date of derivation.

Tales deriving from the Babylonian Talmud have been identified as stemming from Babylon, although this is a matter of some scholarly debate, since they probably originated in ancient Israel. The Talmud consists of two parts, the Mishnah and the Gemara. The Mishnah was written down in ancient Israel, but the Gemara, from which the fairy tales included here have been taken, was set down in Babylon, and therefore the tales have been attributed to that country. Medieval tales from the Holy Land have been identified as coming from Palestine. There is some debate over the Palestinian origin of "The Princess with Golden Hair." This origin is the conclusion of Moses Gaster, who discovered this early version of the tale in the manuscript he titled *Sefer Maaysiot*. His dating of this tale to between the ninth and the twelfth centuries has also been questioned.

The tales identified as coming from Eastern Europe have not been linked to a particular country because of the shifting boundaries in Eastern Europe, those of Poland in particular, and due to the fact that the Jewish communities, which shared the Yiddish language, formed something of an extranational culture.

While most of the fairy tales collected here have been recorded in only one version, a few of them, such as "The Beggar King," can be found in one or more variants. In these cases I have adapted episodes from the variants to create an amalgam which is as inclusive as possible. In a few instances, especially involving oral sources, where a fine tale had a missing episode which could not be supplied by an existing variant, an attempt has been made to recreate such episodes for the sake of rendering a complete and coherent narrative. Two of the tales, "The Eternal Light" and "The Golden Bird," have been more freely adapted from their sources than the other tales in the book.

Elijah's Violin (Egypt)
> From *Hodesh Hodesh Ve-sippuro: 1968–1969* (Hebrew), edited by Edna Cheichel (Haifa: Israel Folktale Archives, 1969). IFA 8133, collected by Ilana Zohar from her mother, Flora Cohen.

The Witches of Ashkelon (Babylon)
> From the Babylonian Talmud, tractate Sanhedrin (Aramaic).

The Golden Mountain (Morocco)
> From *Shivim Sipurim Vesipur* (Hebrew), edited by Dov Noy (Jerusalem: Israel Folktale Archives, 1964). IFA 3911, collected by Jacob Avitsuk from Shlomo Alozh.

The Princess and the Slave (Morocco)
> IFA 6414 (Hebrew), collected by Yakov Laseri from his father, Machlouf Laseri. Previously unpublished.

King David and the Giant (Babylon)
> From the Babylonian Talmud, tractate Sanhedrin (Aramaic).

The Princess in the Tower (Palestine)
> From *Midrash Tanhuma* (Hebrew), edited by Solomon Buber (Vilna: 1885). A variant of "Rapunzel" from *Grimm's Fairy Tales.*

King Solomon and Asmodeus (Babylon)
> From the Babylonian Talmud, tractate Gittin (Aramaic).

The Beggar King (Babylon)
> From the Babylonian Talmud, tractate Gittin (Aramaic). Episodes have also been culled from *Midrash Mishle,* edited by Solomon Buber (Vilna: 1893); *Yalkut Shimoni,* compiled by Shimon Ashkenazi (Frankfurt: 1687); *Emek ha-Melech,* by Naphtali Hirsh ben Elhanan (Amsterdam: 1653); and *Beit ha-Midrash,* edited by Adolf Jellinek (Jerusalem: Bamberger and Wahrmann, 1938).

The Eternal Light (Palestine)
> Based on *Aggadta di B'nai Moshe* from *Beit ha-Midrash* (Hebrew), edited by Adolf Jellinek (Jerusalem: Bamberger and Wahrmann, 1938). Also *Etz Hayim* by Rabbi Hayim Vital (Jerusalem: 1866).

Sources

The Mysterious Palace (Palestine)
From *Maaseh ha-Nemalah* in *Beit ha-Midrash* (Hebrew), edited by Adolf Jellinek (Jerusalem: Bamberger and Wahrmann, 1938).

The Flight of the Eagle (Spain)
From *Mimekor Yisrael* (Hebrew), edited by M. J. Bin Gorion (Tel Aviv: 1966). This version is based on the retelling by Rabbi Yakov Asharaf, collected by Menachem Bar Ari, IFA 4735. Previously unpublished.

The Wooden Sword (Afghanistan)
From *Otsar ha-Maaysiot* (Hebrew), edited by Reuven ben Yakov Naana (Jerusalem: 1961). Collected by Reuven ben Yakov Naana; told by Shlomo Shalem. A variant of this tale has been attributed to Rabbi Nachman of Bratslav.

The Magic Flute of Asmodeus (Persian Kurdistan)
From *Min ha-Mabua* (Hebrew), edited and annotated by Eliezer Marcus (Haifa: Israel Folktale Archives, 1966). IFA 6053, collected by Rivka Ashkenazi from her father, Sasson Ashkenazi.

Partnership with Asmodeus (Libya)
From *Shiv'im Sipurim ve-Sipur mi-Pil Yehudey Luv* (Hebrew), edited and annotated by Dov Noy (Jerusalem: World Zionist Organization, 1967). IFA 3523, told by David Hadad.

The Demon Princess (Byzantium)
From *Maaseh Yerushalmi* (Hebrew), edited by Yehuda L. Zlotnik (Jerusalem: Palestine Institute of Folklore and Ethnology, 1946).

The Enchanted Fountain (Byzantium)
From *Mishlei Sendabar* (Hebrew), edited by Abraham M. Habermann (Tel Aviv: 1946).

The Nightingale and the Dove (Greece)
From *Judeo-Spanish Ballads from New York* (Judeo-Spanish), edited by Samuel G. Armistead and Joseph H. Silverman (Berkeley: University of California Press, 1981). Collected by Mair Jose Bernardete.

The Golden Tree (India)
From *Shomrim Neemanim* (Hebrew), edited and annotated by Dov Noy (Haifa: Israel Folktale Archives, 1976). IFA 8181, collected by Zvi Haimovits, from Yitzhak Sasson.

The Golden Feather (Greece)
From *Notzat ha-Zahav* (Hebrew), edited and annotated by Dov Noy (Haifa: Israel Folktale Archives, 1976). IFA 10102, told by Moshe Atias. A variant of "The Golden Bird" from *Grimm's Fairy Tales*.

Sources

The Mute Princess (Yemen)
From *Hadre Teman* (Hebrew), edited by Nissim Binyamin Gamlieli (Tel Aviv: Afikim, 1978). Collected by Nissim Binyamin Gamlieli; told by Ovadia Zandani.

The Princess on the Glass Mountain (Iraqi Kurdistan)
From *Hodesh Hodesh Ve-sippuro: 1964* (Hebrew), edited by Ziporah Kagan (Haifa: Israel Folktale Archives, 1965). IFA 6084, collected by Marcella Noah from her sister-in-law Rachel.

The Wonderful Healing Leaves (Iraqi Kurdistan)
From *Hodesh Hodesh Ve-sippuro: 1974–1975* (Hebrew), edited by Dov Noy (Haifa: Israel Folktale Archives, 1975). IFA 10125, collected by Ofra Elias from her mother, Rachel Elias.

The Princess with Golden Hair (Palestine)
From *Sefer ha-Maaysiot* (Hebrew), in *The Exempla of the Rabbis,* edited by Moses Gaster (New York: Ktav, 1968).

The Enchanted Journey (Eastern Europe)
From *Eretz ha-Hayim* (Hebrew), collected by Hayim Liebersohn (Przemyśl, Poland: 1926). Also including episodes from *Rosinkess mit Mandlen: Aus der Volksliteratur der Ostjuden* (German), edited by Immanuel Olsvanger (Basel: Schweizerische Kommission für Jüdischen Volkskunde, 1931).

The Magic Mirror of Rabbi Adam (Eastern Europe)
From *Sefer ha-Maaysiot* (Hebrew), edited by Mordecai Ben-Yehezkel (Tel Aviv: Dvir, 1929).

The King's Dream (Eastern Europe)
From *Eretz ha-Hayim* (Hebrew), collected by Hayim Liebersohn (Przemyśl, Poland: 1926). Also including episodes from *Shivhei ha-Ari* (Hebrew) by Shlomo Meinsterl (Jerusalem: 1905).

The Boy Israel and the Witch (Eastern Europe)
From *Shivhei ha-Besht* (Hebrew) by Rabbi Dov Baer Ben-Samuel, edited by Samuel A. Horodezky (Berlin: 1922).

The Lost Princess (Eastern Europe)
From *Sippure Maasiyot* (Hebrew) by Rabbi Nachman of Bratslav, edited by Rabbi Nathan Sternhartz of Nemirov (Warsaw: 1881).

The Prince Who Was Made of Precious Gems (Eastern Europe)
From *Sippure Maasiyot* (Hebrew) by Rabbi Nachman of Bratslav, edited by Rabbi Nathan Sternhartz of Nemirov (Warsaw: 1881).

The Water Palace (Eastern Europe)
From *Sippure Maasiyot* (Hebrew) by Rabbi Nachman of Bratslav, edited by Rabbi Nathan Sternhartz of Nemirov (Warsaw: 1881).

Sources

The Pirate Princess (Eastern Europe)
From *Sippure Maasiyot* (Hebrew) by Rabbi Nachman of Bratslav, edited by Rabbi Nathan Sternhartz of Nemirov (Warsaw: 1881).

The Golden Bird (Eastern Europe)
Based on a Hasidic legend from *Midrash Ribesh Tov* (Hebrew), edited by Lipót Abraham (Kecskemét, 1927). A variant of "The Golden Bird" from *Grimm's Fairy Tales.*

The Imprisoned Princess (Eastern Europe)
From *Yiddisher Folklor* (Yiddish), edited by Yehuda L. Cahan (Vilna: 1938).

The Exiled Princess (Eastern Europe)
From *Yiddishe Folksmayses* (Yiddish), edited by Yehuda L. Cahan (Vilna: 1931). Including an episode from *Rosinkess mit Mandlen: Aus der Volksliteratur der Ostjuden* (German), edited by Immanuel Olsvanger (Basel: Schweizerische Kommission für Jüdischen Volkskunde, 1931). A variant of "Cinderella" from *Grimm's Fairy Tales.*

The Underground Palace (Eastern Europe)
From *Rosinkess mit Mandlen: Aus der Volksliteratur der Ostjuden* (German), edited by Immanuel Olsvanger (Basel: Schweizerische Kommission für Jüdischen Volkskunde, 1931).

The City of Luz (Eastern Europe)
From *Dos Bukh fun Nisyoynes* (Yiddish), edited by Israel Osman (Los Angeles: 1926). The earliest references to the city of Luz appear in Genesis. The nature of the city is expanded on in the Babylonian Talmud, tractate Sota, and further embellishment is found in Genesis Rabbah. The injunction for the use of the blue dye *(tekhelet)* derives from Numbers.

Glossary*

Aggadah   a term referring to the nonlegalistic material in the Talmud, primarily of a legendary character. In a broader sense, usually lower-cased (plural *aggadot*), it refers to the post-biblical legends found in both the Talmud and the Midrash. In the broadest sense, it is the kind of legendary material found throughout Jewish literature.

Asmodeus   the king of demons, a familiar figure in Jewish folklore.

Beit Din   a court of rabbis.

Book of Raziel   a legendary book given by the angel Raziel to Adam at God's command, from which Adam learned of the future generations. A book of the same title, *Sefer Raziel,* appeared in the Middle Ages; it consists of charms and spells and merely took the title of the legendary book.

drash   an interpretation of a passage in the Bible.

dybbuk   the soul of one who has died that enters the body of one who is living and remains until exorcised.

Gehenna   the place where the souls of the wicked are punished and purified.

Gemara   literally "to study" in Aramaic. The commentaries surrounding the Mishnah.

Hasidism   a Jewish sect founded in Poland in the eighteenth century by Israel ben Eliezer, known as the Baal Shem Tov. Hasidim are usually associated with a religious leader, known as a rebbe.

* The terms included here are Hebrew unless otherwise noted.

Lamed Vav; Lamed-vav Tzaddikim according to the Jewish tradition, there are thirty-six (*lamed-vav* in Hebrew) Just Men in every generation, and the world continues to exist because of the righteousness of these hidden saints.

Lilith Adam's first wife in Jewish legend. Later she became identified as a night demon who attempts to seduce men and strangle newborn infants.

maaseh (plural, *maaysiot*) a tale or story, often a folktale.

maggid a wandering preacher who confined his talks to easily understood homiletics.

Midrash a method of exegesis of the biblical text. Also refers to the post-talmudic Jewish legends as a whole. A midrash (lowercased, with the plural midrashim) is an individual midrashic legend.

Mishnah the earliest portion of the Talmud, consisting of six orders, each divided into tractates. The Mishnah is believed to contain the Oral Law transmitted from the giving of the Torah at Mount Sinai.

mitzvah (plural, *mitzvot*) a divine commandment. There are 613 *mitzvot* listed in the Torah. The term has also come to mean a good deed.

shammash literally, "servant." The beadle of a synagogue.

Shekhinah literally, "to dwell." The Divine Presence, usually identified as a feminine aspect of the Divinity, which evolved into an independent mythical figure in the kabbalistic period. Also identified as the Bride of God and the Sabbath Queen.

tallit a four-cornered prayer shawl with fringes at the corners, worn by men during the morning prayer services.

Talmud the most sacred Jewish text after the Bible. The term "Talmud" is the comprehensive designation for the Mishnah and the Gemara as a single unit. The material in the Talmud consists of both halakic (legal) and aggadic (legendary) material. There are Babylonian and Jerusalem Talmuds, which have different Gemaras commenting on the same Mishnah.

tefillin phylacteries worn at the morning services (except on the Sabbath) by men and boys over the age of thirteen.

tekhelet a blue dye which Jews were enjoined to use to color a thread in the fringes of the *tallit* (Numbers 15:37–38). By the talmudic period it was no longer known which creature supplied the dye nor how to make it, and the rabbis decided to leave the thread white rather than to dye it incorrectly.

tikkun   restoration and redemption.

Torah   the Five Books of Moses. In a broader sense the term refers to the whole Bible and the Oral Law. In the broadest sense it refers to all of Jewish culture and teaching.

Tzaddik (plural, *Tzaddikim*)   an unusually righteous and spiritually pure person. Hasidim believed their rebbes to be *Tzaddikim.*

Yetzer Hara   the Evil Impulse.

Yenne Velt (Yiddish)   literally, "the other world." The world in which demons and other spirits live.

Zohar   literally, "illumination" or "splendor." The central text of kabbala, written in the thirteenth century by Moshe de Leon, but attributed to the talmudic sage Simeon bar Yohai.

Howard Schwartz was born in St. Louis in 1945. He attended Washington University and at present teaches at the University of Missouri–St. Louis. He is the author of two books of poetry, *Vessels* and *Gathering the Sparks,* and of four books of fiction, including *Midrashim: Collected Jewish Parables.* He has also edited three anthologies, *Imperial Messages: One Hundred Modern Parables; Voices Within the Ark: The Modern Jewish Poets* (with Anthony Rudolf), and *Gates to the New City: A Treasury of Modern Jewish Tales.* A new collection of his stories, *The Captive Soul of the Messiah: New Tales About Reb Nachman,* will be published in 1983.

Linda Heller grew up in New York and studied at the Rhode Island School of Design. She has illustrated many children's books and is the author as well as the illustrator of *Alexis and the Golden Ring* and *Lily at the Table,* among others.

Tsila Schwartz was born in Jerusalem in 1952. She is an artist and calligrapher who specializes in *ketubot* (traditional Jewish wedding contracts) and Jewish amulets.